-5 DEC 1981

20. NOV 1981

Suffolk
6/6/02

COUNTY
RESERVE STOCK

D1580109

RETURN TO
COUNTY LIBRARY BOOKSTORE
TAMWORTH ROAD
HERTFORD, HERTS. SG13 7DG.
TEL. 56863

7/12

B) THE   4389396   JB/THE

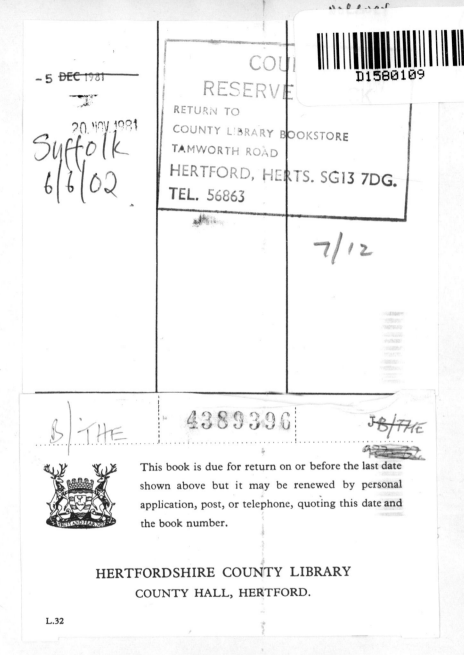

This book is due for return on or before the last date
shown above but it may be renewed by personal
application, post, or telephone, quoting this date and
the book number.

HERTFORDSHIRE COUNTY LIBRARY
COUNTY HALL, HERTFORD.

L.32

Warrior in Chains

By the same author

Naomi Jacob: The Seven Ages of 'Me'

WARRIOR IN CHAINS

St Thérèse of Lisieux

JAMES NORBURY

WILLIAM KIMBER
46 WILTON PLACE, LONDON SW1

© William Kimber & Co Ltd 1966

This book is copyright. No part of it may be reproduced in any form without permission in writing from the publishers except by a reviewer who wishes to quote brief passages in connection with a review written for inclusion in a magazine or newspaper or a radio broadcast.

B66 22899

HERTFORDSHIRE
COUNTY LIBRARY
JB/THE
4389396

Printed in Great Britain by
The Millbrook Press Limited, Southampton
and bound by Kemp Hall Bindery, Oxford

Contents

Frontispiece: St Thérèse of Lisieux from an original painting by Benedicta de Bezer.

For

Geoffrey Handley-Taylor

— in friendship and admiration —

Introduction

The story of Thérèse Martin, better known to the world as St Thérèse of
Lisieux, has been told many times before and will probably be told many
times again. What justification then has any author for entering into the field
of those who strive to portray this strange and complex character to his
readers unless he can claim to bring something new, something exciting,
something unusual to the telling of such an oft-told story?

What I have attempted to do is rub off the varnish that clings to her statues,
to take away the smell of stale rose petals that surrounds her image, and to
present her as she was, a living person in many ways much greater than her
life and death and its aftermath have been portrayed by most of my predecessors. One great advantage I have had is that she lived close enough to
us in time to be looked upon almost as a contemporary. One great dis-
advantage I have had to face is that she is too near to us in many ways for
much of the accumulated rubbish that had collected round her image to have
been blown away by the winnowing fans of time.

After a careful, and I hope critical, study of all the facts about her life and
death and character I have come to the conclusion that here, in a simple
Normandy girl, we are presented with one of the greatest saints in the
Christian calendar. In an age of darkness she was a centre of light. In a period
of doubt she became a symbol of certitude. In an era of decay she was a
renewing power. In our own day and generation she strives still to fulfil her
mission, the healing of all nations and the unity of all men who strive in their
lives to express and embody the love of God.

I would like to express my thanks to Major Hugo Tobias and his friends
in Lisieux who gave me so much assistance when I visited the places associated with the earthly life of Thérèse Martin; the Mother Prioress of the
Carmelite Convent at Golders Green; Father de Felici of the Church of St
Edward the Confessor, Golders Green; and the many Catholic friends who
have inspired and encouraged me in the writing of this book. At the same
time I would like to make it perfectly clear that I alone am responsible for
all the ideas and opinions I have expressed in these pages.

My special thanks are due to Anthony Pegrum who has corrected and
edited the manuscript and prepared it for publication.

J.N.

I come in the little things,
Saith the Lord:
My starry wings
I do forsake,
Love's highway of humility to take:
Meekly I fit my stature to your need.
In beggar's part
About your gates I shall not cease to plead —
As man, to speak with man —
Till by such art
I shall achieve My Immemorial Plan,
Pass the low lintel of the human heart.

—Evelyn Underhill

Part One

The Forcing House

'The dazzling genius of St Augustine, the luminous wisdom of Thomas Aquinas have shed forth upon souls the rays of an imperishable splendour, through them, Christ and His doctrine have become better known. The divine poem lived out by St Francis of Assisi has given to the world an imitation, as yet unequalled, of the life of God made man. But a little Carmelite who had hardly reached adult age has conquered in less than half a century innumerable hosts of disciples. Doctors of the law have become children at her school; the Supreme Shepherd has exalted her; and even at this moment there are millions of souls from one end of the earth to the other whose interior life has received the beneficial influence of her little book *The Story of a Soul*.'

– POPE PIUS XII

CHAPTER I

Souls in Exile

At the close of the eighteenth century the spiritual crisis that had split the country asunder during the aftermath of the Revolution was proving the focal point of internal dissension that might well divide France into two warring factors, thus giving rise to a secondary upheaval. The downfall of the monarchy and the collapse of the houses of the nobility had not solved the country's internal problems. In fact it would be true to say that if it had done anything at all about the stresses that always endangered the well-being of the working classes it had merely been to accentuate them. Many of the common people were murmuring in the taverns and market places that a bad monarchy was better than no monarchy at all. Civil strife always brings problems in its wake.

The new aristocrats, products of the machinations of Madame Guillotine and the Revolutionary struggle for power, found themselves faced with either a divided nation or an offering of a half-hearted support to the upstart whom none of them really liked and whom most of them positively hated. The old faith, that had made much of the glorious history of the nation, was threatened on all sides, and the new philosophy of radical scepticism did not find a ready acceptance among the masses of the common people.

The Papacy, who still tried to play a dominant role in the affairs of Europe, was fully conscious of the danger zone into which France was drifting, and with that genius for compromise that has so often made her politically suspect among the non-adherents to her tenets was already considering what steps it would be called upon to take to protect the faithful from the open attacks upon their religious liberty that were already becoming an obvious part of French policy.

There was uneasiness everywhere, a sense of discontent tormented most of the thinking men of the time and the doubtful directives from the leaders of the Republic found little or no response in the hearts of the common people. The working men and women and the rising middle class shared equally the fear that overshadowed the whole of the community. All they sought was that the even tenor of their life might be maintained and that their existence might still move in the simple pattern that had been their strength and mainstay throughout the centuries. They were nominally Catholic but had within their natures an inherent nationalism that placed France first and Rome second.

15

The fascination of the watchmaker's workroom so interested the young man and enchained his imagination, that before long he had decided that the following of this worthy profession was to be his future career. No doubt his father had mixed feelings when his son's decision was communicated to him, but his mother was delighted at the thought that her third born had decided to follow a peaceful and creative occupation. He became apprenticed to his father's cousin but soon moved to Strasbourg, where another friend of the family was a noted clockmaker.

One day, when he was carefully examining the mechanism of the famous cathedral clock in that city, the solemnity of the quiet atmosphere of the building seemed to release some inner urge in him towards a life of deeper and more profound spirituality. He was already a member of one of the religious confraternities, that constantly strove to recall the layman to an awareness of the fact that heaven was his true destination. The disciplined life of prayer and daily meditation, the regular attendance at the Sacraments, and the reading of religious books created in him a sense of discontent, a thirst and a longing for a deeper awareness of the power of God in his own soul, and in August 1843, when he was twenty years of age young Louis, for in many ways he was young for his age, set out on the first of many pilgrimages he was to undertake throughout his life. This first one was to the famous monastery on Mount St Bernard where he decided to withdraw from the world for a time, and while there in retreat to try and discover what it was that would bring a fullness of satisfaction to his heart.

We can easily discern in the pattern of his life the discontent that is the common lot of all adolescents. The growing awareness of sexual desire is so difficult to master. The narrow and almost puritanical restrictions of his upbringing where ignorance was proving far from bliss, and a sense of shame allied to a shadowy fear that seemed to haunt him even when he was on his knees or wrapt in meditation, these factors urged him into seeking a release and an escape, which he hoped might open up to him in the solitude of the mountains. We must strive to see his life at this point in its true perspective, otherwise we shall entirely misunderstand the many strange events that were to follow.

In his age ignorance was considered a virtue, and even succumbing to the minor temptation of masturbation was looked upon as a major triumph for the powers of darkness. There was little free or open intercourse between the young of both sexes, and not only were girls completely unaware of the pains and joys of the marriage bed, but the young men in turn had no sound biological knowledge of the processes of procreation and reproduction.

The wild and tempestuous urges of the flesh must be disciplined and controlled, and it is doubtful if in the Catholic atmosphere they inhabited there was anyone willing to or capable of advising them as to how to meet the stresses of their developing manhood. After all it is not very long ago that in our own country, where puritanical slavery had replaced catholic ideas, that a whack across the bare behind and a cold bath were considered the most potent weapons against the possibility of falling foul of the sins of the flesh.

The Monks of St Bernard were Augustinian Fathers, one of the oldest orders in the Church and one of the first to live by the reformed rule of the great St Benedict. They lived as a community, their daily lives divided between work and worship and the aid of lost travellers, who went astray in the rough pathways that led across the pass on the mountain side. These men, hardened and vigorous in the service of God and their fellows by the strictly ordered routine of their communal existence, met many who aspired to follow in their wake. But few proved capable of that singleness, that unreserved integrity that was the foundation of their calling.

Louis Martin did not realise that a desire for solitude in itself was a selfish thing, that a striving for personal satisfaction was no justification for a hair shirt and a monk's habit. The monastic calling must be rooted in fulfilment and not looked upon as a way of escape. The Prior, relying on an innate wisdom born of years of experience in a life of disciplined austerity, was sympathetic towards the aspirations of the young man who expressed a desire to be received as a novice that he might dedicate his life to the service of his Maker. So many came to seek what he sought but did not realise they could find their solace in the world, and because of this were not destined for the life of the cloister.

'Return to Normandy, carry on with your studies, pray that God's will be made manifest to you, and having done these things return here again and I will admit you to the novitiate.'

On returning to Alençon Louis immediately placed himself under the direction of an old *curé* who was to teach him the rudiments of Greek and Latin. Illness dogged his footsteps. He found it more and more difficult to settle down to the enforced discipline his studies demanded, and at last broken completely by these new trials he left for Paris to carry on his work as a watchmaker in that city.

There is an element of mystery, almost a conspiracy of silence about his life in the French capital. We have no direct evidence that he fell from grace, but there are suggestive phrases in one of his wife's letters to her own brother, who was at the time resident in that city, that Louis Martin had suffered some kind of severe shock during his stay there. Had the weakness of the flesh, in a moment of dire temptation overcome him? We shall never know the answer to that question, but we do know that by the time he returned home to Alençon, to set up in business on his own, he had of his own volition taken a vow of perpetual celibacy.

The Guérin family were well known and well-respected in Alençon and its neighbourhood. Deeply religious, clinging tenaciously to the old faith during the years of persecution that had followed the Revolution, their devoutness had become a byword in the neighbourhood. The elder daughter of the family at the time of which I am writing later became a Visitation nun, the second daughter Louise died in early childhood, and the third daughter, Zélie Guérin, presented herself as soon as she was old enough to the Sisters of St Vincent to offer herself in the service of the Order.

Zélie had been given a sound education, and was in many ways a typical product of the more prosperous members of the middle classes of her day. I have already warned you that an element of the miraculous will run through these pages, and when Zélie presented herself to the Mother Superior of the order she was given short shrift and told in categorical terms that the Almighty had already decided there was other, and equally important work for her to do for Him in the world.

For those who are privileged to look backwards from the end to the beginning of the story this sturdy nun's remarks undoubtedly have a providential justification, but to the disappointed girl who saw herself duly clothed and received into the convent to devote her life to the service of the poor the words offered little, if any, consolation.

The young woman, on returning to her father's house, 42 rue St Blaise, found herself at a loose end. What could a French woman of middle class stock do in those days when the Church had refused the offer of her life? Have a husband found for her, keep house, and produce children was the only answer. Zélie was not, however, cast in the mould out of which the vast majority of the women of her time were made. She possessed a more than ordinary intelligence for a woman of her time, she had a precociousness and determination that surmounted all obstacles, she had a deep-rooted and genuine piety that gave to her an inner knowledge that in some way her life was meant to be dedicated to the work of her Maker. Whether it was in a spirit of rebellion against the round of drudgery that would have been her lot had she merely remained an obedient daughter of the family we do not know. Whether it was a desire to better herself in order that she might be a worthy example to the women of her time we cannot say. All we do know is that having decided the convent walls and the daily service of the poor were not her vocation she knew that she must seek the married state, and she also realised there was not sufficient money in the family purse to offer with her a worthy dowry.

So Zélie became a pupil at the famous school where the rudiments of the lacemaker's art were taught. The work itself is difficult and calls for endless patience. The patterns must be pricked out on paper first. Next the separate pieces, the leaves, flowers and abstract motifs that form the foreground to the patterning must be made and mounted on the fine material onto which the outlines have been marked from the pricked holes in the paper. Finally the pieces must be assembled that form the lace itself, the pieces being joined by carefully executed cotton meshes and fillings that are the apex of the lacemaker's craft. Zélie assiduously studied each phase in this traditional craft and once she was proficient lost no time in setting herself up in her father's house as a maker of fine laces.

One thing must be understood at the outset, this was a communal undertaking. Zélie would obtain the orders and design the patterns. She would then employ workers who made the basic shapes, teach them how to assemble them and herself put the finishing details to the final product. Obviously she had a natural genius for this work, and before long she was getting more orders than she could fulfil, and steadily acquiring for herself a nest egg that should be her dowry.

Zélie's attitude in setting herself up in business in the family house may seem strange reading seen against the background of its period. Were we face to face with a potential rebel? Was the demand for woman's rights already asserting itself in Alençon at such an early date? The answer is that Zélie was neither a rebel nor a new woman, she was merely a girl who had always failed to get on with her mother, in fact it would be a fair statement of fact to say that at this period there was an active and an acute dislike existing between them. The reason for this enmity is not at all evident in the scant, and sad to say carefully censured, records that have been left to us from that time. The daughter we know had a wilful and stubborn streak, the mother a quick temper and sharp tongue, and these factors may well have been the cause of family conflict. On the other hand it might have been that the mother resented her younger daughter attempting to enter a religious order, while the daughter resented in her turn that so much had been spent on her sister's and brother's education that there was little of the family fortune left when it came to the question of her own dowry.

There may have been another reason altogether, and that is that the mother saw in the daughter's spiritual strivings an element of priggery. Her father, a retired gendarme who seems to have been somewhat of a nonentity in the household, encouraged his daughter's aspirations. Whatever the cause, the rift in the smoothness of family life gave Zélie just the opportunity she needed to strike out as an independent business woman in the ancient French market town.

Modern usage is always dangerous when it is applied to times and places outside the orbit of the present century. To classify Louis Martin as a sex-starved bachelor constantly living on the edge of frustration that he strove to balance out by a disciplined observance of his religious way of life is only to move the problem one stage further back and not to seek for its resolution. To classify Zélie Guérin as a disappointed woman who had failed to justify to her Superior her own desire to follow a spiritual vocation and who in violent reaction to this disappointment had set herself up as a woman very much of the world with one dominant desire and that was to find a husband and establish a family, would be equally futile. These two characters, and they are in every way the central and cardinal figures in the opening phases of our drama, were each in their differing ways convinced that they had a unique part to play in God's plans for the salvation of mankind.

We are moving here on dangerous and delicate ground, and neither the microscope of the scientist nor the text books of the psychologist can give us a complete and satisfying answer. To be God-possessed is to move at a slant to time, to live just beyond the orbit of ordinarily understood experience, and just as it would be ridiculous to suggest that Florence Nightingale merely faced the rigours of the Crimea and the filth and grime of many of the hospitals of her day to satisfy her own ego, so it would be as foolhardy to try and cancel out the inner call these two human beings felt in terms of neurotic repressions and compulsory reflexes.

We are too apt these days to replace one set of terms by another, thinking that this in itself will give us the meaning and purpose of men and their actions. Even Freud was forced to admit in the end that there were imponderable elements in human behaviour that did not always respond to analysis, and Jung has stated quite categorically that a disciplined and directed spiritual impulse may reveal to us regions of consciousness outside the field of clinical research.

There is one other point that we must take into consideration and that is that faith is often upheld by ridicule and religion enriched by persecution. Both these forces were present in the France of this time, for Napoleon had introduced an oath of allegiance that every priest was expected to take, and most of them refused to consider, which would oblige them to recognise the power of the state before the rights of the church, and the intellectual sterility of the church at the time had led to a nonconformity and scepticism that still has its repercussions in our own day.

The most difficult problem that anyone is brought face to face with who attempts to write a new evaluation of Thérèse Martin is that one is hedged in on every side by almost impassable barriers of either prejudice or special pleading. It is so very easy to get lost in the maze of a miasma of piety, or on the other hand to be betrayed into the aura of prejudice that has surrounded her from those who seek to detract from her greatness and belittle her sanctity. The uninhibited praise of her camp followers and the unrestrained sneer of her detractors must both be constantly combatted if one is to strive to arrive at a balanced verdict on her life, her death and the mission that followed after.

It is important therefore to get as clear a picture as possible of Louis Martin and Zélie Guérin at the period I am writing of that was in every way the turning point of their own lives. How were they seen by the people around them, and what was the impression of their fellow citizens in the small town of Alençon?

Louis Martin was undoubtedly looked upon by many of his contemporaries as an amiable crank with a touch of religious mania. He was a reticent and in many ways a somewhat morose individual, who would readily have been accepted had he been a village *curé* but frowned upon to a certain extent when seen as merely one of the laymen of the community. There is nothing more calculated than what is openly spoken of as an overdose of good works to give to the outside observer a touch of spiritual constipation.

In most of the cafés and bars this slightly timorous, yet at the same time seemingly arrogant, jeweller and clockmaker appeared on the surface to be much too good to ring true. Goodness, that inherent quality out of which a deep-seated integrity is born, is always looked upon with a slightly jaundiced eye. It may be an acceptable thing for God, who after all is in heaven, but it has little place in the life of the average man who is very much of the world. The monastery and the cobblestoned roadway of Alençon belonged to a different order, both recognised as having a rightful place in society, but when one sought to intrude upon the other, well, this spelled quite a different story.

His reading, and the content of this was obvious to all who got into conversation with him, appeared to be far too preoccupied with the New Testament and the lives of the saints. His hobbies, if one dare label his interests and activities by such a frivolous phrase, centred far too much on visiting the sick, striving to assist the poor, and going to church far too often. The Society of St Vincent de Paul, the Confraternity of the Blessed Sacrament, and the Catholic Club of which he was one of the leading figures, commanded from him all of his spare time.

The kindliest view taken by most of his contemporaries during this period was that he was a harmless fanatic, whose cranky outlook on life found little favour with those who were flowing with the rising tide of scepticism that was to play such an important part in the life of France for the next fifty years. At the opposite extreme were those who openly laughed at him, labelled him a kill-joy, a lick-spittler of the parish priest, a harmless and idiotic neurotic who would be much better for a good tumble in the hay with one of the buxom wenches from the villages in the nearby countryside.

Zélie Guérin was considered by her neighbours in quite a different light. Goodness, always a doubtful proposition in a man, was seen from quite a different slant when it manifested itself in a woman. Zélie could be gay and vivacious, she had a sharp tongue that she was always trying to keep in check, she had a slightly rebellious disposition that was revealed in her constant skirmishes with her mother, and a ready wit that soon put everyone who tried to intrude into her inner privacy in their right and proper place. If she attended daily Mass, well what better place was there for a woman than the church? If at times she cast sad and longing eyes at the convent door, well, it was wiser to be a nun rather than a loveless spinster. Her kindness, her generosity, and her willingness to go to anyone's aid who called upon her for assistance were sterling qualities that won her a good name in every part of the town.

We cannot doubt the fact that there were many parents who saw in this attractive young woman the perfect match for one of their sons. She was known to be a hardworking follower of her chosen craft, the making of Alençon lace. It was common knowledge that her savings must be considerable, that meant she would enter no prospective bridegroom's house empty-handed, Her domesticity, her thriftiness, and her genial nature argued well that here was the perfect wife for the man who was lucky enough to win her admiration and affection.

We must never lose sight, however, of the cardinal point that can never be overemphasised in the story we are telling and that is that both Louis and Zélie were convinced that providence had singled them out for a supernatural destiny. Voices from beyond themselves would direct their footsteps, visions from another order would reveal to them the way they must travel. Their whole beings were centred on seeking and finding the prophetic utterances that would guide them in all that they undertook to do, and it is to one, and in some ways the most significant of all, these spiritual encounters that we must now turn our attention.

Both Louis and Zélie's mothers found themselves constantly in each other's company, and what could be more natural than each of them should talk to the other of the virtues of their respective children. Louis's mother felt that her son had remained a bachelor for far too long. Zélie's mother knew that her home would be a pleasanter place if her daughter was out of it, as she was tired of the daily bickering and quarrelling that went on between them.

Little did either of the mothers realise how fortune was to take a hand in bringing their much discussed plans to the rightful fruition. Although Captain Martin's wife had already made tentative suggestions to Zélie Guérin that her son would make her a perfect husband her suggestions were met by a certain aloofness and a calculated restraint by the daughter of her friend Madame Guérin. It was not that Zélie disdained the idea of marriage, or sought to run away from the duties of the married state. But she had an innate conviction that her marriage would be ordained by heaven, and she was not at all sure that Louis Martin was the man who had been selected by the Almighty that His ways might find their completion and fulfilment from such a match.

The matchmaking mothers found themselves in a very delicate and extremely tricky position. Each of them was wise enough to know that both Louis and Zélie had a stubborn streak in them that would never be overcome by force and that might not easily yield to the most carefully thought out persuasion. They were both individuals who had a very clear concept of what they were seeking to find in life. One had seen the doorway of a monk's cell closing itself against him when he had striven to fulfil what he inwardly felt was his true vocation, and the other had been turned away sorrowfully from the convent in which she had hoped to find the proper sphere to busy herself with good works. But as she crossed the bridge of St Leonard one evening she could not help noticing a young man who gave her a curious look as they met. His calm manner and his dignified demeanour impressed her, but none of these things were sufficient in themselves. But, without warning another Voice spoke within her, 'This is he whom I have prepared for you'. She knew then without doubt that marriage to Louis Martin was destined for her in the writings of heaven.

Louis and Zélie became formally engaged almost at once, a spiritual betrothal took place a few days later, and at midnight in the Church of Notre Dame, on 13th July 1858, they were married with due solemnity by the Abbé Hurel, Dean of St Leonard. There were no doubts at all in Zélie's mind as to what was the true meaning and purpose of this ceremony. Her vocation was to be the mother of sons who in their turn would each be dedicated at birth to God, to serve in the mission field and to help to gather in His harvest of redeemed souls. While there was no doubt in her mind of the worthiness of her new calling, the voice on the bridge had omitted to inform her of a trivial detail that challenged the plans and dreams that appeared to open out to her such a wondrous future. It was Louis's, her husband's, voice that uttered the words that apparently, temporarily at least, turned her plans to dust and her dreams to ashes.

'I have decided after devout prayer and deep thought that my vocation in marriage is to remain true to the celibate state.'

Poor Zélie Martin, like many a woman before and after her, went to her marriage bed in tears, for it looked as though she had been betrayed into a forced acceptance of a married life that was to be marriage in name only, and might well make her the laughing stock of the whole town.

CHAPTER II

A Marriage made in Heaven

Whatever can be said in Louis Martin's favour, and at the best it might be that he was a misguided bigot, the fact remains that he was a pious prig, whose outlook approximated much more to the mind of Calvin although his heart might be deeply rooted in the teachings of the Catholic Church. He was a domineering, vain, and pompous man, who had a strange and at times bewildering inner feeling that he had been called by God to fulfil a particular mission in life.

That he was a master craftsman has never been in doubt. That he was an impeccable member of the establishment has never been in question. His real need was for a love he would seek for throughout his life and never find because he was completely incapable of being objective either about himself or those he came into contact with. He made very few friends, for to do so might lead him into a life of worldliness that terrified him. The world was not for him since it had all the appearance of a diabolical playground of the senses. The flesh was the great betrayer that must be curbed and leashed at all cost. The devil lurked in every cloud and every shadow and kept up a never ceasing vigil in order to lure him into its trap.

There can be no doubt at all that his marriage to Zélie Guérin caused a great deal of gossip in the taverns and cafes of the town of Alençon. He might be a cold and aloof sort of fellow but he knew a nice bit of skirt when he saw it were words that were constantly being heard among his contemporaries. If some of the stories told of him are of a libellous and scandalous nature Louis Martin has no one but himself to blame. At heart he was a Victorian prude who felt that the conjugal relationship between man and woman, even in the sanctified marriage bed, was to be tolerated but never enjoyed. What he saw in Zélie, his wife, in the early days of their association together, and I hesitate to call it a marriage, was a friendly companion, an admirable housekeeper and a business woman who, through her activities at lace-making would be able to contribute a useful addition to the family income. He had somewhat begrudgingly agreed to marry her because he felt it was the will of God, but he had definitely decided that nothing would tempt him away from the celibacy that he felt was his soul's true vocation.

Louis was still able to play at being a monk and Zélie could still dream of the days she would like to spend in a convent. In fact it is almost impossible

27

to discover who was to blame for the sterility of their married state for in a letter to Pauline many years later her mother says:

> You, Pauline, who love your father so much, will think perhaps that I was making him unhappy and that I had spoiled our wedding day for him. But no, he understood me, and consoled me as well as he could, for he had similar inclinations.

It is difficult to surmise where this stifling, and, as I see it, soul-destroying state of affairs, might have led to had it been allowed to go on indefinitely. Fortunately a wise confessor stepped in and reminded the Martins of their marital duties as good Catholics, and Louis found consolation in the words of Père Sertillanges, 'when kept in its place the flesh does not offend the spirit, it serves it'.

The danger of a misguided and unrestrained spirituality based on a false premise is that once one is released from its bondage the tendency is to move in exactly the opposite direction, and all the evidence at our disposal certainly suggests that this well might have been the case with Louis Martin. For once he had submitted to the demands of the flesh he was destined to drive his wife into an early grave largely due to the constant strain of childbirth, a strain that continued even when she was in the first stages of being ravaged by the cancer that led to her death.

If Louis Martin is an enigma, in many ways his wife is to a certain extent a problem child of her period. On reading Zélie's letters, and she was a vociferous letter writer, you get the glimpse of a gay and vivacious woman, whose tongue and pen had a tough acidity in them, and whose commentaries on the changing social scene going on all around her were worthy at times of the pen of Jane Austen. No woman dare wear a slightly outrageous hat without it calling forth a caustic comment from Zélie Martin. A dress cut too low or a skirt raised too high were easy targets for her somewhat sarcastic and ready wit.

If Louis had not constantly tightened the bearing rein he might well have found himself trying to handle a spirited filly who would take him, almost before he was aware of what was happening, into the golden fields and green pastures of the world from which he was constantly seeking to escape. The inherent puritan in him, the 'thou shalt not' outlook that characterised the whole of his outlook upon life, was to prove triumphant throughout the whole of his days. He ruled his home with an inflexibility and sternness that almost verged on cruelty. He dominated the life of his wife and later on of his children in such a way that none of them can be said to have had a life of their own. He was the self-elected agent of God and his wife and daughters were the counters of the celestial draughtboard over which he brooded year after year.

Once the decision had been made to embark upon their duty as good Catholics and to have a family another decision was made at the same time, and that was that their offspring should be God's children, not in the particular way in which we are all called upon to be inheritors of the Kingdom of God, but in a special way that closed the doors of the convent on them almost before they had uttered their first cry as they emerged from their mother's womb.

' "My ways are not thy ways," saith the Lord,' seems to have had no place in their conception of their home and their offspring. If nature was to ordain that Zélie Martin was to give birth mainly to daughters, and if the sons who were born to her were to die in infancy, these things did not deter the parents from their objective of producing servants of God. The sons, the ones who died, had been dedicated to the priesthood and mission field before they had spoken a single word so that they could not say either yea or nay, and the daughters each of whom in turn was looked upon as a potential saint were destined for Carmel from the earliest days of their childhood.

In spite of these things the Martin home was in many ways a happy household. If life is so circumscribed for you that you are only allowed to survey it through one narrow window, the little world that opens out to you can become a complete world, a satisfactory world, simply because you have known no other. God must be the centre and circumference of your whole existence, and if the centre is your father's interpretation of God's will for himself and you, and if the circumference is your mother's determination that she will breed and house a brood of saints there is nothing left for you to do except either accept or rebel, and acceptance in the main was the keynote of relationships in the Martin family circle.

The townspeople of Alençon, ordinary folk in the main who had discovered through bitter experience that probably the most expedient thing in life was not to take it too seriously, could not help but have a sneaking admiration for the stalwart Christian virtues that were so obvious in the lives of Louis and Zélie Martin. Louis was meticulously honest in pursuing his craft as a watch and clockmaker and his trade as a jeweller. Zélie was noted for the generous way in which she treated her servants, and the fairness she meted out to the lacemakers who delivered their work to her every Thursday.

Their home, the church, and the various organisations and associations or religious activities among layfolk was their world, and in it they found a satisfaction and completeness that may seem very strange, if not a little bewildering when we survey it through the more enlightened eyes of the twentieth century.

Both Louis and Zélie were overjoyed when they realised that soon they were going to have a child. As they sat in the stuffy little parlour at the back of the shop in the shadows of late evening their whole conversation centred on their ideals and plans for the son they hoped for and so ardently prayed for together each evening. He was not their child, he was a creature God was loaning to them that they might guide it to the fulfilment of His will. He would be a priest, he might even become a valiant worker in the mission field winning other souls into a following of his Master. He might even, the thought brought with it a hint of that diabolical temptation pride, become a bishop one day.

Whatever else might happen to him, of one thing they were both certain and that was that they were to be the instruments Divine Providence would utilise in the making of a saint. All their thoughts must be sublime that they might prove worthy of their high calling. All their words must be noble that they might properly fulfil their high vocation. All their deeds must be above reproach that nothing should mar their child's ability to fulfil its divine calling.

The Martins' first child, a girl, was born on 22nd February, 1860, and if both parents felt a sense of disappointment and frustration at its not being the son they had lived and hoped and prayed for so ardently, they nevertheless knew the child must be dedicated to the service of the Queen of Heaven and christened her Marie-Louise. Louis himself was overjoyed as he took on his new role of a Catholic father and exclaimed to the priest at the christening, 'It is the first time you have seen me here at a baptism but it will not be the last'.

Many will read this as a happy and joyous exclamation, capturing in words his exalted mood at the time, others, the more cynical perhaps, knowing how passionately he wanted a priest in the family might read into it the old adage, 'If at first you don't succeed try, try again'. The one thing we can say about Louis Martin is that he was constantly trying, even when his wife was too weak and ill to face the agony of further pregnancies.

On 7th September, 1861, Marie-Pauline was born; on 3rd June, 1863, Marie-Léonie was baptised, but by the time Marie-Hélène was born on 13th October, 1864, Zélie Martin was no longer capable of breast feeding her latest infant. The constant supervision of the home, the never ceasing application of her labours to the making of Alençon lace, the strain of too frequent childbearing were already taking their toll, and it was soon after the birth of Hélène that the first signs of the cancer that was to lead to her comparatively early death manifested themselves.

It is easy enough writing today to blame the husband for the sad plight in which his wife found herself in, but the fact is that her life was no better and no worse than that of most married women of her time. The majority of middle class wives found themselves in a similar position. They were household drudges catering for the whims of their male partners. They were his constant bed companions, with whom he sought sexual and sensual satisfaction irrespective of the ravages it might make upon the woman's health. They were domestic slaves, whose basic duty it was to obey their husbands in all things no matter how great the cost to themselves. The only difference between most of them and Zélie Martin was that the majority of them had not married husbands who lived with their ears constantly glued to the keyhole of heaven.

Louis Martin does not seem to have been particularly disturbed at the first signs of his wife's breakdown in health, in fact it was only after her death that a guilt was to take possession of him that was in my opinion one of the factors leading to his own insanity. He saw himself as the man of action, the practical idealist whose duty it was to see that the right kind of milk flowed through the breasts of the woman who was to be honoured by being allowed to wet-nurse his daughter. Obviously she must be an upright and pious woman without a touch of guile in her nature. His knowledge of biology was scant to say the least, and psychology, a science then in its swaddling clothes, was completely unknown to him. In Louis Martin's opinion the character of the nurse flowed out through her nipples, and if she was stained with mortal sin it might well endanger the immortal soul of his own infant.

There was one constant source of consolation in Zélie Martin's life and that was the deep and abiding friendship she had built up with her sister who was a Visitation nun in a convent at Le Mans. Here was the Mother Prioress she had sought and never found. Here was the cloistered security that had been the constant hope of her girlhood dreams. Every incident in her daily life, her children's smiles, her hopes for their futures, her joy at hearing them speak for the first time, her worries if they seemed even in the slightest way to be slipping from the path of virtue, were all duly reported to the convent.

By April of the following year, 1865, Zélie Martin appears to have realised that there was something radically wrong with her for she is writing to her brother who had studied medicine reminding him of a blow she had had in the breast when she was a child, and describing to him the glandular swelling that was becoming more obvious in her breast. Her husband seems to have been almost completely indifferent to his wife's illness. It is true that he sought advice from the local doctor and that he wrote to his brother-in-law, Isidore, to see what his thoughts were upon the matter, but he does not seem to have taken any definite action to help to alleviate his wife's suffering.

I know that his apologists try to explain his apparent indifference away by emphasising that in those days X-ray was unknown, surgery in a very primitive state, and cancer was a killer no matter what treatment was used to alleviate the more dreadful aspects of this horrible disease. The fact is that after the tentative enquiries I have referred to Louis Martin took no further action for eleven years, and when he did so his wife was already almost in the grave.

Let us pause for a moment and take a look at this family as they were at this time. Louis and Zélie still longed for the son that nature had not seen fit to grant them. Marie, the eldest daughter was growing into a quiet, solemn little girl whose old-fashioned ways endeared her to her elders. Pauline on the other hand was already showing signs of that domineering and deter-mined character that marked her out as a future Prioress of the Carmelite Convent at Lisieux. And Léonie, the grey sheep (there would be no black ones in the Martin family) was exhibiting that waywardness and rebellion that singled her out from the rest and that even caused her mother to describe her as a 'difficult and unruly child'. It did not seem to strike anyone that the father's own character was such that it might be driving Marie far too much inside herself, and his indecisiveness about practical affairs might be forcing Pauline to assume a worldliness beyond her years. As for Léonie's rebellious attitude, what wild bird has not sought to escape from its cage if it finds it too hampering and limiting as it grows to full flight and maturity?

On 26th June, 1865, the shadow of death fell across the Martin household for the first time. From the day of their strange marriage Louis and Zélie had lived with the husband's parents, sharing a communal house attached to the shop where Louis himself carried on his business as clockmaker and jeweller. His father, a noble patriarch looking very like an Old Testament prophet as he strode through the streets of Alençon, had been suddenly struck down with a stroke. The doctors had only given him a few weeks to live and at his death Zélie wrote to her brother:

> I own to you that I am terrified of death. I have just been to see my father-in-law. His arms are so stiff and his face so cold! And to think I shall see my loved ones like that, or that they shall see me!

The shock of coming face to face with the physical fact of death had a profound effect upon Zélie Martin. She was a woman who had, as we have seen, a profound sense of the presence of God in the common day to day experiences she was called upon to pass through, and rather than run away from this fear that was holding her in bondage she opened herself up to its frightening embrace and in so doing conquered it. Her philosophy of death became as simple as her philosophy of life. It was the will of God, it was part of His divine pattern for the soul's perfection, and when a person died in the cradle, in the first flush of youth or in the fullness of old age, it simply meant that God desired them for Himself.

In trying to understand and reconstruct the lives of these two people, so strangely alike in some ways and yet so completely alien to one another in others, it soon becomes obvious that Zélie was in many ways the greater of the two. Her sense of humour was always bubbling up beneath the surface and gave at times a real zest to her letters. Her practical attitude in the running of the home and caring for her children and her implicit trust in the ultimate goodness and wisdom of Divine Providence single her out as a creature whose nature had a great deal in it of natural sanctity.

The constant thought that formed a deep bond between the parents was a mutual desire for a son. The priest who was to be, the one who would offer the daily sacrifice of the Mass and who would be flesh of their flesh, blood of their blood, was forever in their thoughts. After four pregnancies, each of which had ended in the birth of a daughter, Zélie decided that natural means were not sufficient in themselves to bring about what she had come to regard as a near miracle. To her, any apparent failure in the natural sequence of events called for the need of supernatural intervention, and to make this possible she instructed her daughters, who had grown old enough to understand a little of the meaning of prayer, to offer up to St Joseph petitions every night that he would plead that they might have the one gift they desired above all others, a baby brother. Zélie herself offered up an almost unceasing series of supplications through the saint whom she almost saw as a battering ram against the gates of Heaven itself, striving with her to see that God's will was aligned to her own wishes.

As soon as she knew she was pregnant again her happiness knew no bounds. In the quiet of the evening her talk was constantly of the day they would see him at the altar, and of the joy they would know when they went to hear him preach. He should have the finest vestments her nimble fingers could devise and his alb, designed and made by herself in Point d'Alençon, would be a masterpiece in design and workmanship. By the time the unborn had quickened in her womb her sense of contentment and her deep feeling of happiness knew no bounds for she had an inner certainty that here was a direct answer to her own, her husband's and her children's prayers.

Storming heaven had justified itself, and on 20th September, 1866, a son, Marie-Joseph-Louis was born to them. Here was the fulfilment they had both sought after and desired so ardently through the early years of their marriage. Here was the perfect justification of their belief that they were people who had been called out and set aside to fulfil some special role in the working out of God's plans for men. Here was the event, insignificant perhaps in itself, but full of significance for the future that more than compensated them for not being able to follow the religious vocations each had desired in their younger days. But alas, here too was the first testing of their faith, for on 14th February, 1867, the long hoped for son died before he was quite six months old.

Even at this distance in time from the event we can capture something of the heart-rending agony that engulfed Zélie Martin. The Lord had given and the Lord had taken away, such easy words to utter but such difficult words to accept when the hopes and longings and desires of so many years had seemed at last to be coming to their fulfilment. A few days after her son's death her sister, writing from the Convent of Visitation, tells of how when she was kneeling at the Communion rail she had prayed that she might understand how this heavy burden had been allowed to fall across her sister's shoulders and tells her:

> I seemed to hear interiorly this answer, that He wished to have the first fruits, and would give you another child later on, who would be such as we desire.

Now we must remember that to Zélie her sister's words were like those of the Delphic Oracles were to a pagan world. If God desired her first-born son then it meant that he was already living with Him in glory. Sanctification, that was the whole objective of living and purification was meant to be the keynote of our worldly pilgrimage. Marie-Joseph-Louis was already of the elect, and what was more simple than to prove it by getting her daughter Hélène, suffering from an ear complaint that gave her a great deal of pain, to pray to her little brother that he would seek for healing grace on her behalf. The prayer was offered up, the pain vanished immediately, and the trouble in the ear cleared up. What better sign could the Martin family have that their deeply-mourned child was in heaven itself, and that they had seen through his intervention the performance of a miracle?

Since God had desired little Joseph for Himself, and since her sister had assured her that she would be granted the favour of another son, what was more natural than that Zélie should pray again to St Joseph that he would be instrumental once more in pleading before the Divine Grace that her hopes and longings should find their proper fulfilment.

On 19th March, 1867, the feast day of the saint, she ended a long novena to him and on 19th December of the same year, exactly nine months to the day her second son Marie-Joseph-Jean-Baptiste was born. Surely even the most sceptical amongst us will realise that Zélie Martin saw in the birth of this second son a direct answer to her prayers?

Her tragedy was that she could no longer feed her own infants and they had to go out to be wet-nursed. Hopes and fears tormented every hour of every day while the child was away. All she could think of and dream of and delight in was the knowledge that each week that passed brought her nearer to the day when he would be at home with her and she would be able to look after him herself. There is a sadness, a pathos in her own words, 'It is so sweet to attend to little children. If only I had that to do, I think I should be the happiest of women.' That might be the dream but there were also the practical realities of living to be faced and so she goes on, 'But their father and I must work to earn enough for their dowries, otherwise when they are grown up they will not be pleased.'

When the child was three months old the mother realised that all was far from well. He was racked with recurring attacks of bronchitis and would lie panting and exhausted in her arms. There lay ahead of her weeks of daily heartbreak in spite of her faith which grew deeper and stronger as she followed her second son hourly to the gateway of death. On 24th August, 1868, her son died in her arms. His death agony was frightening, he seemed to be suffering so profoundly that Zélie prayed with tears in her eyes for his deliverance from the bondage of the flesh.

There were moments when Zélie found herself wondering whether this second bereavement was a punishment for her striving to bend the ways of God to her own will. The fact that she herself had been weak and ailing through the long months of pregnancy, and that the child itself had little or no resistance to the illness that destroyed him never entered her thoughts. The natural order had long ceased to be her habitation. If there were moments when she had doubts about their death and found herself wondering why St Joseph had not taken better care of his protegés she never expressed them to anyone.

In spite of the fact that his wife was worn out with overwork and the strain of constant pregnancies, and knowing that the cancerous growth was spreading yet apparently doing nothing to see if anything could be done to alleviate the ravages of the dread disease, Louis Martin talked quite openly of their having more children. His only proviso was that neither himself, his wife, nor the nun sister should seek in any way to intervene with the workings of providence, they should leave it to God to decide whether they should be sons or daughters.

Not long afterwards Zélie Martin's aged father died and it seemed to her that she must be doomed to a life lived in the shadowy places of suffering and death. On 28th April, 1869, another daughter was born, Marie-Céline, and although there were times when Zélie doubted whether she would live she grew stronger month by month and the mother's happiness seemed complete, and she could jokingly say, 'At present I have everything but trouble'. There would almost appear to be an underlying note of irony in the words, for in February of the following year, Marie-Hélène, who had been a strong and healthy child and had hardly had a day's illness since she was born died suddenly. The doctor who had been called in to see her because she was unwell had not himself recognised the seriousness of her condition.

The mother partly blamed herself for what really was negligence on the doctor's part. The elder children were distraught when they heard the news of the loss of a sister who had become so much part of their own lives. Louis Martin, who had made no secret of the fact that Hélène was his favourite, felt that his own heart was breaking at this new sorrow that had entered into the family circle. He would sit for hours, withdrawn from the rest of the family, in that aloneness that is the companion of a deep and exhausting sadness, and would repeat to himself the words of Chateaubriand:

> Ah, who will give me back my mountain,
> And the ancient oak and my Hélène?
> Their memory fills me every day with pain.

There is an almost frightening poignancy in a letter that Zélie wrote at this time.

> Sometimes I imagine myself slipping away very gently like my little Hélène. I assure you I scarcely cling to life since I lost that child. However, those who remain need me and for their sakes I pray that God will give me a few years longer in this world.

Doubts were there, taunting her all the while with the terrifying thought that perhaps she had been mistaken in her assurance that God had a special meaning for her marriage and a special purpose for her life. Despair sought to destroy her faith as she pondered on the mysteries that death had opened up to her. The two elder girls, Marie and Pauline, had settled down happily at the boarding school at Le Mans run by the Visitation nuns, and were under the vigilant eye of her saintly sister. Her two sons and her darling Hélène were in the grave. Léonie was becoming more of a problem child than ever, and she herself knew that as the swelling increased in her breast, and as she found herself facing constant recurring bouts of pain her days were definitely numbered. Even her daily attendance at Mass, which had become part of the pattern of her spiritual life, and her constant recourse to prayer had in them an aridity and sterility that almost made a mockery of her faith in the One to whom she had entrusted the care of herself and her family.

Her purpose, in fact it would be true to state that it was the whole object of her marriage, the making of a saint seemed doomed to frustration. Had she been mistaken? Was it all an empty dream in a world of menacing shadows? The question seemed to be always haunting her and out of the gathering darkness that surrounded her there seemed to be no answer forthcoming. In spite of the fact that she had proved herself a willing wife and a perfect mother, and had built up a very successful business as well as fulfilling all her marital and domestic duties, Zélie Martin knew and understood perfectly that her kingdom had never been of this world. At the altar on the day of her marriage she had vowed herself to be a dedicated vessel for the Lord's will. In those early months of enforced celibacy she had bent her will to the greater will that she believed had within it the ordering of her days. In the birth of her first three daughters she had seen a taunting and testing and in the death of her two sons she had been perplexed at the vicissitudes that dogged her steps.

Can we wonder that she should have knelt in prayer asking in the simplest terms for some sign, some revelation that her ideals and hopes and aspirations were not all part of an empty and idle dream? The answer came once more from the cloisters of the convent, from her sister, who was for her the veritable voice of divine wisdom.

> One day your faith and trust that never flinched will have a magnificent reward. Be sure that God will bless you and that the measure of your sorrows will be that of the consolation reserved for you. For after all, if God is pleased with you and wills to give you the great saint you have so desired for His glory will you not be well repaid?

How had Louis Martin, the background figure who always appears in half-light in all the biographies of this perplexing and bewildering family, fared when faced with the vicissitudes that fate seemed to pursue him with throughout the years? It is an obvious question to ask, but an extremely difficult one to answer as we have little upon which to base our attitude and outlook towards the father of the Martin family. He never appears in the round as a whole and complete portrait in any of the scrappy accounts we have of his own life. The short biography of him by his daughter Céline, Sister Geneviève of the Holy Face, must be studied with many reservations for it is so obviously a piece of carefully manufactured near-hagiography that it would not be admitted as evidence in any court of law. When Céline wrote this little monograph her sister had already been canonised and there were already those who thought that the cause of her parents ought to be entered as well.

Let us try and catch a glimpse of the real man behind the over-sanctified exterior that has been created of him so that we can fully understand the many tangled threads that go to the make-up of this amazing story. At this time he was 44 years of age, a well built austere figure who might well have been mistaken for a schoolmaster, a church warden, or a minor dignitary of the town. He was well liked by the few who knew him intimately, but his popularity was not of the boisterous, hail-fellow, well-met type for he allowed no one to approach him with any undue familiarity. His charitable words were a basic part of his Christian vocation and if they led to a certain amount of smugness in his character this means that he was no worse and no better than many of his Catholic contemporaries.

I do not think we have any evidence at all to suggest that he was either a happy or a contented man, and from reading the few contemporary documents that exist about him he obviously had no sense of humour. His God smacked far too much of the 'Vengeance is mine' figure of the Old Testament rather than the Galilean carpenter's son who was the embodiment of the all-embracing love of the Gospels. Like Kierkegaard his inner life was always on the edge of fear and trembling, and his ears were constantly listening for the sounds of doom and damnation. If he was self-centred it was largely because of the constant frustrations that surrounded his days.

His selfishness, his arrogance, and his domineering manner would be seen today not as inherent faults in his personality, but as defence mechanisms that were essential to him if he was to adjust himself to the dark places that always seem to be threatening him with destruction. When he thought of his youth, of that high vision of the mountain top that had led him to seek entrance to the monastery of St Bernard, he found himself wondering why God had not found him an acceptable disciple for his profound inner call of the spirit.

When he considered the bewildering nature of his call to the married state that seemed by its very nature to have robbed him of his self-dedication to celibacy, its major objective seemed doomed to failure as he considered the early death of his two sons who might have replaced him at the altars of the church. When he pondered about his daughters he could not escape from a consideration of the worldly temptation to which women seemed in his eyes to be particularly heir to.

If the gateway to the cloistered seclusion had been closed to him he had found something of its meaning in his long walks, his hours fishing on the river bank, and the spiritual pilgrimages that had become part of the pattern of his life. If he had been refused the sanctuary of a monk's cell, he had built for himself a hermit's retreat in the Pavilion, the little two-storied haven to which he stole away so often to lose himself in prayer, in meditation, and in the reading of the spiritual classics of the inner life. Had he not been a loyal and obedient son of the church he might well have become a quietist, listening only to the inner voice of the spirit, and relying on its messages entirely in mapping out his pathway to heaven.

We must, in all fairness to Louis Martin, recognise that in all matters appertaining to the spiritual life he sought the advice of his parish priest, and in all problems relating to the dangers of sin he acted upon the guidance of his confessor. Human beings are fallible, and while it is obvious that the clerics to whom Louis Martin constantly turned for advice strove to assist him to the best of their ability they could not be expected to fully comprehend the tortured way he had made for himself out of the pathway of the spiritual life.

The prophetic utterance from the sister-nun in the convent at Le Mans had a profoundly calming effect upon the life of Zélie. The dead had buried their dead and her duty was with the living, her hope lay in the future. Europe might be in the throes of conflict but the house at Alençon was a still centre, a hallowed place that had been specially selected by God for the unfolding of His will.

Early in 1870 she knew she was pregnant again and although she still longed for another son she was quite happy to accept whatever God should send her. The only thought that troubled her was her inability to nurse her own babies, and she had hopes of finding a wet-nurse in the town so that she could take her into her own home and thus supervise the upbringing of her infant from its first days in the cradle.

On 17th August, 1870, Marie-Mélanie-Thérèse was born, and in spite of her own suffering the mother decided to attempt to nurse the child herself. Her attempts, that verged on folly in view of her shrunken paps and diseased breast were completely abortive and the baby's health steadily declined. A woman was found in Alençon who claimed she could feed the child, but whose avariciousness had led her to lie about her supply of natural milk for the puny infant. It was only when it was too late that the mother discovered that the so-called nurse was starving the child, drastic steps were taken to try and remedy the harm that had already been done. In the early hours of the morning of 8th October Louis Martin set out for Heloup in order to try and find another nurse. The woman he sought out was sick herself and when he arrived back home it was to find that the two-month-old baby had died on her mother's lap after a two-hour death agony. Zélie's sadness was too deep for tears. Was heaven mocking her? Were the scales of providence weighted against her?

By the January of the following year the war in Europe had reached the outskirts of Alençon itself. The National Guard of which Louis Martin was a member had been called out. Enemy soldiers had been billeted on the Martin household. The nine men appear to have been the usual motley mixture one always finds among troops who are on the move. One, who was gentle and more reserved than the rest, gained Zélie's sympathy and she gave him some of their own food to help out his meagre rations. Another attempted to steal jewellery from the shop but Louis successfully fought with him, got the articles he had stolen back from him and threw him out of the house.

These things served to turn Zélie's attention away from her own sorrows and led her to consider the tragic situation that appeared to be threatening her own little town. Once more she looked for and hoped and prayed for a miracle. The same day on which the soldier, who had attempted to steal the jewellery was tried, 17th January, the Blessed Virgin appeared to two children at Pontmain, and the whole of the town rejoiced feeling that salvation had come to them through Divine intervention as it had done to France centuries earlier through the sanctified valour of Joan of Arc. The three years that followed were not easy ones for the Catholics in France. The Pope was a prisoner in the Vatican, the anti-clerical movement seemed to be gaining new force everywhere, and the spread of atheistical socialism brought dismay to the hearts of the faithful all over the country.

At the time of the apparition at Pontmain Louis Martin, himself a French patriot who saw his country as destined by heaven to save Europe from the materialism that threatened on every side, often spoke of the Maid of Orleans and of the need for another saint, who should embody within herself those virtues that would uplift the people of France and give a new vision of God's meaning and message to the world. And Zélie pondered these things in her heart and found herself wondering if God had taken away her sons in order that one of her daughters might prove to be the saint for whom she and her husband longed.

If this were true, if this was the thing to which they had been called then all the pain, all the sufferings, all the bereavements might be part of a splendid purpose that one only dare whisper about with bated breath. Was her own illness, the dreadful disease that was slowly eating her away, part of the necessary purification for such an event? Was her strange and in some ways bewildering marriage to find its meaning and spiritual fruition in a destiny so overwhelming that it could only be contemplated in the silent sanctuary of her private prayers?

In July 1871, Louis Martin, who had sold his jewellery business and moved into the house that Zélie's parents had left them in the rue Saint Blaise. His earnings together with the additional income his wife had brought into the home with her lace-making had enabled them to put by sufficient capital for both of them to move into an easier way of living. Zélie would still continue to employ her lacemakers but even she could take life more quietly and ease off a little from the long and arduous labours that had been so much part of her married life.

By the early autumn of 1872 Zélie knew she was pregnant again. Her neighbours, seeing her physical condition, whispered among themselves about the scandal of a husband whose wife had had eight children, four of whom had died in their infancy, and who was herself a very sick woman indeed, burdening her womb with yet another child. Louis himself was worried and it needed all the reassurances of his wife to console him. Zélie knew that the little home on the rue Saint Blaise was about to be enriched by a 'great event'. She had, in some mysterious way a foreknowledge that she was in perfect union with God and had been called out by Him for an end that she herself could not comprehend.

As she whispered the words of the Magnificat they seemed to have a meaning especially for her alone. The father, the mother, and the future incarnate as seen in the child; the mystical union of Christ with His Church; the vows of the nun as she pledges herself to her Celestial Bridegroom, these were the thoughts that were constantly in Zélie Martin's mind during the closing months of this, her final pregnancy.

On Thursday, 2nd January, in the year 1873, the one who was later to refer to herself as a 'little winter flower', Marie-Françoise-Thérèse Martin was born. The news of the birth spread rapidly through the streets of the town. In one house, a father who had been saved from starvation by the kindness of the Martins handed to his son a slip of paper and instructed him to take it round to the house on the rue Saint Blaise immediately. It was addressed to Louis and Zélie Martin and on it were written these words:

> Smile, grow up with speed.
> All summon thee to joy;
> Gentle care, tender love,
> Yes, smile at the dawn,
> Bud just enclosed,
> Thou shalt be a rose someday.

Idle phrases, cheap doggerel, sentimental balderdash! As you will, but the hand of God had moved across the earth, and a saint had been born in a little house in Normandy whose roses were destined to shed of their fragrance to the whole world.

CHAPTER III

The Divine Holocaust

Zélie Martin had reached a crisis in her personal and spiritual life. Her marriage, that she had seen as an act of obedience rather than the call of personal love appeared to have been beset with doubts and difficulties. The sons both she and her husband had hoped and prayed for her had died in infancy. These, who were to have been her Samuels, her offering to God for His ministry, were in heaven. Louis had his own life, the quiet peace of his long walks in the countryside; the solitude of fishing as he sat watching his rod and line and pondering upon the eternal verities; his spiritual pilgrimages when he went in search of divine favours and heavenly grace; and above and beyond all these the beloved Pavilion, the hermit's cell, the thing that was in many ways the Alpha and Omega of his existence.

Her daughters Pauline and Marie were progressing well as boarders at the school run by the Visitation Sisters at Le Mans. Léonie was still the problem child of the family, not the black sheep for the Martins did not even accept the possibility of an outcast such as this forming part of the family circle, but a grey lamb that needed careful guidance if it was to find its proper place in the family circle. Céline, who filled the house with happiness and laughter was a joy to all who knew her. Thérèse, her mother's eyes filled with tears of joy as she looked at her lying in her cot, this was her saint, this was the infant who had sung to her while it still lay in the womb.

She was a sick woman, a little tired of the burden of living and of the strain of constant childbirth. Thérèse had been God's gift, His benediction fulfilling the hopes of the passing years. If this were so, and within her heart she accepted it as such without question, why had He not given her the full breast of a triumphant mother so that she might enjoy to the full her parenthood by suckling the infant at her own breast? The tumour in her breast had grown much worse and she could not help but notice the red swelling as she attempted to nurse her new-born child. Her task was a hopeless one at the outset, and within a few days it seemed as though the infant might end in a similar way to her two brothers and two sisters, and die before she was a few weeks old. There was not enough milk in the mother's breast to meet the baby's needs, and probably the little there was was of a poor quality owing to the state of the mother's own health. The baby sickened, vomiting and diarrhoea racked its little body with pain, and one

43

evening as Zélie sat watching it struggling for breath in its tiny cot she knew that her attempts to rear it herself were doomed to failure.

All night long she was pursued by shadows of hopelessness and frustration that seemed to people the room like ghostly shapes mocking at her inner conviction that this child was one who had been given special graces by the angels at her baptism. Death seemed so near and there was nothing to ease her own sense of frustration and heartbreak. Long before dawn broke she had wrapped up the child in blankets, laid it in its cot, and set off to walk to the village of Semalle to seek the service of Rose Taille, the robust wife of a farmer who had wet nursed another of her children. It was a long and lonely road, robbers it was said often hid in the wooded places to attack the unwary passer-by, but to Zélie the possibility of death by violence was nothing compared to the need to save her ailing child.

At first Rose was unwilling to take on the duties of wet nurse. It meant leaving home and neglecting her own husband and family. Her husband was adamant about the idea of her going back to Alençon even to save the life of an ailing infant. Zélie pleaded with both of them and in the end, a little ungraciously, Rose agreed to go back for one week and then to bring the baby back with her to the farm in order that she could tend to its needs and at the same time help her husband and look after her own family.

They were hardly half a mile away from the farmhouse when Rose's eldest boy came running up to them and stated that his father had changed his mind and that Rose must return home immediately. At that moment the life of a future saint hung in the balance, but fortunately Rose scolded the boy and told him to go back home and inform her wayward husband that she would be back as she had promised in a week's time. When they arrived at the house on the rue Saint Blaise at Alençon, Rose gave one look at the frail-looking infant and muttered that here was a hopeless task, adding that soon another infant would join its brothers and sisters in the little cemetery on the edge of the town.

Leaving Rose to attempt to revive the child with the warm milk from her healthy breasts Zélie crept upstairs and offered a special prayer to St Joseph, pleading his help since she was sure that this child had been bestowed even before its birth with special graces. The pious ones will look upon what followed as yet another miracle; the sceptics will see it as the rational outcome of the healthy ministrations of the farmer's wife, but the wiser ones will recognise that both heaven and earth played their part in these vital moments in this drama. When Zélie returned to the living room Thérèse had had a sound feed and was lying peacefully asleep in Rose's arms.

As the week progressed the child grew stronger each day, and a wonderful light of thankfulness shone out of Zélie's eyes. She knew that she must accept the inevitable and let Rose take Thérèse back home with her to the farm but the very thought of parting, even if only for a short time, with this the last and in some ways her loveliest of her offspring was an agony and a heartbreak to Zélie Martin. Even the happy company of little Céline could not rob the home of an emptiness once Thérèse had gone back to Semalle to become part of the farmer's own family.

It would be impossible for anyone who has studied the life of Zélie Martin to suggest that she was anything other than an eminently practical, simple, down-to-earth woman, whose life was lived in complete obedience to the teachings of the Catholic Church and the guidance of her confessor. As a craftswoman she excelled, as a housewife and mother she was a paragon of perfection, as a woman she lived in as perfect a charity towards others as it is possible for any human being to do. The workers she employed all recognised in her an honesty and fairness in her dealings with them that made her an outstanding example of Christian benevolence. Her servants loved and respected her and her neighbours saw in her the embodiment of love and understanding. The fact that she went to Mass every morning at five-thirty called forth a certain amount of sarcastic comment among some of the townspeople, but then, they said when they considered her good works, 'Everybody has some idiosyncrasy and Zélie Martin certainly does no one any harm, and if it gives her pleasure who are we to say nay to it?' Her daughters, particularly the two eldest ones, found in her an endless source of comfort and understanding and her husband saw in her the perfect wife, the congenial companion and the one who shared with him a deep and passionate desire for spiritual perfection.

In spite of the above facts, and I have stressed them to give due emphasis to the next phase in our story, I am convinced that Zélie Martin during the final phase of her life passed through a series of crucial experiences that have been defined by writers on mystical theology as 'the Dark Night of the Soul'. Those who experience this very profound development of their own inner life know it as a period of interior purification that is always accompanied by intense suffering. In this state they realise a sense of aloneness, an isolation that is terrifying to the normal self. They fulfil the promise that there are those 'in the flesh who shall see God'.

One important point that must be fully recognised if we are to enter into and try to understand this aspect of the soul's pilgrimage is that the Catholic Faith has always denied any form of dualism. There are not two realms, one of God and the other of the Devil. There are not two spheres, the one of good and the other of evil. There are not two worlds, the spiritual and the material. All is part of one ordered existence and everything that happens is an opportunity to know within oneself the fullness of the love of God. The Creator and the creature are part of a perfect unity, 'the Word was made flesh and dwelt amongst us' we must remember, and the Word, the proclamation of and the promise of redemption, finds its perfection as the creature strives with the whole of his being to embody in himself the will of his Creator. Life is no longer a pendulum swinging between the heart and the mind. It is a constant and deliberate focussing upon the Good, and even the most trivial event in the daily round is disciplined in such a way as to contribute towards a final harmony.

Zélie Martin sought, and I am convinced found, this truth in her unflinching acceptance of what each day brought to her, seeing in each moment of the day an opportunity to play her part in what was the fulfilment of her own vocation, the making of a saint.

For a few weeks all went well at the farmhouse, and then late one night Zélie was summoned as the child seemed to be sickening to death once more. The doctor who accompanied her on this journey expressed grave doubts as to whether her child would live, but it recovered and once more all seemed well.

No sooner was the baby out of danger than another fear entered the mother's heart. This time it was the serious illness of her eldest daughter Marie, who had been stricken with typhoid while at school at Le Mans. She was brought home to be nursed, and Pauline, the second daughter, had to stay on at the convent for her Easter holidays. For the five weeks that the girl was in danger the mother hardly left her bedside.

Death that she had seen so often seemed to hover like a grim shadow over the household once again. Louis Martin made yet another of his spiritual pilgrimages, this time to a sacred shrine fifteen miles away from home to intercede to the heavenly powers to save the life of his child. Whether it was careful nursing or divine intervention is a question that will never be answered. The fact is that by Ascension day his daughter had recovered and was well enough to go out for a short walk in the town.

Thérèse Martin was growing into a buoyant and healthy child in the clean air and open fields of the farm. When Rose went to help in the fields she trundled her along with her in a wheelbarrow and made her a bed in a mound of hay. When at morning and in the evening she went along to milk the cows she tied the baby on to the beast's back where it lay and gurgled contentedly while Rose carried on with the milking. A deep bond of affection had grown up between the foster mother and the Martin baby. Wherever Rose went Thérèse must go with her, and if she was left behind she cried vociferously until Rose appeared again.

There was always to be one person who mattered supremely to Thérèse throughout her all too short life. Rose, her foster mother, to whom she was a paragon in every way, her mother, Zélie, to whom she was a little angel, her father, Louis, who looked upon her as his little queen, her sister, Pauline, who saw her as a daughter bequeathed to her by God that she might aid in perfecting His will in the unfolding pattern of sanctity, but above and beyond all these even from her earliest infancy, Jesus, the Bridegroom she would seek for, pledge herself to and serve until that final and perfect consummation in a divine marriage.

Zélie found herself suffering from constant headaches. The days seemed to drag out to infinity and the nights appeared to have neither beginning nor end. Questions, doubts, fears, all battering in on her from every side. A loneliness, a standing apart from all she loved in a dreaded isolation that seemed to open up to her the veritable pit of hell itself. Her prayers, the consolation she had found in them throughout the troubled years seemed to have become an empty jumble of words, idle phrases terrifying in their meaningless repetition. It was only her resolute will and her inner knowledge that in God alone would she find her ultimate consummation that she found the strength to say to herself 'though He slay me yet will I trust in Him'.

Zélie Martin knew that she was slowly dying and yet in spite of this, in moments of tranquillity, she would still daydream of the time when all her children were grown up and capable of fending for themselves, and would find a passing happiness in thinking, that then perhaps, in the eventide of life, she might find the peace of the religious vocation that had eluded her in her earlier years.

Pauline, probably in some ways the most practical and matter of fact member of the whole family, had already sensed within herself a move towards the religious life. Marie had come home for good and had agreed to act as teacher to Céline. Thérèse, who was not three years old, had decided that she too must take part in the lessons as well.

Let us take a glimpse into the schoolroom where the two children were Marie's pupils. Céline sat engrossed in the book she was learning to read, or listening attentively to her teacher's words, while Thérèse, wide blue-eyed and golden haired, sat bolt upright on the table enthralled at all she heard, proving in spite of her tender years that she was a very apt pupil. In the early evenings Zélie and Louis would listen to her reciting her alphabet or singing the simple songs she had learned in the schoolroom that afternoon.

A deep bond of affection had sprung up between Thérèse and Céline. They would play together, they would discuss the doings of each day and occasionally would argue about their religious ideas. Quite often the adults who heard them were astounded and bewildered at the profundity of Thérèse's replies to Céline's questions.

'How can God be in such a tiny Host?' Céline asked Thérèse one morning.

Without a moment's pause the apt reply came, 'That is not strange at all for God is almighty and can do whatever He wishes'.

The most learned theologian in the church could not have found an easier, a more logical or a more satisfactory answer.

There was a pleasant custom in those days among Catholic families of taking a loaf of bread with them to Mass in order that the priest might bless it for them. This was to serve as a reminder that every meal is, or ought to be a sacrament of thanksgiving. When Thérèse was too young to go to church with the family on Sunday morning she would wait patiently until she heard familiar footsteps approaching the door of their home. As soon as the door opened she would rush to Céline calling out in a rapturous voice, 'Quick, where is the blessed bread?' and when it was shown to her would take a little, and after a few moments' prayer would eat it believing as she tells us that 'this was her Mass as she was too young to go to the proper service'.

One Sunday no blessed bread was forthcoming. For a few moments Thérèse was disconsolate, her day seemed spoiled, the bread of heaven had not passed her lips to bring leaven to her soul. Desperate needs call for equally desperate remedies and before anyone else realised what was happening she exclaimed, 'We must make some,' and taking a morsel of bread she knelt in prayer, made the sign of the cross over it, and found comfort in the thought that God was everywhere and hence must be in the crumbs that had passed her lips.

Trivialities, childish prattle, foolish games, the sceptic may exclaim. These might be a partial answer if we were dealing with an ordinary child, but they do not explain why in everything she did from the age of three onwards Thérèse's heart, and later her mind, was centred utterly and completely on the love of God. The sacrifices she made might be, in fact many of them were, insignificant in themselves but they all formed part of a pattern of sanctity that was the mainspring of her life.

Although Thérèse Martin's earlier biographers have disagreed about most of the incidents in her life and the religious interpretation that has been placed upon them, they all accept the fact that even in early infancy she was an extremely intelligent child for her age. Some claim she was smug and precocious, others state that she was priggish and wilful, and others still that she was stubborn and spoilt by her parents.

After having carefully studied all the evidence upon which these claims are based I am convinced that none of those who have written about her hitherto have arrived at a proper conclusion about her spiritual development. She was shy and diffident, and this made her appear at times to be a little too self-assertive. She was full of a deep and abiding tenderness, and this was wrongly interpreted as pious humbug. She had a simplicity and innocence that seemed far too precious and otherworldly for most people. Of one thing I am perfectly sure and that is that she was 'God-possessed from the moment of her emergence from her mother's womb'.

When she stated quite calmly that she wished her mother and father would die she was neither careless nor vindictive in her use of words. Death for her had no existence in the eternal order that was her perpetual habitation, and since in human life it was a gateway to complete and perfect happiness it was her desire that Louis and Zélie should know this happiness that led her to make such a strange and bewildering statement. When her sister Léonie pointed to a heap of toys, dolls and doll's clothes that she had outgrown, and asked Thérèse to pick the one she would like, when she exclaimed, 'I choose everything,' this was an involuntary statement of the totality of her need for the love of God.

When after her mother's death she chose Pauline for her second mother it was because she knew that in the perfecting of human relationships we see reflected the divine glory. When she built her little altars, decorating them with flowers from field and hedgerow, and lighting candle stumps before the little cross she had placed there, this was no childish whim but was in fact a conscious exercise in personal sanctification. The idea of God was to her a concrete reality that could only be partially known and experienced in this world, and the whole of her striving towards personal perfection was an expression of her seeking in life the fullness she would only know in its totality beyond death.

In the late autumn of 1876 Zélie Martin visited her sister at the convent at Le Mans for the last time. The nun had been ailing for some months, and it soon became obvious both to the doctor who attended her and the Mother Superior of the Visitation that the consumption that had claimed her for a victim was moving into its final stages. The knowledge that her sister's death was imminent was a terrible blow to Zélie. She realised that she was going to lose the one who had been a source of strength, of courage and of spiritual direction to her for so many years. The bitter gall of unending sorrow seemed to be filling the cup of life for her to the brim.

There is a pathetic ring in a few phrases from a letter she wrote to her daughter Pauline at about this time:

> I do nothing but dream of solitude and the cloister. Now I want to live until I am very old. Then, when all my children are established I can retire into solitude.

The pathos in those lines reveals to us quite clearly the depth of suffering through which this noble, strong and courageous woman was passing. And yet she does not plead for death that would have been a happy release, nor does she ask for life for its own sake, all she desires is to live longer that she might the more fully dedicate herself to the will of God.

On 24th February, 1877, her sister died. The news of her passing, although not unexpected, seemed to create a void, an emptiness for Zélie that nothing would ever fill. There was a quiet happiness as well, a movement towards an inner tranquillity when she read the words of the nun who had sent her the sad news.

> The life of our dear Sister Marie-Dosithée, that was so edifying, closed this morning by a death one might envy. She was quite conscious and preserved an admirable calmness to the end. One evening, almost the last before her death she whispered to our Mother Superior, 'O Mother I have no other thoughts but of love, trust and abandonment. Help me to thank God for it all.'

Love, trust and abandonment, those were just the words that Zélie Martin needed to hear, and it was these things that she strove to embody in her own life in the all too short time that lay ahead of her, Love, the giving of one-self utterly and without reserve into the hands of God. Trust, the willingness to accept without reservation all that came to her knowing it to be the will of God. Abandonment, the complete surrender of herself to the workings of divine providence that she had sought to know and understand all her life.

There was not to be long for her to wait before she would have to put these virtues to their ultimate testing. The growth in her breast grew worse, and there were signs that it was spreading to her neck. The pain became almost a perpetual agony. At last she decided to go and see the local doctor. He was staggered when he saw the calm look in the deep-set eyes of this woman who had come to him to hear her own death warrant. He talked to her about her illness, discussed with her the nature of her pains, and smiling as though to disguise the reality that he realised she knew only too well, said, 'I will mix you a bottle of medicine that you can take every day'.

In an almost cold, and completely unflinching voice his patient asked him, 'Will it do me any good?'

The way the question was asked and the steel-like courage of the woman before him forced the truth out of his lips. 'No, but most of my patients feel I ought to give them something.'

On returning home she told her husband the doctor's verdict and immediately wrote to inform Pauline of the day's news. 'Day's news' may seem an odd phrase to use in circumstances such as I am relating, but that was exactly how Zélie Martin herself treated the matter.

Her husband, who had failed to recognise how ill his wife really was, immediately decided that she must go to see her sister-in-law at Lisieux, and that her brother Isidore Guérin, the chemist, should make an appointment for her to see a famous physician and surgeon who dwelt there. Even the suggestion has an ironical twist for had he suggested this some years before when first the presence of the growth manifested itself an operation might have been possible, and although it would not have cured Zélie it would in all probability have extended her life by some years and eased her suffering to a considerable extent. To Zélie herself the proposed consultation seemed a fruitless errand and when she saw the doctor he simply confirmed what the local doctor had already told her with a bluntness that would have upset most patients that it was too late for anything to be done and that at the most she had only a few months to live. It is worth pausing for a moment to consider the full implications of this statement for the sick woman. Sedatives in those days were a thing of the future, pain-killing drugs completely unknown, and she knew quite clearly and accepted the fact quite dispassionately that before her lay the end of a journey in which every day would be one of ever-increasing agony.

On returning to Alençon from the visit to the doctor at Lisieux, Zélie told her husband of the death sentence she had heard passed upon her the previous day. The very calmness of her announcement cut like a barbed steel into Louis Martin. Zélie, had he simply taken her for granted all these years? Had he been selfish and inconsiderate in his attitude towards her? These thoughts seared his very soul and his own helplessness, when faced with the inevitability of coming events, became a torturing and menacing burden from which there was no escape. All that was left was a feeble flickering flame of hope, Lourdes, the grotto, the pool of miracles, that might be the answer.

Pilgrimages to Lourdes at the time of which I am writing were a much more exclusive and expensive business than they are today. Nowadays it is a common practice each year for every Catholic Church in the country to run tours to Lourdes, Lisieux, and Rome; every diocese in the country organises special weeks for visiting the Holy Places, and even the ordinary tourist agency can cater for the individual needs of any persons who wish to pay a visit to these places. In the closing years of the nineteenth century such a pilgrimage was a very special event and normally only the wealthier members of the Catholic community in the country where it was being organised could afford to take part.

Fortunately for Louis Martin at about the same time that the doctor had given to his wife what was more or less a death warrant, a pilgrimage to

Lourdes was being organised by some of the more influential clergy in the diocese in which he was able to secure places for his wife and the three daughters who were to accompany her on the journey.

Even when his wife was in this desperate state the situation had its ironical twist, for there was some argument between husband and wife as to whether they could afford to pay for the daughters to go as well. Zélie won this battle and on 18th June, 1877, the four of them set out on the journey upon the results of which Louis and the children had set such hopes. Although as an invalid seeking a miraculous cure Zélie Martin could have asked for special travelling concessions, she refused to and instead travelled with the ordinary passengers, many of whom saw the journey more as a pleasure trip than a seeking of spiritual experience.

The passengers who shared their carriage were in some ways a gay and boisterous crowd. The jolting of the railway carriage was very painful indeed to Zélie Martin, the girls were sick for most of the trying journey, and some other occupant of the railway coach who was making coffee on a spirit stove spilled boiling water over the Martins' clothes and belongings. It was a journey on which everything seemed destined to go wrong, for when they arrived at Lourdes they discovered the lodgings that had been allocated to them were so bad that they had to look for somewhere else to stay, a difficult enough task at a time when the town was packed with visitors to the famous grotto. The food was poor, and then Zélie Martin slipped on the roadside tearing her dress and twisting her neck. The latter accident caused her a great deal of pain and discomfort for the cancerous tumours were already spreading through her body and one of them was causing a swelling in the throat.

Each day for four days the Martins took part in the afternoon procession, joining in the litanies, the prayers and the hymns. The mother bathed in the icy cold waters while the three daughters knelt very near to the spot where Bernadette Soubirous had had her apparitions, and prayed to the Lady for their mother's recovery. Each time Zélie was plunged into the water she herself prayed that a miracle might occur. It was not that she was afraid of death but simply that she wanted to live longer if possible to look after her husband and see her daughters settled in the world.

The four-day petitioning, bathing, praying, and hoping were over and no miracle had occurred. Marie, Pauline and Céline, the three girls who had accompanied their mother, were distraught at the savage turn that events had taken. They knew of their mother's goodness, of her unceasing kindness to all who appealed to her for help, of her unfailing charity that was a shining example to all her friends and neighbours. Surely if anyone had a right to a miraculous cure it was Zélie Martin?

The only one who accepted the situation cheerfully was Zélie herself. 'I am learning through Our Lady the lesson that Bernadette had to learn from Our Lady's own lips and that is that I shall know no more happiness on earth and that my true happiness awaits me in heaven.'

The journey home was a sad and depressing business. All of them wondered how their father would react when he faced the fact that a miraculous cure had not been vouchsafed to his wife, and each of the three girls wondered if their own faith was going to prove strong enough to face up to such a bitter disappointment. The most cheerful member of the party was their mother herself. Perhaps a miracle had occurred, the miracle of complete reconciliation of the fact of death that was in itself a source of deep and lasting consolation to the suffering woman. She talked to her daughters quite cheerfully throughout the journey, she even tried to make them laugh occasionally by telling them jokes.

The sad and serious looks on their faces disturbed and alarmed her, and when they spoke to her in grave tones of how difficult they were finding it to sustain their faith she had said quite simply, 'The Blessed Virgin has said as she said to Bernadette, "I will make you happy not in this world but in the next".'

Louis Martin, sustained by an inner strength that had upheld him throughout the years, accepted the disappointment of his wife's returning in a much weaker state than when she left for Lourdes. Marie relied on the assistance of divine grace in order that she might be reconciled to the inevitability of her mother's death. Céline and Thérèse were too young to understand the full implications of the situation that was to face them during the coming months. Léonie, to the surprise and consternation of her relatives, seemed to be indifferent to it all, but the fact is she was hiding her own agony behind a screen of apparent indifference in order not to add to the heavy burden her father was carrying. Pauline still remained rebellious, so much so that on her return to school her mother wrote to her: 'Do not hope for too much happiness on this earth, you will meet with only disappointments. I know by experience the fickleness of earthly joy; if my hope were not indeed centred on heaven I should indeed be unhappy.'

The weeks dragged on and each day saw Zélie Martin growing a little worse. Pain racked the whole of her body. She could not lie down in comfort, yet she could find no ease sitting on a chair. The nagging, gnawing, ruthless pains of the slowly corroding growths in all parts of her body were merciless in the toll they demanded from her. In spite of this she still dragged herself to early Mass, finding comfort and inspiration in receiving the Sacrament from the hands of the parish priest. One Friday she stumbled and fell as she left the church and it was obvious, even to herself, that this would be the last visit she would be able to make while still alive to the place that had meant so much to her.

There was one moment of joy or perfect happiness that was to ease for a moment the dreadful plight of the dying woman. Marie, who was still teaching the two little ones, Céline and Thérèse, arranged a prize-giving for her pupils in the sick room. She decorated the room with flowers and arranged two chairs, draping them with curtains so that they looked like miniature thrones for her mother and father. Bringing the two little ones in they knelt at their parents' knees while their dying mother gave them their prizes and their father his blessing.

During the last few weeks of her illness Thérèse and Céline were sent away each morning to spend the day with a kindly neighbour to avoid their being constant witnesses of their mother's suffering. On 16th August Zélie Martin commenced to make the final preparations for her last journey. She wrote to her brother Isidore at Lisieux, asking him after her death to do all that he could to help to console Louis and the children. Ten days later it was obvious that the end was very near. Pauline had been called home from school, and with her husband and all her children kneeling round her Zélie Martin received the last rites of the Church, its final absolution and solace for a soul about to seek its heavenly habitation. On 28th August, 1877, Zélie Martin died one hour and a half after midnight. She was only forty-six years old.

Thérèse, who was only four years old, showed no fear at all of death. She quietly kissed her mother's corpse on the cheek, and calmly surveyed the coffin as it stood on end in the passage, having to stand on her toes and look right up in the air to see the whole of its lined interior. Louis Martin was distraught at the loss of his wife and it seemed as though no one would be able to comfort him.

After the funeral, as the five girls stood together round the grave the maid said, 'Poor little darlings,' as she looked across at Céline and Thérèse, 'you have no mother now.'

'Yes I have,' said Céline, 'Marie is going to be my new mother.'

Thérèse looked across at Pauline, 'I have a mother too,' she quietly exclaimed, 'Pauline shall be my mother.'

Louis Martin had given up his business after his wife's return from Lourdes and had decided to settle down to a quiet retirement, enjoying the solitude of the Pavilion, the delights of walking and fishing, and above all seeking the spiritual contentment he found in making pious pilgrimages to shrines in the surrounding countryside. After the funeral his brother-in-law wrote and suggested that the family should leave Alençon and come and settle at Lisieux, where he and his wife would be able to help him in the bringing up of the younger children who had always enjoyed playing with their own two children when they had visited them with their mother. At first Louis resisted the idea. Alençon had been his home for so long, his roots were there and the few friends he had made were very precious to him in his bereavement. He considered the possibility of sending the younger children away to school, but his religious scruples led him to reject one school after another.

Marie and Pauline were all in favour of their uncle's idea, and under pressure he finally decided to let his brother-in-law find a house for him at Lisieux, and to go and settle down there for the rest of his days. Louise, the maid, would go with them, Marie could take her mother's place as house-keeper, Pauline could finish her education at the Visitation, and the two younger children could go to the school run by the Benedictine nuns that their cousins attended. And so it was that in November, the same year as his wife's death, Louis Martin and his daughters left Alençon to settle down at Les Buissonnets at Lisieux, this was to be his home until he had to be taken away to an asylum some years later.

CHAPTER IV

The Pathway to Grace

No one with any sense of taste would call Les Buissonnets a pretty house. It is one of those ugly, rather ornate buildings so dear to the heart of mid-Victorians, and you find them sprinkled over the Normandy landscape just as plentifully as you see them in the southern part of England. The house is approached by a narrow straggling pathway leading up from the main road.

Today souvenir stalls stand on the side of this lane and the house itself has become a museum as well as a place of pilgrimage. High walls hide it from the curious gaze of the passing public, and it stands in a pleasant garden rising in terraces to the front of the house and with pleasant lawns at the back. It is much as it was when Louis Martin and his daughters resided there, and it embodies within it an aura of middle class respectability. At the top of the house, reached by a winding stairway is the Belvedere, the private sanctuary that replaced the Pavilion at Alençon as a spiritual retreat, a place of study and meditation for Louis himself.

Louis accepted the move from Alençon to Lisieux with certain reservations. A conservative by nature he disliked the idea of uprooting himself from the place he had lived in for so long and that had so many happy associations for him. His daughters on the other hand were delighted at the thought of their new home. They would be near their aunt and uncle, the Guérins; there would be the little cousins for the younger children to play with, and there was a fine school run by the Benedictine nuns that would be perfect for Céline and Thérèse. One pattern of life had been broken by death, another must be created to serve the needs of the living.

The new developments in their family life had a very profound effect upon Louis Martin. The grief he felt at his wife's death, the sense of guilt he had developed through that event, forced him to recognise that he must take a more active part in looking after the children. I do not wish to give the impression that he was an indifferent father, what I am trying to convey is that he had been so lost in the miasma of other-worldliness that he had not perhaps paid sufficient attention to the practical affairs of his own family. He had built up a good business as a jeweller, watch and clockmaker. He had, in latter years, taken an active part in his wife's lace-making ventures. He had saved enough money to settle down to the completion of his daughters' education and a comfortable retirement. He was in every sense of the word a perfect example of middle-class respectability at its best and its worst. A devout Catholic, subject at times to periods of spiritual melancholia; an engaging companion when travelling, and travel was one of his main joys, next to reading and fishing; an honest and upright father, once one accepted his limitations, but at heart a selfish man when his own interests were threatened.

Zélie Martin's death had had a strange and in some ways bewildering effect on Thérèse herself. The physical fact of death did not frighten her, but it left her with a sense of emptiness and a feeling of desolation. The need for personal love was always to play a dominant role in her own spiritual development, while the realisation of its inadequacy, even when it found its expression on the highest level, was one of the major factors that led to her sanctification. The more she moved outwards to find pleasure in earthly things, only to find them turn to dust and ashes, the more she was driven inwards to seek heavenly joys that she knew were the only things that were everlasting.

I feel that I must digress a little from my main story to say something about the whole process that I have called sanctification. It is the ultimate objective of the soul's quest and within it is contained the vision of the artist, the dream of the poet, the consolation of music, and the complete fulfilment of the innermost needs of the human spirit. Man, as I see him, is a religious animal, and if God had not existed man would have invented him to make life tolerable and give it meaning.

Most of us, if we are prepared to be completely honest with ourselves, recognise the frailty of physical sensation even at the most refined level to give us any lasting satisfaction. The consummation of physical love is a death and resurrection, and unless out of it we build emotional reserves of friendship, tolerance and understanding, we soon find our appetites satisfied, and seek some new object with which to continue our experimental search for ultimate fulfilment. Even the deepest and most profound emotional experiences are not sufficient in themselves to satisfy the heart's longings. A change of mood, even a change in situation can have a devastating effect upon our deepest associations. The mind striving perpetually in a philosophic gymnasium cannot give us that wholeness we seek. Even a sceptical materialist like Bertrand Russell admits that 'the good life is one guided by love and upheld by knowledge'. The poet John Keats came much nearer to the heart of the matter when he exclaimed, 'I believe in the truth of the imagination and the holiness of the heart's affections'.

Timelessness, that inner serenity that is not plagued by either the rising of the moon or tormented by the setting of the sun is what all of us are really seeking. We may deny it, denounce it, try to curse it out of existence, but the very bitterness of our denial, the savage irony of our denunciation, the arrogant blasphemy of our words; all these things are in themselves a negative affirmation of its ultimate claim to our allegiance. The saints are those who give an unreserved affirmation to the supremacy of the life of the spirit and whose sole objective is to embody that life in its fullness in themselves.

Every student of sanctity knows perfectly well that age, family background, physical environment, have nothing to do in themselves with the unfolding of sainthood. They may in some ways be detrimental to self-fulfilment as in the case of St Francis of Assisi. On the other hand they may aid the saint every step of the way as did the family of Thérèse Martin. There may be those who will argue that this girl was too young in years, too inexperienced in the way and discipline of the inner life to have been aware of her purpose at the tender age of four and a half years. I am convinced they are wrong for after a very careful and detailed examination of all the relevant facts I am sure that even at that age she had within her the capacity for singleness, for seeing the part as only finding itself within the whole, for recognising the need for an unceasing disciplining of the body, the emotions and the mind. It is true that she writes of her own spiritual development in candy-floss and sugar-flower phrases, but her inadequacy to find literary expression that will satisfy the 'savants' does not in any way invalidate the reality of the experiences about which she is writing.

The family soon settled into their new home. Marie took over the duties of housekeeper, Pauline helped with the education of the two youngsters, Léonie became a pupil at the Benedictine convent school, and Louis Martin idolised his little Thérèse whom he called his 'little queen'. Sedate parties at the Guérins, occasional holidays at Trouville, visits to old friends at Alençon all formed part of the pattern of their days. There was one thought that overshadowed Louis Martin's own life and that was the fear of loneliness, for he knew that Pauline was already contemplating following a religious vocation and he had an inner feeling, an irritating intuition that his other daughters might well follow in her wake.

How Thérèse loved the walks they took together, the swing her father had erected for her in the back garden, the little altar she had built against the far wall. Her pets, the parrots, the birds in the aviary, the silken-coated rabbits, and joy of joys, Tom, the faithful spaniel that had been given to her by her father as a present.

There seemed to be so much goodness, so much tenderness, so much happiness in the world that very often the tears would run down her cheeks at the wonders each day brought to her. Tears would run for other causes as well, for since her mother's death she had become strangely indrawn, extra-sensitive, and the least thing she did that she thought might bring pain or hurt to others would cause her to dissolve in torrents of weeping. These things, tiny acts of disobedience, the occasional assertion of self-will, or the odd fits of moodiness that sometimes possessed her all assumed a tremendous importance in her childish eyes. All she sought after, all she desired was love, and anything that brought pain to anyone around her was a sin against that perfection in love that she had made her life's goal.

First thing every morning she would rush to her father's room to hug and kiss him and assure him of her undying affection. Pauline, the new mother she had selected for herself, was perfect in all things and what she did must be imitated by her in her own little way. Céline, dear sister Céline, the perfect companion both in the schoolroom and out in the garden sharing in her games. Above and beyond all these, outside the orbit of earthly affection with its failings and shortcomings, Our Lady, the Mother of God Himself, to whom she gave an unstinted devotion.

The whole of the day was hedged in and surrounded by simplicity. Morning prayers, the daily dedication of oneself to God. Lessons to be undertaken very seriously as through these she could learn to read the books in her father's shelves up in the Belvedere that held an endless fascination for her. The daily visit to one of the churches in the town, her favourite of which was the one dedicated to Our Lady of Victories. Swinging so high when her father gently pushed her into the air that at moments she felt she was almost touching heaven. Making endless little sacrifices, unknown to anyone except herself in the dawning realisation that it was only through personal suffering that one could aspire to personal purification. A strange kind of life you may think for a child of such tender years, but remember Thérèse Martin was no ordinary child, she was a God-possessed creature who in humility and love strove every moment of the day to subject herself to the will of her Creator.

The picture of family life, and I assure you it is not overdrawn, is one that is as near to perfection as human beings can make it. Marie busy supervising the running of the home; Pauline painting exquisite miniatures on wood and ivory; Céline trying very hard to master the principles of drawing and painting, and Thérèse working at some easy piece of embroidery at which the older girls were already experts. Those wonderful winter evenings when as dusk fell and the lamps were trimmed and lighted Thérèse would rush upstairs calling out as she went, 'Papa, papa, the lamp is lit' and wait anxiously for her father to come down from his attic room where he had been lost in study and meditation to either have a game of draughts with one of his older daughters or read to them from one of the spiritual books of which he was so fond. Dom Gueranger's *The Liturgical Year* was a favourite with all, and Pauline would often explain to Thérèse in simple language the things in it that she was too young as yet fully to understand.

When late spring and early summer days came along there would be meals in the garden, treasure hunts among the rockeries and shrubberies, fishing in the streams of the neighbourhood, and above and beyond all these occasional pilgrimages to local shrines. 'These were supremely happy days,' Thérèse was to write many years later. . .

. . . when my dear 'King' as I called him went fishing and took me with him. Sometimes I tried my hand with a small rod of my own, but more often I preferred to sit on the grass at some little distance. My reflections would then become really deep, and without knowing what meditation meant my soul would be absorbed in prayer.

These were indeed her 'very heaven' moments and she was to know all too few of them in this world. Soon the time arrived when Thérèse and Céline had to go to school and after a family consultation the father decided that they should go as day scholars to the school run by the Benedictine nuns that their cousins the Guérins attended. Thérèse was good at her lessons and meticulous in the work she had to take home to complete. In some ways she was an unpopular child with the other girls for she took no part in the round games and childish pranks that formed part of their own lives. She always seemed a little away from it all, and her mood was undoubtedly very much that of the child Jesus when he said, 'Wist ye not that I must be about my Father's business?'

There was, however, no false piety or sanctimonious humbug about her. When one starry night she looked up into the sky and saw Orion with his girdle of stars she mistook the formation for a letter 'T' and said in all seriousness, 'Look papa, my name is written in heaven!' A childish whim or a prophetic voice echoing into the future? This is a question to which we shall never know the answer.

By the spring of 1882 life seemed to have settled down to a simple and pleasant routine in their new home. Pauline gave to Thérèse all the love she needed and more, Marie ran the house very successfully for them all, Céline was busy with her painting lessons, and even Léonie appeared to be taking a much more serious interest in the spiritual factors that formed a solid background to all their lives. Happiness, a deep and abiding sense of inner contentment reigned everywhere. Her father loved taking her for long and solitary walks or, when she had a holiday took her with him for a day's fishing. The joy of playing at being solitaries, the pleasure of spending hours on end with her cousins the Guérins, the ecstasy of decorating the Virgin's statue with spring flowers she had plucked from the fields and hedgerows around Lisieux. All seemed to move to perfection in the white and green splendour of the Normandy countryside. The apple blossoms were like clouds of silver radiance as they swayed gently in the afternoon breeze, or took on the reflected glory of the evening sunshine. Willow catkins tossed their golden heads nonchalantly in the morning hours, harebells hung sedately from their fragile green stems in the hedgerows, and always that incessant splendour of the lark's song from the first flush of dawn to the last violent orange-flamed sky of dusk.

It is true that in many ways their lives were lived out in a very limited environment. Sanctity was the beginning and end for each and every one in their father's view, and it was a sanctity that must be guided and guarded against the snares of the world, the flesh and the devil. Young men were not encouraged to visit them, their social life was restricted to church concerts and socials, their friends were carefully selected for their primness and piety. A narrow world you may think, but to the Martin family it pointed from temporality to the limitless horizons of eternity. Heaven was their immediate destination and every step they took must be disciplined so that it formed part of a continuous journey.

The inner life of Thérèse Martin although she was only a girl of thirteen was having a profound formative influence on her day by day activities. She was gay and abandoned in her sense of a not yet fully realised vocation. She was forever seeking inside herself and through her conversations with her beloved Pauline to find her way towards a dimly sensed but nevertheless very real call to the cloister.

How had the desert fathers of old found God? Why had the hermits withdrawn themselves from the world to live lives of solitary contemplation? What went on behind the high walls of Carmel that she often gazed upon with a mixture of fear and wonder as she passed them on her way to school? Her father talked to her of the meaning of the life of prayer. Her sister told her in simple phrases something of the hidden mystery of a nun's search for perfection. Her confessor explained to her why the soul must constantly seek rededication and repurification if it was to find and lose itself in the Love of God. All these things had a personal message and a profound meaning for little Thérèse. One day, very quietly, but with a persistence in her tone that surprised the listener she confided to Pauline that her whole heart was set on entering Carmel. Only there would she find solace and satisfaction, refuge and release. Only there would she learn to enjoy that divine felicity that was the source and the goal of her soul's pilgrimage.

Strange thoughts, odd ideas, we may think for so young a child. Was she becoming slightly unbalanced? Was her adolescent religious fervour surrendering her to a fantasy that might in the end destroy her? Had the hot house of her infancy forced the growing plant to what might turn out to be a freak blooming? The answer to all these questions and the hundred others that torment us when we consider this, the most formative period of her life, is a definite 'No'. Thérèse Martin, child of Zélie and Louis Martin, already saw herself as a daughter of heaven whose whole life was to be spent in adoration and pursuit of a heavenly bridegroom. Sanctity was her natural habitation, and in the years that lay ahead it was to lead her to her celestial splendour.

Even Pauline, who probably knew her better than any other member of the family was a trifle nonplussed at the turn that events were taking. She discussed the problem with her father. She talked it over with her elder sister Marie. She sought advice from the parish priest and in the end decided to seek an interview with the Mother Superior of Carmel to see what advice she had to offer. Thérèse walked beside her sister with a light heart and dancing feet when the morning came for her to go along with Pauline to the parlour of the convent where they could discuss her hopes and dreams of the future with the Mother Superior herself. At first the grille frightened her a little. It made that inner world she longed for seem something she was barred from, a faraway and distant place into which she would never find an entrance.

The Mother Superior talked first of all to Pauline, questioning her very closely about the whole of Thérèse's life. Then she turned and with a supreme gentleness talked to the child herself. The simple and direct answers that Thérèse gave to her questions startled and stimulated her. Thirteen, a tender age indeed to seek admittance to one of the most austere orders of the Church. Eighteen at the earliest was the usual age for novices. With a wisdom and directness far beyond her years Thérèse pleaded her case and in the end the Mother Superior agreed that if she was still as certain of her vocation when she was sixteen she would consider allowing her to enter the convent as a novice.

Meanwhile the winds of change were blowing around Les Buissonnets. A subtle, almost imperceptible feeling of dissatisfaction with life as it was, was causing each member of the household to react in a different way to the changing circumstances that surrounded them. Marie, running the home felt a sense of imprisonment and wondered where if anywhere there was an escape from the ceaseless round of chores. Pauline, very much her mother's daughter, knew within her own heart that she too was being called to Carmel. Céline, clever with her pen and brush found refuge in an inner realm of fantasy where she saw herself as an artist, a social butterfly, perhaps eventually to take the salons of Paris by storm. Léonie, rather plain and definitely matter-of-fact, was still the outsider, the one who did not quite fit in to Louis Martin's ideas of the pattern for the perfect family.

Even the most generous of their critics, if he impartially examines the facts at our disposal, will be forced to admit that the Martin family were all disciplined into what for most people would seem an abnormal way of life. The world pressed in too closely upon them, its temptations beset them at every side. Their father was determined that it should not claim them for its own, and with the best of possible intentions denied them the normal companionship that most girls and young women find in life. Boy friends were frowned upon; the only members of the male sex they came into contact with were at the social functions run by the church. Their reading must be carefully selected and it must never be lighthearted or frivolous. Their leisure hours must be spent in painting, embroidery, and in prayer. They were hedged in by prejudices that were not of their own making and no one can be surprised to learn that all of them took to the cloister in the end.

One of the major difficulties that faces any author who attempts in all honesty to tell this strange, fascinating, and as I see it enlightening story, is that all the witnesses are engaged in a series of special pleading that swaddles up the truth and at times distorts the facts in such a way that you end in a kind of exasperated stupor. The mother's and father's life was not written until many years after their death, and then by one of their daughters who had entered Carmel. They emerge from her writing of them as ghostlike figures belonging much more to the sentimental world of an old maid's memories than from the real world in which they lived.

The books written on the family as a whole all suffer from the same error. They are determined, at all costs, that none of the Martin family shall escape beyond the incense-hung cloudiness of a darkened sanctuary. There is no danger of your being called upon to entertain angels unawares, you are all too aware of the fact that they have become crystallised into angels and as such appear to have little truck with the mortal clay out of which we all are made.

By reading and re-reading the letters that have been preserved, by seeking for furtive hints and half-formulated statements about them in the many biographies that have been written, you do occasionally come across a creature of flesh and blood and are then faced with the equally difficult task of tracking down this creature until it becomes a person in its own right and not a glorified name in a gaudily illuminated address.

It is imperative at this point to take a much closer look at Pauline Martin as she is destined to be one of the major figures in our story. Some of those who have written of her have portrayed her for us as a sort of female Machiavelli, a diabolical woman using all her power to gain her own ends, the glorification of her own family. They point out that she prompted Thérèse to defy the orders of the parish priest, to stand out against the authority of the Bishop, even to challenge the authority of the Pope himself.

Didn't Thérèse write her famous biography under her direct instruction? Wasn't it Pauline, as Mother Agnes of Jesus, who censored it before she allowed it to go out to be read by the outside world? Didn't she persuade the convent authorities to allow her sister Céline, herself a nun, to have a camera in the cloister and take endless photographs of Thérèse when she herself had assumed the religious habit? Hadn't she had these same photographs retouched to present to the world a completely false picture of her sister? Hadn't she misused her authority as Mother Prioress of Carmel at the time of the opening of her sister's cause to force some of the nuns in the community to falsify their evidence to the commission set up to examine the evidences for Thérèse's sanctity? Didn't she even try to get her father and mother canonised as well, and with this object in view persuaded her sisters to write distorted and garbled versions of their lives?

Formidable questions these, and relentless arguments against the whole case of Thérèse Martin's saintliness if they are true. The simple fact is that all of them are distortions of the real facts, and all of them have been used in turn by those who would seek to destroy the spiritual wonder that lies in the life and legend of the Little Flower of the Child Jesus, the name by which Thérèse Martin is more familiarly known.

Pauline Martin's own life falls into four distinct periods, each one developing from and growing out of the others. In her girlhood she was her mother's confidante, the one to whom Zélie Martin poured out so much about her own hopes and fears in life, and to whom she entrusted the secret that an inner voice had told her that the baby Thérèse would grow up to become a saint. In her late adolescence and early maturity she was the second mother to Thérèse whose one objective was to do all in her power to act as Zélie herself would have done to further the spiritual unfolding of the child. In her early years as a Carmelite she was the spiritual guide and mentor of Thérèse after she herself entered the convent. After Thérèse's early death the rest of her life was spent working for her cause, living to see it come to its glorious conclusion and acting as a stalwart missionary to bring her sister's graces and favours to the whole world.

A woman who pondered deeply on every subject before coming to any final conclusion, a woman of indomitable will where truth was concerned, a well-disciplined and deeply loved Mother Prioress in Carmel. A generous hearted and simple soul knowing no guile but striving at all times to sift the

E

wheat from the chaff in the souls placed in her care. A devout religious, a wise counsellor and a patient teacher, she possessed just those qualities that were needed in the all inspiring task that was to be her life's work – assisting in the moulding of a saint and then striving to make that saint's virtues known to the whole world.

Thérèse herself, writing of her sister Pauline says,

> Oh, how I love you. But that is not all I want to tell you. You will know only in heaven what poetry your soul has put into mine. What a wonderful thing it is to be your little sister, your little mother, to feel that I am loved by you. Thank you for all your attentiveness to me. Oh, take me away from earth with you.

And to these words Pauline replies:

> You can know what you are to me only in heaven. You are a lyre, a song, even when you say nothing. There are not two like you on earth.

A trifle gushing perhaps, too precious and sentimental to have any true value. Even allowing for this we can see in them the seeds of a perfect relationship, and they prove conclusively that many of the charges made against Pauline by her later critics will not stand a moment's critical examination. One can sense behind the personal adulation an impersonal desire for perfection in both of them, and one is forced to recognise that to each of them perfection in love was the way by which the soul developed in its awesome, frightening and desperate journey towards eternity.

Perfection in love, yes, that was Pauline's aim and the whole of her life must become centred on its realisation. How could that be achieved? What were the practical steps she must take to make this possible? The question that had faced her as a schoolgirl at the Visitation convent at Le Mans and had haunted her adolescent years now seemed to demand from her an urgent and decisive answer. Her daily reading from *The Liturgical Year*, her constant attendance at Mass, her discussions with her sister Thérèse about the latter's own vocation for the religious life all seemed to point in one direction. More than any of these things however there was a voice, a quiet tired voice that seemed to echo and re-echo through her heart and mind. It was her mother's voice, the memory of almost the last words she had spoken to her as she lay dying that finally led her to seek the road to Carmel. 'Oh, my Pauline. You are my treasure. I know very well that you are going to be a nun. You will become a saint. I am unworthy to have a daughter like you. You are my glory and my joy.'

Therein lay both her secret and her solace. Her secret, the dominant desire to further the task that her mother had undertaken, to produce a child who should be a saint; her solace the knowledge that it was Thérèse who had been chosen and that it was her vocation to seek to aid the storming of heaven to make the fulfilment of her mother's dream a possibility. Whatever might happen to her, no matter how hard the road or how difficult the way she would surrender herself without reservation to this one increasing purpose. Carmel, the life of solitude, the quest for sanctification through constant prayer, the search for the proper means by which she could assist in leading her sister's life to its perfect end, this she knew was destined to be her calling.

There was sadness in her heart as she climbed the spiral staircase to the Belvedere to seek her father's permission to take this step. She knew how much he had come to depend upon her since her mother's death. She realised that in their happy friendship he had found a sense of understanding, of inner completeness that meant so much to his own interior life.

The pained look in his eyes as she spoke to him very gently but insistently of the decision she had made was the first of the arrows of anguish that were so constantly to pierce her own heart. The old man's helplessness stunned her, he seemed so fragile, so lonely and so desolate as he gave his permission for her to seek admittance to the convent. And yet his pain seemed to fade into insignificance when she found herself face to face with the baffled anguish in Thérèse's tear-filled eyes when she spoke to her of the step she was going to take. Her Pauline, her 'little mother,' beloved one going away, leaving her to face life with a loneliness of heart, and agony of spirit she had never known before. Peace, that well might be written in the stars of heaven for her, but pain, an ever recurring and ever increasing pain, seemed all that was written for her in the dry stones of earth.

In October 1882 Pauline Martin entered the Carmel at Lisieux as a novice taking the name in religion of Sister Agnes of Jesus. Thérèse was heartbroken when the time for their separation came. Was love always destined to betray her? Was the affection she sought after so deeply always to prove as dust and ashes? Was the cup of sorrow always to be filled to the brim for her to drink from? Was an inner crucifixion to be all that life really had to offer her? Young girl as she was these thoughts always seemed to be pressing in upon her. Rose, dearly loved Rose, the foster mother who had seemed more than her real mother in the first two years of her life had been taken away from her. Her own mother, the dearest, the kindest, the gentlest of mothers had died leaving in the child's heart an emptiness that nothing else seemed able to fill. Pauline, her second mother, the one she had consciously chosen to take her dead mother's place, was now enclosed behind the forbidding walls of Carmel. Her father's face had taken on a mask of sadness that hid the cheerful light in his eyes and shrouded the laughter on his lips. All that was left was her true mother, the Blessed Virgin, and it was to her she would turn in perpetual adoration.

A slight fear, a tremor of doubt assailed her, for with that deliberately sought after and clearly found insight that was to prove her touchstone in life she knew the answer was a cross – a crucified man, a suffering God striving to win the world back to Himself through a deepening and widening and overwhelming love. How easy it seemed to make that love her goal and to strive to embody its meaning and its purpose in her own life; and yet how difficult it was to prove itself to be, to apply the hidden meaning of that love to the hourly and daily happenings, to the often humdrum and seldom exciting things that made up the pattern of ordinary human existence.

After Pauline's departure from the home all the family became very worried about the change that was taking place in Thérèse. Her happiness seemed to have gone for ever. The cheerful laughter, the joyous pranks, the romps with her dog Tom and the pleasure-laden hours she spent in the garden all seemed to belong to the past. She became listless and languid. She lost interest in everything that at one time had been a constant source of delight to her. Even the walks with her father brought no comfort, and playing with her two little cousins, the Guérin children, was no consolation. She would sit silent and alone, withdrawn from all that was happening around her, constantly recalling the day when Pauline had listened to her explaining how one day she would like to withdraw to the desert taking Pauline with her, and how full of splendour and promise it had seemed when Pauline had gaily replied that they would do it one day and that she herself would wait until Thérèse was old enough for them to go away together. She wrote later, when recalling these times:

> How can I describe the anguish my heart endured? In a flash I beheld life as it really is, full of suffering and constant partings and I shed most bitter tears.

Strong sentiments for so young a girl, too full of self-pity and selfish pathos one might be inclined to say. We must remember however that Thérèse Martin was no ordinary child, she was already becoming conscious of being God-intoxicated with divine love, and young and frail and overwrought as she might seem to those around her, within herself she was building up a composure far beyond her years. For hours she sat pondering over the many things that Pauline had told her. For weeks she considered the implications of the many discussions they had had together about the meaning and purpose of human life.

Later when she herself recalled what all these months of agony and suspense had meant to her she tells us,

> One evening, when pondering all alone on the picture you (Pauline) had drawn for me, I felt that Carmel was the desert where God wished me to hide. I felt it so strongly that there was no room for doubt. It was not the dream of an impressionable child, but the certainty of a divine call, and this sensation, which I am unable to describe, brought with it a wonderful peace.

There is a strength, an assurance in these words that none but a fool can ignore. They elevate the writer to the heights on which the great mystics have always dwelt. They are that eternal yes to life that eludes most of us. They form part of the pattern that the late Studdert Kennedy, the beloved 'Woodbine Willie' to the soldiers of the first world war, captured in one of his poems when he wrote:

> Peace does not mean the end of all our striving,
> Joy does not mean the drying of our tears;
> Peace is the strength that comes to soul's arriving,
> Up to the heights where God Himself appears.

A similar thought is also expressed in the noble and sublime words, 'In the flesh they shall see God'. Most of us know and experience such a moment in our own lives, but we seek to erase their meaning, to cast aside their purpose for we prefer the market place to the mountain tops, and choose to live in society rather than in solitude.

The truly dedicated soul, whether he is a scientist, a doctor, an artist, a writer or a mystic knows that the price of singleness is unselfishness. Love always strives to give, never to gain, and it is only as we release ourselves from the fear-ridden stresses of possessive love that we can rise to the fullness of being that is the source and the goal of man's deepest longings and highest aspirations. Thérèse Martin knew this in that terrible winter of 1882, when timorously and hesitantly she set out on the road that was destined to lead to her own personal Calvary.

Once the family in the home at Lisieux had adjusted themselves to the fact of Pauline's absence from their midst things resumed their normal pattern. Céline carried on with her drawing and painting lessons. Louis took to his fishing, his country walks and religious pilgrimages. Léonie became more integrated into the family circle and Marie took over Pauline's responsibilities for the practical running of the home. The same, but not quite the same, for Pauline's decision was soon to have its effect upon Marie, who followed her sister's footsteps into the Carmel at Lisieux a year later.

The void was growing larger and deeper and the inner anguish of Thérèse was deepening in its hold over her. Human frailty is our common heritage, and, when this second blow fell so quickly after the first, the headaches that she had suffered from since the day Pauline had entered the enclosure increased in intensity. Her face grew pale and wan, she stumbled as she walked about the house, and before anyone realised it she fell into a state of nervous collapse that led to a very serious illness indeed. Even the doctor who was called in and attended her was unable to completely diagnose the cause or find a cure. As the day approached for Pauline's clothing the family were all sure that Thérèse would not be able to be there but to their surprise and consternation when the morning arrived of the day in question she was fit and well again and able to join in the family's joy at being present on such an important and impressive occasion in Pauline's own spiritual life. Alas, Thérèse's recovery was short-lived, and within a few days she was in bed again so weak and tired and ill that the family and the doctor all despaired of being able to save her life.

The child's sufferings struck terror into the hearts of all who visited her. She suffered from hallucinations. She fell into fits that racked her body with distorting pains. She beat her head against the wooden frame of the bed, and on one occasion, more terrifying to the onlookers than all the others, she flung herself bodily out of the bed onto the floor before anyone could save her. Fear peopled the room with demons. She felt she was standing on the edge of dark precipices and was at any moment likely to be plunged into an all-enfolding darkness. The family were constantly at her bedside facing the heart-breaking anguish that there was nothing they could do to ease the pains that racked the body of the demented child. Louis Martin himself was completely distracted and sent a purse of gold pieces to Paris asking that a novena of Masses might be said for Thérèse's recovery at the shrine of Our Lady of Victories. Marie, who naturally wondered how far her own decision to enter Carmel had contributed to this frightening turn of events, hardly ever left her sister's bedside.

The crisis grew in its magnitude. The prayers of the nuns in Carmel, the prayers of the family round the bedside, the prayers of the parish priest in the sanctuary all seemed of no avail. All human effort had failed and it almost seemed as though all appeals to the divine mercy of God was to fail also. And then it occurred, the event no one can understand but to which everyone always seems ready to give an answer.

It was an evening in late spring. The humming of insects, the gentle love-song of the birds at mating time, the perfumes from the garden below all filled the sick child's room with a sense of serenity and peace. Léonie sat by the bedside taking her turn as one of the nurses who were in constant attendance upon the invalid. Death seemed to be imminent at any time for the doctor had stated quite frankly that there was nothing else he could do to cure the illness or delay the ravages it was making upon the patient herself. Suddenly Thérèse turned her face to one side, gazed blankly at the spot where her sister was sitting and started to moan softly and insistently 'Marie, Marie, Marie'. The uttering of the name was interspersed with cries of agony and moans of pain. 'Marie, Marie, Marie,' a note of hysteria could be detected in the whimpering voice.

Léonie was distraught, and gently lifting the weakened and frail body of Thérèse into her arms carried the patient to the open window hoping that the sight of Marie in the garden below would soothe Thérèse and ease her sufferings. There was no response from the invalid and in utter despair Léonie carried her back to the bed and laid her down again between the cool sheets. 'Marie, Marie, Marie,' the cries went on, breaking the silence of the sick room like a constantly recurring death knell.

In the corner of the room, standing on a corner bracket was the statue of the Madonna that had belonged to Zélie Martin. It was a copy of the statue by Bouchardun that had stood in the Church of St Sulspice in Paris until the time of the French Revolution. Marie, who had been summoned by Léonie from the garden entered the bedchamber where Thérèse was still pitieously calling out her name. She moved over to the child whose body was convulsed with pain and for the first time since the beginning of her illness Thérèse failed to recognise her. Marie, convinced that this was the beginning of her death agony, whispered something to Léonie and then moved out of the room quickly to summon the rest of the family. Léonie once more carried the child to the window and Marie called out to her from the garden below, 'Thérèse, my little Thérèse,' but her words called forth no response.

A few minutes later Marie re-entered the room followed by Céline and calling Léonie across to them they all knelt in front of the statue and prayed for their sister whom they were convinced was dying. At that moment the child lying on the bed opened her eyes, smiled at her three kneeling sisters and quietly announced that her pains had vanished and that she was completely cured. Within a few days she was up and about again. The doctor could not offer any explanation of this amazing recovery and the relatives and friends of the family were equally nonplussed to find an explanation for this inexplicable event that had brought so much happiness back into all their lives.

A week or two later Thérèse was sitting talking to Marie about her desire to offer herself completely and unreservedly to God for the special grace He had sent to her as she lay on her sickbed. I will let Thérèse tell you once more in her own words what happened to her on that spring evening when Marie, Céline and Léonie were kneeling in prayer before the statue of Our Lady.

> Utterly exhausted, and finding no help on earth, I too sought my Heavenly Mother's aid, and entreated her with all my heart to have pity on me. Suddenly the statue became animated and radiantly beautiful – with a divine beauty that no words of mine can ever convey. The look upon Our Lady's face was unspeakably kind and sweet and compassionate, but what penetrated to the very depths of my soul was her gracious smile. Instantly all my pains vanished, my eyes filled and big tears fell silently, tears of pure, heavenly joy.

It is easy to scoff at this statement but if you read it carefully and ponder over its words there is no escape from its ring of truth. It is simple to call it a sentimental description of a childish hallucination but how can you explain the sick child's immediate recovery of which ample evidence is available? It is futile to try to pass it over as a form of auto-suggestion or a psychological turn of events for neither statement is sufficient to deal with the fact that Thérèse's recovery was immediate and lasting. A miracle, a dangerous word for modern ears, but as far as I know it is the only word that will explain all the facts. Saints do not follow the well-worn tracks walked along by ordinary men. Theirs is a narrow path with a razor's edge sharpness and simplicity about it that both astounds and bewilders us when we come across it. Piety always makes us uncomfortable, since it is a mirror that reflects our own shortcomings and makes us face up to the unpleasant truth that most of us are much less than we ought to be in the ways of the spirit of truth.

It is obvious that there is something here that neither the cynicism of Sackville West nor the sanctimosity of Monseigneur Laveille can explain to us. Miss Sackville West views her far too much from the near side of earth and Monseigneur Laveille far too much from the near side of heaven. The one strives to materialise her spirituality too much and the other to spiritualise every material event in her life so that she becomes a kind of animated celestial puppet. I am convinced that the clue to her life and the only thing that will give a full meaning to her story is the fact that her greatness lay in her simplicity, and that that simplicity was never 'childish' as so many of her detractors have tried to claim but failed to prove, but had a childlikeness that bewilders and frightens us when she forces us in her day to day way of life to face up to its full meaning and significance.

Thérèse Martin, like Francis of Assisi, like John of the Cross, like Catherine of Siena, was one of those rarified and sanctified souls whose objective in life is showing heaven to those who follow after. Like Joan of Arc she was a warrior, but alas, a warrior in chains that were never of her own making.

The summer of 1883 was one of the happiest periods in Thérèse's life. Recovered completely in health, looking forward eagerly to her first communion, settled in the fact that one day she too would enter Carmel, each day brought a deeper joy to her heart. Together with her father and her two sisters they visited friends in Alençon and there she learned to decorate earthenware pots with clay flowers. Pauline, who was settling down with a naturalness to convent life that was an ample witness to the truth of her vocation spent many hours preparing the manuscript she intended to send to Thérèse to help her to prepare for the great day when she would kneel in silent adoration waiting for that wondrous moment when she would receive the body of her Lord. The sun seemed to be shining brighter than ever before. The green fields of Normandy had a radiance she had never seen in them in the past. The bird songs were clearer and more harmonious, the apple harvest was full of promise for the autumn, while even the stars in the summer night seemed to have taken on a more luminous quality for her.

As the day of her communion arrived it took on a very special significance for it was also the day on which Pauline was to take her final vows and was to become a fully professed nun. They would each be offering themselves to Christ in a very special way and there seemed to Thérèse a special significance that both herself and her beloved Pauline would each be making a thanksgiving and a heart's offering to the One whom both of them sought to serve. There is once more a prophetic ring in the words she wrote before setting off to Mass on this day, that so far was the most memorable day in her young life.

> I will never be discouraged; every day I will say a Memoria; I will try to humiliate my pride.

No words can describe the ineffable joy that this moment in her life meant to her. The One she sought to love above all else in life was with her. The One she was to seek to offer herself to in perpetual adoration set the first seal on that divine union that was the source and goal of her own spiritual aspirations.

'I love Thee and I give myself to Thee for ever,' a simple phrase and yet it had for her such a profound meaning that in fulfilling it she was to find her own Calvary and her own crucifixion. This was the first phase in the mystical experience that was to colour her whole life. It was the initial step outside the limits of time into that order of being where everything was to be offered completely and without reservation in a sacramental act of abandonment to divine love.

That same afternoon Thérèse accompanied her father to the Carmel at Lisieux where Pauline was to make her profession. There was once more an unearthly loveliness in the service in the convent chapel. How other-worldly Pauline looked in her bridal gown, her flower white veil and the wreath of roses that was always worn at the nuptials of a nun with her heavenly bridegroom. Thérèse and her sister met in the parlour for a short time after the ceremony both dressed in the white robes of their innocence and each of them crowned and veiled. All she longed for, all she hoped for, was to join her sister in Carmel as soon as possible. The words she herself used to describe what the day had meant to her express much more ably than any I can find the second step in her ascent of Mount Carmel.

How sweet was the first embrace of Jesus. It was indeed an embrace of love. I felt that I was loved and I said, 'I love Thee and I give myself to Thee for ever'. Jesus asked nothing of me and claimed no sacrifice; for a long time He and little Thérèse had known one another. That day our meeting was more than a simple recognition. It was perfect union. We were no longer two. Thérèse had disappeared like a drop of water, lost in the immensity of the ocean; Jesus alone remained, He was the Master, the King.

It seems almost incredible, in fact to many it will be looked upon as an impossibility that so young a child could enter so fully into a knowledge of the heart and mind of love. The truth is that the incredible had happened, the impossible had been realised and from henceforth nothing could bar Thérèse from moving towards her ultimate destiny. 'I choose all' – her own words take on a new significance for us as we move through the next six years of her life. Apparently insurmountable obstacles were to be placed in her path. Every month some new difficulty had to be faced and overcome. Neither the anger of priests, the jovial asides of bishops, nor the restraining voice of the Pope himself were to be allowed to deter her in fulfilling the interior vows she had made that they might become actual and concrete realities.

The happiness of that summer holiday, the joy of her first communion, the ecstasy of her Confirmation were all to be swept away in the divine holocaust that awaited her. Every thought, every emotion, every word, every action were to be submitted to a scrupulous examination before the bar of her own conscience. Her own imperfections in everything she sought to accomplish tormented her. Even the gentle words of her confessor did little or nothing to ease the burdens that troubled her restless soul. The devil was to her a roaring lion going about seeking whom he could devour and there was nothing anybody could do to still her fears of falling into his clutches. Once more we are brought face to face with the dilemma that runs through her whole life. We cannot understand her outlook or her attitude. We, the ordinary people who prefer to live in a second-rate world and make the most of second-best, cannot understand those who have only one objective in life and that is the seeking of a flawless perfection. They are the lights that shine out on the mountain tops to guide those of us who are struggling in the shadowed places in the valleys. We see in them what we know in our own hearts we are meant to be, and like all who have been privileged for a brief moment to glimpse the Face of God we are afraid.

CHAPTER V

Storming Heaven

On Christmas Eve, just before her fourteenth birthday, Thérèse Martin placed her slippers on the hearthstone to be filled with the usual gifts that were always placed there by angels to mark the birthday of Christ. It was a very ancient custom and is still carried on in households in Normandy to this day. As she walked upstairs, she heard her father say to Céline, 'It is time Thérèse had grown out of these babyish habits. This is the last time she will find gifts in the slipper.'

The words were like a knife thrust into her heart. Her father, her Little King, whom she loved so deeply and so devotedly could speak of her like that. The tears welled up in her eyes, and then suddenly, with such a decisive feeling that she always referred to this moment later as her 'conversion', she saw clearly that this was a double attachment, to the gifts in the slipper and to the need for her father's love.

The gifts were not wrong, there was nothing sinful in loving one's parents and in their returning one's love, but all must be surrendered if one was to become truly worthy of the love of God in the special way she was seeking that love. For her the call was quite clear, she must know and embody within herself the full meaning of the words, 'Unless a man forsake his father and mother and follow me he shall not be worthy of the Kingdom of Heaven'. Thérèse Martin also knew the significance of taking the Kingdom of Heaven by storm, and this was the next step she took in testing out the inner truth of her vocation, which she knew by now lay within the walls of the Carmel at Lisieux.

Lying in a Paris jail, awaiting his execution lay the murderer Pranzini. This loathsome and wretched creature, a native of Alexandria, had lived by his wits all his life and had robbed and murdered a poor old woman who kept a small shop in one of the back streets of the city. His capture and trial had been one of the major sensations of the day and was openly discussed in every cafe and bar throughout France. He was an atheist, a blasphemer, and had added to his notoriety by translating obscene books while he lay in prison awaiting the morning when they would escort him to the guillotine. There was apparently nothing to be said in his favour. He had cut himself adrift from the world of decent men and had cast aside the help the prison chaplain offered him that he might die in the knowledge of the mercy of God.

Thérèse Martin found her thoughts constantly turning to this wretched creature, and as she pondered upon his plight she found herself thinking of the thief who had shared a death on the cross with the Saviour of men. He had repented and had been forgiven. He had even been promised that on that very day he should enjoy the green and golden pastures of Paradise. Why not Pranzini?

Once Thérèse Martin had come to a decision nothing could deter her from seeking to see that it was carried out. God wanted her for Himself, she needed God's help for the miracle for which she was praying. If her life was to be dedicated to the salvation of souls then she would seek a sign from Heaven that this was her destiny. Kneeling down before the Blessed Sacrament she pleaded that this murderer, this monstrous and corrupt man lying on the verge of execution should be her 'first child'. If God willed that her mission was the salvation of souls, then surely God must by virtue of His goodness and mercy will the salvation of Pranzini.

The morning of the execution arrived. The prisoner was dragged to the plank on which he was forced to lie down, cursing and blaspheming with every step he was forced to take. He hurled obscenities at his gaolers. He shouted blasphemies at the priest escorting him to the scaffold. He laughed derisively at the prayers that were being said for the good of his soul. He was flung down and bound to the plank. The newly sharpened knife of the guillotine glimmered in the first splashes of morning sunshine. Then a strange hush fell over the death party. Even the priest ceased praying for a moment. Suddenly, the roped prisoner who had also stopped cursing and blaspheming, reached out, snatched the crucifix from the hands of the priest and reverently kissed the wounded side of the figure on the wooden cross.

The day after the execution when Thérèse heard from her father what had happened on the previous morning in the prison yard on the outskirts of Paris, a joy and serenity filled her heart such as she had never as yet experienced. Every day, for the rest of her life, she was to pray for the soul of this wretched creature whom she always referred to as her firstborn, and each year on the anniversary of his execution she would see that a Mass was said for him in the tiny chapel at Carmel.

Thérèse knew now that she must tell her father of her decision to enter Carmel at Christmas 1887, the anniversary of her final conversion. Although Louis Martin was only sixty-four years of age he was already starting to look a frail old man. The break-up of the family had been a terrible strain to him and in May 1877, while on his way to Church to attend morning Mass he had had a minor stroke that left him partially paralysed but from which he appeared to make a complete recovery. It was true that he seemed a trifle vague and that he spent more and more time brooding and meditating in the silence of his beloved Belvedere. His relatives and friends who had always had a profound respect for his piety saw in this a soul moving nearer to God, whereas in actual fact it was the first signs of a man moving towards the fringe of insanity which was soon to claim him as its victim.

Whit Sunday that year had been one of those perfect days when the spring sunshine seemed to wash the fields and houses of the Normandy countryside with liquid gold. The grasshoppers were chirping merrily in the fields, the larks' song cascaded through the blue brilliance of the clear skies, the apple buds were just forming in the heavily laden orchards. There was a peace, an awe-filling stillness over the garden at Les Buissonnets as the soft folds of a turquoise and amber twilight enshrined the scene with an almost unearthly beauty.

Louis Martin, who had recovered from his illness, was walking among his shrubs and flowers thinking over the words of the sermon he had listened to at Vespers. Thérèse crept quietly up to where he was sitting on a wooden seat on the back lawn and told him very quietly but very firmly of her wish to enter Carmel that Christmas.

Something within the frail old man seemed to curl up. Was another sacrifice to be demanded from him so soon? Was God now asking for his Little Queen as He had previously asked for her two sisters? The tears rolled down his cheeks as he told his pleading daughter that he was prepared to make yet another sacrifice if she was sure that this was the will of God for her.

When his brother-in-law Isidore Guérin was told of Thérèse's decision he was amazed and annoyed. A lot of arrant nonsense, a child of her age to think of becoming a nun, what she needed was a good thrashing to beat such silly ideas out of her. He would see the priest and forbid it. If that failed he would appeal to the Bishop himself, and if the worst came to the worst he would see that the naughty child was kept under lock and key until she had mended her ways.

Thérèse listened to this tirade but remained completely unperturbed. If God wanted her, and she was certain He did, what could her uncle do to corrupt His will? All she did was to withdraw from the rest of the family and seek consolation in prayer. Our Lady, the smiling Madonna who had healed her in her childhood, would surely come to her aid in what threatened to become a major crisis in her life. That night a feeling of confidence filled her soul and the next day her uncle apologised for all he had said and promised to do all he could to further her vocation. Her father had agreed, the one relative who could have opposed her entry into the convent had acquiesced, the Mother Prioress had consented to receive her at Christmas, all that remained now was for her to obtain formal permission from the Superior of Carmel, the parish priest of St Jacques, Monsieur Delatroette.

The parish priest of Lisieux was like so many of his kind, a bewildering mixture of arrogance and humility. He could be magnanimous when he chose, sceptical when it suited his purpose, a benign pastor when tending his flock and a domineering dictator when he felt that his authority was in any way being challenged or threatened. He was an austere, tight-lipped cleric, well versed in scholarship, well tutored in moral theology, believing that his authority, next to that of the Pope himself, must be the final word for his parishioners.

The Martin family were well known to him, in fact he had been a little doubtful of the wisdom of the convent in accepting the second daughter from the same family as a postulant. He also looked upon Louis Martin with suspicion, since in his opinion no layman had the right to practise the extremes of piety for which Louis Martin was so well known in Lisieux.

These were the thoughts that were passing through Monsieur Delatro-ette's mind as he paced round his study awaiting a visit from Louis Martin and his youngest daughter Thérèse, who had asked for an appointment to see him to discuss a personal matter. However rumour had it that the child wanted to enter Carmel at Christmas just after she had celebrated her fifteenth birthday. Gossips around the town were never tired of repeating a wild story that when she was much younger she had seen the Virgin Mary, that some statue or other had come to life and the Madonna had smiled at her. Cant and humbug, he was sure of that, almost every town in France had some over-zealous soul or other who claimed to have private visions and personal revelations from the Almighty. It was true that the Mother Prioress had spoken to him of the girl's wishes in the matter and had advised him, as the spiritual superior of her convent, to accede to her request. He didn't like it, the whole matter verged on adolescent hysteria and he was going to have no part in it.

Thérèse Martin and her father were announced by his housekeeper and entered the study. Louis inclined his head reverently to the standing priest while Thérèse dropped a charming curtsy to witness her respect for the man and his priestly calling. She was afraid of those deep-sunken eyes, those furrowed brows, those tightened lips. Her heart almost seemed to stop beating, and when looking straight at her the priest said, 'Well child' in a tone of angered command, she found that her throat was parched, her lips seemed to be sealed and she was unable for a few moments to utter a single word.

'Come child,' the priest called out with a definite note of impatience in his stern voice, 'have you lost your tongue or your wits or both? What is it that you require from me?' Louis Martin tried to intervene but a gesture from the priest commanded his silence.

Suddenly Thérèse looked up at the standing priest. The clear-eyed innocent look in her eyes for a moment disarmed him and put him off his guard. 'Tell me, child,' he said in a more kindly tone than he had used before, 'what is it that you want from me?'

'Your permission to become a postulant at Carmel next Christmas, Reverend Father,' Thérèse answered.

'Next Christmas' – there was a definite note of sarcasm in the priest's voice – 'and how old will you be then, in fact how old are you now?'

'I was fourteen on the second of January,' answered the kneeling child.

'Fourteen, fourteen, have you lost your senses? I consider eighteen young enough for any girl to enter upon such an austere life and in the case of an immature child like yourself I am not prepared to consider the matter until you reach the age of twenty-one.'

There was a finality in the words and the way he had uttered them that would have deterred most people from any further discussion with him on the matter. Not so with Thérèse Martin. She may have been tongue-tied when she entered the study but now the words were pouring out of her lips. 'I know that God wants me there, I am sure that I am acting on our Lady's orders, I am convinced that my goal in life is to become a Bride of Christ in the enclosure at Carmel.'

'You know, you are sure, you are convinced,' the priest's voice rose to an almost strident shriek as he threw her own words back at her, 'and who are you to know and be sure and be convinced that you have the right to challenge the power invested in me by the Holy Mother Church and entrusted to me by the Prioress of Carmel?'

The priest knew that there was a falseness, a lack of the truth about the situation as he shouted these words at the kneeling girl and her aging father. The Mother Prioress had pleaded with him to give his consent to Thérèse Martin's request. When her words had failed to convince him the saintly old Mother Geneviève had added her pleading to that of the Prioress. He had lost his temper with them just as he was losing his temper with the girl now. He was determined not to relent from his decision, but something inside him, a strange uneasiness, a bewildering suspicion that he might be in the wrong, forced him to tell the father and daughter that if they were not satisfied with his decision they had the right to appeal to the Bishop on the matter.

On the way home Thérèse was very quiet. She was lost in mental prayer, seeking a guidance from beyond the heart and mind of man, looking for assistance where she was sure she would find it. When they reached home her father patted her head lightly and tried to get her to see that the priest might be right, she might be too young, there would be no harm in waiting for a year or two longer. Thérèse was adamant.

'I know that I am right and that I am following the will of God for me in seeking to enter Carmel this year. I shall appeal to the Bishop, I am even prepared to plead with the Holy Father himself if necessary. I may look young, people may take me for a child, but I am sure that no human power can deny or destroy or corrupt the call I have to follow, my vocation.'

Louis Martin stood amazed as he listened to these words. They were spoken with such quiet conviction, they carried with them such a weight of assurance that he immediately wrote to the Bishop of Bayeux to ask for an interview with his Lordship for himself and his daughter.

Some months were to elapse before her father could arrange for them to travel to Bayeux for their long awaited audience with the Bishop. It is somewhat difficult to understand the cause for this long delay. Was the father hoping that the rebuffs his daughter had received from the parish priest would shake her convictions and thus alter her course of action? Had he a secret, an unspoken wish that she would remain at home with him to be the companion of his declining years? Was there within him an unspoken rebellion against God for demanding another sacrifice of this kind from him?

Bishop Monseigneur Hugonin had ruled over the See of Bayeux and Lisieux for over twenty years. He was a happy, easy going cleric, noted for his human qualities and admired for his scholarship. He saw himself in every sense of the word as a pastor of souls, and on the day at the end of October when Thérèse Martin and her father called to keep their appointment with him he was determined to listen to them without prejudice in order that he might arrive at what he considered to be a just and proper conclusion to this difficult and delicate matter.

Sinners, yes he understood and sympathised with them all right, they were the common flesh of humanity. Potential saints, and that was what he had heard whispered was what this girl who was coming to see him well might be, that was quite another matter. The common yardsticks of moral theology were of little use in measuring her stature, while the authority of the church itself must be wielded with great care when dealing with such a question as sublime sanctity. He found himself thinking of Joan of Arc, a saint to whom the girl from Lisieux was supposed to have a particular devotion. How wrong the bishop who had sat in authority at her trial had been, and how right she had been to uphold the rights of conscience against the judgement of the Inquisition. This was the hair's breadth line that so many people outside the Catholic Church, and many inside it for that matter, found so difficult to understand. The Pope, the cardinals, the bishops, the priests, all of them were men having authority to rule and to govern, but not one of them had the right to violate another person's conscience. That was man's private domain, his fragment of Eden, where he could still walk with God in the cool of the day and listen to His voice. Practically all heresies had arisen from a misunderstanding of this aspect of the church's teaching and many of the persecutions that had rent the church asunder were due to a refusal to recognise the unique quality of each individual soul before its Maker.

From where did Thérèse Martin obtain that tenacity of purpose that brooked no obstacle but persisted all the while in pursuing its end? Let her answer this question for herself. 'All the time deep down in my heart reigned a wonderful peace, because I knew I was seeking only God's will.'

On the day of their audience with the Bishop Thérèse had put up her hair for the first time in the vain hope that it would make her look much older and more mature than she had appeared when she had visited the parish priest. In fact this ruse had just the opposite effect and she appeared to the Bishop rather like a child trying to play an adult part in a game of charades. His smile of welcome and the friendly tone of his voice gave her some sort of reassurance. Perhaps this was her day, God's day, and she would leave the palace with the permission she had come to plead for to enter Carmel at Christmas.

After genuflecting to the Bishop and kissing his pastoral ring she stood silent and withdrawn until he spoke to her.

'Sit down child,' he suggested.

'No thank you, Sir, I would rather stand,' was her humble and courteous answer to his suggestion.

'The first thing a good religious has to learn is obedience,' the Bishop retorted in a much firmer voice.

Hanging down her face to hide the blushes Thérèse sat in one of the large easy chairs in the study, sinking into its leather until she was almost obscured by the high arms of the chair itself. In the simplest of terms, with a clarity that both surprised and disarmed the Bishop she stated her case. There was no hesitation, no doubt in her voice, when she came to the crucial point of the day's proceedings and asked his Lordship to direct the parish priest to give her the permission she was seeking. No bishop would override the findings of a priest who was the religious superior of Carmel. Thérèse knew that, but she also realised that a bishop might be prevailed upon to intervene on her behalf and that his intervention might change the whole course that events seemed to be taking.

The girl's simplicity, that was an obvious fact the Bishop could not ignore. The girl's sincerity, that shone out clearly from her deepset blue eyes and echoed through every word she spoke as she made her request. The girl's sanctity, well, that was another matter. Many young girls sought to enter a convent, it had a spectacular appeal, a sense of adventure in it that easily captured their newly awakened emotions and imagination. The sad look on the father's face troubled him. In the report he had received upon the two of them great stress had been placed on the goodness of heart and the two sacrifices Louis Martin had made in offering two of his daughters already to the service of the church.

The sadness of the man touched him very deeply, so much so that he felt he must agree with the decision that had been taken by the priest at Lisieux. Before he could open his mouth to say what was in his mind, Louis Martin stated quite simply that he had discussed the matter fully with his daughter, that he was certain of her vocation, that he had given his full permission for her to seek entry to the cloister, and that if his Lordship felt he could not accede to their request, then his daughter would travel with him on a pilgrimage to Rome where they would seek to get a decision from the Holy Father himself on this matter.

This was stalemate and the Bishop knew it. He must have time to consider every aspect of the case. He wanted to seek the advice of others as well, the Mother Prioress, the local priest at Lisieux, and anyone else whom he felt might be helpful in assisting him to give a just verdict on such a tricky case.

'I must have time to think the whole matter over. We can none of us afford to enter into a hasty decision. I will let you know what I have decided when you are in Italy.'

The Bishop blessed them both and found himself troubled at heart at the look of anguish on the girl's face as she left his presence. Turning to his chaplain who had been present throughout the interview he sighed and gently remarked, 'There are things in heaven and on earth that neither you nor I understand, Father, and this little incident today may well be one of them.'

After returning home Thérèse visited her sister Pauline at the convent to give her a full account of all that had happened at the Bishop's palace. The Mother Prioress herself had suggested that Thérèse might make a final appeal to the Pope if the Bishop refused to use his influence to enable her to fulfil her wish to enter Carmel almost immediately. Her sister Pauline was not at all sure that this was a wise or proper step for Thérèse to take, and at the end of their talk strongly advised her against speaking to the Pope about the matter at all.

Later, when the saint had been canonised many charges were made against

Pauline, scurrilous charges that had little or no foundation, and one of them
was that not only had she urged her sister to speak to the Holy Father
himself but had also actually drilled her in the words she was to use in the
audience chamber at the Vatican. The fact is that although in one of her
letters to her sister Pauline had suggested what the approach to the Pope
should be, she was merely repeating suggestions that had been made to her
by the Mother Prioress and that she had been instructed under obedience to
hand on to Thérèse.

Louis Martin had always been an inveterate traveller. He loved foreign
scenes, new faces, famous shrines, and had spent many months even in his
working life travelling to many parts of Europe and Asia. He had stood on
the spot where the Christians had been martyred in Rome. He had followed
the footsteps of his Saviour through Palestine looking with awe on the site
of the stable at Bethlehem and standing in silent reverence on the hill of
Golgotha.

The sadness in Thérèse's eyes troubled him, and he reassured her as soon
as they returned from their apparently abortive visit to the Bishop that he
would take steps immediately to arrange to take part in a pilgrimage to
Rome that was being organised in the diocese of Bayeux. Thérèse and Céline
were to accompany him and he would be able to share with them some of the
joys he had found in his own wanderings during the past years.

The journey to Rome was full of incident. It is true that the boisterous
attitude of some of their travelling companions disturbed them. Prayers, not
playing cards, were surely the finest prelude to an audience with the Holy
Father himself. Hymns and litanies would surely have been more appropriate
to this journey than some of the rowdy songs that filled the railway carriages
with discordant noises. In Paris, where they stayed for some hours, Thérèse
was able to visit Sacré Coeur for the Archbishop's blessing in preparation
for the wonderful things that lay ahead. What she loved more than all else
was the visit she paid to the shrine she already loved so dearly in her heart,
that of Our Lady of Victories. It was here that she gained courage and consolation, for as she knelt gazing at the famous statue it seemed to come to
life, to raise its hand in a token of benediction, and an inner voice assured
her that all would be well.

On leaving Paris they journeyed through Switzerland to Milan, and as
they steamed through the whiteness of the Alps glimmering with silver in the
November night, those white wastes of sheer beauty recalled to Louis
Martin his own frustrated hopes, his own denied dream of a life of solitude in
these isolated places where God might be known and found amidst the
whiteness of the icy caps and the snow clad heights. At Milan the Cathedral

must be visited, for there one would be able to offer up prayers to St Charles Borromeo that he would intercede for the success of their mission. Venice delighted the two girls, who found it great fun to climb to the top of the Campanile while their father wandered among the treasures in St Mark's. A deep sense of joy was enveloping Thérèse. She knew that struggles lay ahead, that there were still obstacles to be faced and overcome, but she felt that the very powers of heaven themselves were guiding and guarding her on this, the most significant journey she had ever taken in her life.

On 13th November, late in the evening, the train steamed into a station and there were many who burst out into a spontaneous hymn of thanksgiving when they heard the shout of 'Rome, Rome' breaking into the stillness of the night. To Thérèse this was one of those near-heaven moments that was to mean so much to her throughout her short life. Rome, the city of the Supreme Pontiff himself. Rome, that had written so many pages in the history of the Church. Rome, where in the Coliseum so many of the early followers of Christ had faced deaths by martyrdom.

For six days it rained without ceasing, but nothing could mar the inner happiness that was flowing through her when visiting the Catacombs on the Appian Way, or lying in the hollow that was said to have been the resting place of one of the early martyrs, or ascending the dome of St Peter's to inspect the cupola erected by Michelangelo as a worthy tiara for the prince of the Apostles. How she resented the fact that some of the sacred places were closed to women.

> Every moment they were telling us: Don't enter here . . . Don't go in there . . . You will be excommunicated. Oh, poor women. How they are despised. Yet they love the good God in far greater numbers than men. And during our Lord's passion the women had greater courage than the Apostles, since they braved the insults of the soldiers and dared to wipe the adorable face of Jesus.

As the day of the Papal audience drew near Thérèse shut herself more and more away from the others seeking guidance and consolation in long hours of interior prayer. Her moment was approaching. Would it be a moment of tragedy or triumph? On 4th November in a letter to her aunt she expressed very definite views on the hazardous venture that lay ahead of her.

> I do not know how I shall manage to speak to the Pope; unless God takes charge of everything I do not know how I shall do it. But I have such great confidence in Him that He cannot forsake me. I leave everything in His hands.

There is an assurance and a simplicity in these words that staggers us as we read them and realise that they were written by a girl of fourteen who was about to face one of the greatest ordeals of her life. She knew that the priest who was leading the pilgrimage was against her. She realised that everything possible that could be done would be done to prevent her opening her lips when she was in the Papal presence. All or nothing, was the price that Kierke-gaard warned us we must pay if we are to truly enter into the heart and mind of the Living God. It is a moment of majesty, a time of terror, a triumph and a defeat, since it must destroy us before it can remake us. The few who have stood in the splendour and agony of this moment of final revelation have recorded for us the bitter cost, the agony they must pass through in time that they, while in the flesh, might know the ecstasy of eternity. Thérèse Martin knew that she belonged to that few, and deep, deep down in her innermost being she also knew that the bronze door that led to the Papal chamber was also the gateway through which she must walk to her personal Gethsemane.

Father Révérony was happy to feel that his arduous and at times delicate task of leading the pilgrimage was nearing its end. What an odd assortment of people had travelled together across France and Switzerland to Rome. The vast majority of them had looked upon it as a holiday, and the fact that an audience with the Pope himself had been thrown in gave them the feeling that they were to be allowed to gaze upon the eighth wonder of the world. The few might have deeper and more profound aspirations, but the many classified the Supreme Pontiff as one of the curiosities of Italy to be classed with Giotto's golden tower in Florence or the famous leaning tower at Pisa. Worldliness was eating like a corrupt and loathsome thing into the vitals of the spiritual life of France, and it was in an attempt to persuade Catholics to take a more vital interest in all that was going on around them that the Papacy had recently introduced the concept of Catholic Action.

The old priest found himself wondering just what these people would get out of the experience of travelling together supposedly with one common purpose, the deepening of their spiritual lives; living together to attempt to experience the inner meaning of a Christian community; and joining in prayer and worship together in order that they should understand a little more clearly their Lord's instruction . . . that they should be as one. He chuckled inwardly as he pondered upon these matters. The cynic in him, and all wise spiritual counsellors must have a sprinkling of cynicism among their pearls of wisdom, told him quite clearly that most of them were only too happy to have discovered that they were a little richer in the things of this world than so many of their fellows.

The Martin family, now they were quite a different matter. In fact he was not sure that their obvious and sincere piety was not even a little more trying than the boisterous gaiety of most of their fellow travellers. There were moments when Louis Martin's deep-set eyes, his moving lips and his hands clasped humbly in prayer, worried him a little. The religious life was for clerics like himself, and the purpose of the laity was to follow where he sought to lead them. If he was really honest with himself this Martin business made him feel a trifle uncomfortable. There had been times during their long journey when they had made him feel almost inferior to themselves. He knew it had been enjoined upon Christians by their Master to pray without ceasing but he was convinced that Christ had not meant the injunction to be taken quite so seriously as the Martin family appeared to.

As for their youngest daughter, Thérèse, she had become a veritable thorn in his flesh. Her simple and implicit obedience petrified him. All this nonsense about becoming a Carmelite by the time she was fifteen ought to have been thrashed out of her years ago. The damnable thing about it all was that he could not find an easy and ready answer as to why she should not follow and strive to fulfil her vocation if she wished to do so.

He was used to listening to the troubles of piety thieves, stupid gossips, trivial liars. He had a deep respect for those pious women who brought flowers for the altar, polished the church's brasses, laundered the choirboys' cottas, and occasionally, if they came from the noble families and wealthier classes, even embroidered vestments for the clergy. These were acts of benevolence and charity that he could appreciate and understand. Their conversations with him had a reverence in them and a respect for him that made the 'Yes Father,' 'No Father,' of their answers fit in perfectly with the expected pattern of Christian obedience that formed the point and counterpoint between a pastor and his flock.

Thérèse Martin was not of their kind. She had a bluntness and a directness in her approach to her own spiritual difficulties that both angered and nonplussed him at the same time. What could you say to a girl who when asked why she wanted to become a nun told you simply and sincerely that she had been instructed to do so by the Virgin Mary? How could you answer the underlying challenge of her words when she told you with such an intensity of purpose that her very presence in the same room as you bewildered you that her one objective in life since the age of three had been to become the Bride of Christ.

He was wise enough in his knowledge of moral theology to know that there was nothing in the teaching of the church to prevent any of her members, even the most humble and unlikely, from having divine revelations providing that the outcome of them was not contrary to the law and the will of the church militant. He recalled the incidents surrounding Bernadette Soubirous at Lourdes. All the forces of the church and state, with the exception of the simple parish priest to whom she had made her regular

88

confessions since childhood, had ranged themselves against her. In the end she had proved to be right and her persecutors had proved to be wrong. The fact that children all over France had suddenly claimed to see visions and hear voices, most of which had proved to be spurious and fraudulent, had not in any way invalidated her claims. Might not Thérèse Martin be of Bernadette's kind? The priest shuddered as he pushed the thought away from him.

The Bishop of Bayeux had certainly been very deeply impressed with the girl when she had called upon him with her father. His Lordship had made it quite clear to Father Révérony that the door to Carmel must certainly not be shut on her but must be left ajar in case it was the will of God that she should pass through it at a much more tender age than that at which most postulants for such an austere life sought entry. Well, with all due respect to the pectorial cross and episcopalian ring he was sure that he knew the girl much better than the Bishop did, and his conviction was that this longing for a life of prayer and solitude was an adolescent whimsy that she would grow out of when the right young man came along. An early marriage and a growing family would probably be the finest thing to put an end once and for all to all this nonsense.

He would keep an eagle eye on the girl once they were in the presence of the Pope, for some had hinted that she intended to make a direct appeal to his Holiness himself. He would seek her out before they entered the audience chamber and forbid her to speak. A chit of a girl from Lisieux would not dare to disobey his orders on a matter such as this. She, a child of the church, a member of the pilgrimage that had been placed under his jurisdiction, would not dare but to keep silent if he commanded her to do so. Why did he find himself thinking of the children who had lined the streets on that first Palm Sunday? Why did the words keep running through his mind, 'If the children are silenced from praising Me even the stones themselves will cry out in adoration'?

He slipped on his soutane, adjusted his cape, placed the chain with its jewelled cross around his neck and hurried along to the Vatican where he had arranged to meet the pilgrims to conduct them through the highlight of their journey.

Thérèse Martin stood very close to her father as they waited outside the bronze door that led into the audience chamber. She was very frightened, more so than she had ever been before in all her life. To make matters worse, even as she prayed there seemed a dryness in the prayer that robbed it of its meaning. Although she could reach out and touch her father's hand he seemed a long way off, a being with whom she had no contact of any kind.

Even when she tried to speak to her sister, Céline, her tongue seemed to be tied to the roof of her mouth and no words would issue forth no matter how ardently she tried to utter them. Herself and God, the loneliness and isolation of the hunter and the hunted, the endless gulf between time and eternity and the abyss of ultimate despair.

The crowd around her were all busy each in his or her separate ways. The women were adjusting the veils on their heads before entering into the chamber, while the men were flicking imaginary dust from their suits that had been carefully valeted for this occasion that had a widely different significance for each of the pilgrims. Some were fingering their rosaries that they wished to be blessed, others were clutching the religious medals and tokens in their hands that they too would offer to their Father of all Fathers that he might touch them for a moment with his gloved hands. Small groups here and there were openly gossiping about what he would wear, what he would look like and what he would say to them.

As Father Révérony joined them an uneasy silence fell across the assembled company. He outlined to them the procedure to be followed. They would walk in an orderly line, each in turn would kneel at the Holy Father's feet and kiss first his slipper, then his ring. They must keep their heads bowed and remain in reverential silence throughout the whole proceedings. Only if the Pope himself addressed them and asked them a question must they speak at all, and then only to answer his question as shortly and simply as possible. Suddenly he paused, and moving across to where the Martins were standing, looking straight at Thérèse he said forcefully and pointedly, 'And I completely forbid anyone, anyone', he repeated to give the word its full emphasis, 'to address the Holy Father on any matter whatsoever.'

The commanding tones in the priest's voice as he uttered these words, the fact that although he had appeared to address them to the whole assembly but had in actuality meant them for her ears alone threw Thérèse into a state of panic. Her body was trembling with fear, her will seemed to be losing its power to impose upon her what she had felt until this moment was her proper course of action. Had Mother Gonzague been right when she had instructed her to make a personal request to the Pope himself about her entry into Carmel? Had Pauline, her dearly loved sister, been right when she had advised caution and had tried to dissuade her from such an extreme course of action? Had her parish priest been right when he had assured her that in all matters appertaining to her vocation she must seek the will of God and then pursue it as directed by her own conscience? Could the Church Militant ever become part of the Church Triumphant unless there were those who were prepared to dare all to answer the challenge of the words 'Follow Me?' These and a dozen other questions were tormenting her brain as the doors were flung open and they silently moved forward into the audience chamber.

The eyes of all the pilgrims instantly turned towards where Leo XIII was sitting on his Papal throne. How tiny he looked huddled up in the huge chair. What an insignificant figure he seemed set as he was against the vastness of the chamber with its long walls and its high ceiling. The jewels in the simple cross he was wearing flashed streaks of coloured light across the rooms as they reflected the morning sunlight that was streaming through the window. The large seal of his office in the ring that he wore made it appear too large and top heavy for his frail hands. His face was the soft yellow of ageing parchment and his eyes seemed to pierce right into your innermost being when he glanced at you as you moved towards him. His hands had a gentleness, a sense of sublime peace in them as he moved them into the sign of the cross and gave you his papal benediction. His voice, so soft that you would have thought it to be inaudible had a resonance that enabled all those around him to hear quite clearly what the Holy Father was saying.

First of all the Chamberlain escorted Father Révérony to the Pope's side and instructed him to remain there throughout the proceedings. The priest knelt for a moment, offered his obedience, explained to the Pope the meaning of the pilgrimage, waiting to rise from his knees until he had been summoned to do so by his Spiritual Father.

Leo XIII raised himself from his throne, stood quite still for a moment, looked round the whole assembled company and then told them how happy he was to welcome them to the city of the apostles. He reminded them of the troubles that had beset their country, of the spirit of arrogant materialism that was threatening to undermine the faith all over Europe. He talked of vanity of men who in their folly sought to persuade others to deny the very existence of God. Action, that was what the church was calling for in this one of its darkest hours. Catholics themselves must seek to know more of the meaning of the faith and be ready to impart the knowledge they had gained to their fellows. Prayer, fervent prayer for the salvation of souls must be their constant offering. Good works, acts of charity, personal dedication to seek to know and fulfil the will of God as revealed through His church, this must be their constant endeavour. There was a note of sadness, a sense of loneliness and longing in his voice as he addressed them.

Each one of the company, even those who only an hour earlier had been full of the worldliness that dominated most of their lives felt that although this was a general citation it had a personal meaning for each one of them. For Thérèse Martin the words, 'Seeking to know and fulfil the Will of God as revealed in one's own heart and upheld by the authority of the Church' had a special significance. A courage not her own, a will to do what she must that did not seem of her own making gave her the strength and inspiration she needed for the difficult task that lay ahead of her. As she moved forward to kneel at the Pontiff's feet a quiet voice from the priest standing beside him said, 'Remember, my child, I have forbidden you to speak to the Holy Father'.

The Pope himself seemed quite oblivious of the words that the priest had uttered. Something inside him disturbed him very profoundly as this child, for she seemed little more than that to him, knelt in humble obedience before him.

Thérèse kissed his slippered foot, raised her head a little to kiss his sealed ring and then gazing straight into his eyes said in clear and unhesitating tones, 'Holy Father, I wish to enter the Carmel at Lisieux at the age of fifteen and seek your permission to do so.'

There was a gasp of consternation from the people standing near her and the Priest at the Pope's elbow immediately said, 'This is a girl from the parish of Lisieux whom I have already forbidden to speak to you, Holy Father. The matter she is seeking to raise has already been discussed by the proper authorities in the diocese and I am sure that you, Holy Father, will assure her that she must wait upon their decision.' There was a coldness, a hardness in the priest's voice that signified quite clearly to all who heard his words the displeasure behind them.

The words had no effect upon the kneeling girl, in fact it seemed to those around her that she could not have heard them. 'Holy Father, in honour of your jubilee allow me to enter Carmel at the age of fifteen.'

This time it was the Vicar General's turn to express his displeasure. 'Holy Father, this is a child who desires to become a Carmelite and the superiors of Carmel are looking into the matter.' By this time Thérèse had clasped the Pope's hand and was holding it in her own. 'Well, my child,' The Pope remarked, 'do whatever the superiors may decide.' Thérèse was terror-stricken. All this way and now frustration. Laying her hands on the Pope's lap she appealed to him once more. 'Holy Father, if only you were to say yes, everyone else would be willing.'

The Pope was nonplussed. He was not used to discussions of this kind during an audience and had never in the past experienced anyone disobeying her superiors in the way this girl had done. There was something about her that made him feel ill at ease. The gentleness, the honesty, the forthrightness and the sincerity that underlay the whole incident moved him profoundly. He was the sanctified instrument of God in His Church. He was the Guardian of its Faith, the Upholder of its Morals. In his hands as he sat enthroned in majesty and power, the humble and willing instrument of the Holy Spirit, were the Keys of the Kingdom. Years of struggle, years of disillusionment, years of bitter conflict between the church and the world had brought to him a realisation that the spirit still moveth where it listeth and he was more impressed at that moment than he dared to admit even to himself at the courage of this child. The Church over which he ruled and presided with such dignity and devotion had made mistakes in the past and would make them again in the future. Its central message, the one factor that gave truth to its divine meaning was the uniqueness of each individual soul before God.

He looked straight into the kneeling supplicant's eyes. Quietly, with a kindliness that infused itself into every word, he said, 'Well child, well, you will enter if it be God's will'. Thérèse opened her mouth to plead with the Pope once more but two of the Papal Guards closed in on her and with the assistance of Father Révérony lifted her to her feet. She seemed like a dead weight and it was obvious to them that unless she co-operated with them they might have to carry her out of the chamber.

Suddenly the Pope motioned to them to remain still. He looked straight into Thérèse's eyes once more, smiled at her gently as he placed his fingers across her lips to silence them, and blessed her. The other pilgrims who were there were all surprised to see that the Pope's eyes followed her all the time she was being escorted out of the audience chamber.

The tears flowed down Thérèse Martin's cheeks. There was nothing now but a sense of despair, an inner feeling of utter failure. Darkness and desolation, a darkness deeper than darkness and a desolation deeper than despair. What could she do, what could she say? 'I am the little plaything of the Infant Jesus and if He wishes to break His toy He is very welcome. Whatever He wishes I wish.'

There is something so terrifying in these words of complete resignation that we need to ponder on them for hours in order to distil from them their full significance and meaning. Thérèse Martin had sought the consent of her parish priest and he had instructed her to seek permission from Father Révérony. Her plea had been discounted and her prayers had seemed all in vain. Thérèse Martin had courageously sought permission from the Bishop of Bayeux whom she knew could override the Superior's ruling on the matter and had failed again. It was true that he had promised to give the matter further thought and let her have his final decision when she was in Italy but there had been no word from him. Probably in the fulfilling of the many tasks that fell to his hands the Bishop had forgotten the Martin child who had amused him a little as she sat buried in the huge armchair in his study. Thérèse Martin had dared everything, even possibly committing the sin of disobedience to appeal to the Pope himself but once more failure pursued her every endeavour. All or nothing, that was what she had longed for, hoped for, striven after and prayed for and it seemed now that nothing was the result and the answer to all the efforts she had made to pursue what she alone appeared to know as her true calling.

The apparent failure of her mission to Rome meant that her high song was over. Failure and despair seemed to have pursued her all that way, and in this, her final effort, even hope itself seemed to have deserted her. What folly it all seemed to be, for her, a simple girl of fifteen to travel half-way across Europe to challenge the authority of the church itself. Dare she, in all honesty suggest for one moment that she was right and the church was wrong? Was she audacious enough to consider the inner voice that had commanded her to give herself wholly and entirely to God was in truth and that the authorities within the church whom she had consulted were all in error? A hopeless dilemma and one that called for the services of a much more profound theologian than the girl from Lisieux to untangle. Perhaps those who suggested the idea was a childish fancy she would grow out of were right. Probably the advice her uncle Guérin had given her in the first place had been the sanest counsel of all – to wait until she was older before taking such a violent and momentous decision.

As she sat in her hotel room drawing close to her the surrounding darkness that she might find some comfort in its silent folds of oblivion to the light, Thérèse found herself thinking how insignificant her simple little altar she had made in the garden at home was to the golden and bejewelled splendour of the high altar of St Peter's.

Outwardly she was in a state of supreme rebellion, inwardly she was completely at peace. All or nothing, why did those words keep haunting her? 'I choose all,' came the triumphant echo of the phrase she herself had uttered so many years ago. Thérèse Martin knew, in spite of her tender years that although there seemed to be no human hand left to help her, the wounded hands of love and pity were still pleading with her to enter into that complete abandonment of perfect trust.

Many heard that voice that whispered so softly that the words it uttered seemed to melt into silence almost before they were spoken, but few were prepared to heed its commands. 'Go, sell all thou hast and give to the poor' was not for the masses. 'If a man seeks thy coat give him thy cloak also' was not said to the masses. 'Unless a man forsake his father and mother, his wife and child, then he is not worthy of my kingdom' was said to the few, that they might journey in loneliness and solitude to the mountain top and from their point of vantage lead others to the land of promise.

During the two days that followed the fateful day in the papal chamber Louis Martin remained in Rome while his two daughters joined the other pilgrims on a journey to Naples and Pompeii. Perhaps the distractions of seeing these two towns would help to heal the wound that he knew had pierced Thérèse right through to the heart. He had ventured all on this request to Rome, to the highest authority in the church and it seemed that the long, trying and at times tedious journey had burnt its high hopes out into the dust and ashes of disillusion. Louis Martin could not escape from the frightening look in his daughter's eyes as he had taken her into his arms and attempted to offer her some words of comfort as they left the papal audience. He recalled all he had tried to do as a layman to help the new approaches that were being made in the realm of Catholic action. He tried to recall whom he knew at Rome who might be able to help and advise as to the best way to deal with the impasse which they had found themselves in.

Suddenly he recalled Brother Simeon whom he had met on a previous visit to the Holy City. He had seemed to be a kind, a gentle and an understanding man and it was said of him that he had great influence in Vatican circles, and that even the Pope himself had consulted him upon important issues before now. He would go along immediately and seek him out and talk the whole question of his daughter's vocation and her desire to enter a convent at the age of fourteen over with Brother Simeon. Second opinions were always useful and at least Louis Martin knew from past experience that he was sure of an unbiased and unprejudiced hearing from this simple monk whose piety was a byword all around St Peter's.

In the meantime Father Révérony was not feeling too happy about the turn that events had taken. The girl's behaviour had been outrageous. It was almost impossible to forgive the manner in which she had openly flouted his authority and that in the presence of some of the highest dignitaries in the church. Still it had needed a great deal of courage to behave the way she had done, and he had had a long enough and profound enough experience as a priest to know that very few people indeed, much less a girl who was little more than a child, would have dared to ignore his admonition to remain silent. What if he was wrong in his assessment of the Martin girl's vocation? It would not be the first time in the history of the church that a painstaking priest had proved to be in the wrong and a potential saint had proved to be in the right. He knew that the rule of morality must not be seen as the manacles placed upon sanctity.

The church in her wisdom laid down regulations for the ordinary, the everyday life and habits of simple Christian souls who sought and found the way to heaven by implicit obedience. What of the extraordinary souls, the ones whose obedience had become such a fine and rarified thing that it moved within the requests of heaven and refused to be confined by the commands of earth. Simple friars had defied popes in the past and proved to be in the right. Simple nuns had stood up to the bishops and princes of the church, calling upon them to see the error of the ways into which the church was drifting. God had given His church the truth and had ordained that it should be protected from error. God had given the See of Peter to the Popes and had placed in their keeping the keys of the kingdom. But God had also throughout history called upon men and women to forsake the common ways and take that razor-edged pathway that led to perfection, and once that call came to them none, not even the Supreme Pontiff himself could say them nay.

Why had Father Delatroette been so sure that he was right, and Mother Gonzague equally sure that he was wrong about the meaning and purpose of Thérèse Martin's calling? Both of them were sound, reliable and sanctified souls, and each of them were seeking in his or her own way to interpret the will of God. The riddle was too much for him, there was only one thing to do and that was seek out Brother Simeon and ask his advice for many said that he was the simplest, the most humble and the most sincere man in Rome.

Louis Martin had hardly finished telling Brother Simeon the full story of his daughter's life and her feelings about her vocation, gaining the friar's assurance that he would certainly try to open the matter again in the right quarters, when Father Révérony entered the room. He hesitated a little, he felt a trifle uneasy at finding himself in Louis Martin's presence. He guessed that they were obviously both bent on the same errand. Almost before the priest could say anything the friar took his hands and said very quietly, 'My brother in Christ, we may both be witnessing a miracle and neither of us have the courage to accept the fact that they still happen in the nineteenth century. In France, you may feel a girl of fourteen is too young to offer herself as a bride of Christ although you would not hesitate to marry her to the man who had her parent's consent to take her as his wife. In Italy we let the butcher, the baker and the candlestick maker each pursue their own ends but we never frustrate the wishes of those who feel they have a different, and dare I suggest it, a slightly higher calling.'

There was a twinkle in the friar's eyes as he spoke these words and an inner joy seemed to fill Louis Martin's heart as he heard them. Father Révérony was much more matter of fact about the whole business. 'It seems to me I have made a mistake. My opposition was rooted in pride. I will try to make amends,' he added, turning to where Louis was standing, 'I will do all I can to assist your daughter to fulfil her wish and enter Carmel by Christmas if possible.'

When Thérèse and Céline rejoined their father in Rome to make the journey back to Lisieux neither of them reacted with any conviction when

they were told of Father Révérony's change of heart. There had been so
many setbacks along the way that it seemed as though the highroad to her
heavenly citadel would never straighten itself out for Thérèse Martin. Even
when the priest himself, who had been so adamant with her suggested to her
that he had reconsidered the whole matter and was now prepared to do all
he could to make reparation for the mistakes he had made during the past
few months, this did little or nothing to lighten the heavy burden that had
settled on Thérèse Martin's shoulders. The antique splendour of Assisi, the
wonder of the leaning tower of Pisa, the arrogant glories of Florence and
the gold and blue and green of the French Riviera did little to bring any
sort of consolation to her. All she wanted was God; and the stumbling block
seemed to be the church to which she had given such unswerving loyalty
and implicit obedience.

The Martin family arrived back at Lisieux to find that the sombre loveliness
of autumn had been replaced by the barren stretches of winter and that each
morning a nip of frost chilled the air. The weeks rolled on, Christmas
approached and still no news from the Bishop as to what decision he had arrived upon about Thérèse's future. Every day she walked to the post office with
her father hoping that the promised letter would be awaiting them there and
every day she came away heavier of heart, and saddened in spirit until at last
she became the victim of an inner despair that was more frightening than
anything she had hitherto experienced. There was no one she could turn to
for consolation and understanding. Her father seemed to be withdrawing
more and more inside himself and spending longer hours each day in the
quietness of his beloved Belvedere. Céline, the deeply loved and affectionate
playmate of so many years, found herself unable to aid Thérèse out of her
fits of moroseness in any way. Even Pauline, who had done so much to
help her and to nurse her developing vocation, seemed to stand away
from the tragedy that was overshadowing her youngest sister's inner life.

A torturing sense of despair, a frightening awareness of defeat, these
things surrounded her in her walks to church, in her wanderings round the
little garden, even following her to the solitude of her own room where
she went to meditate and pray for a single ray of light to illumine the outer
darkness that was clouding her soul with increasing and unceasing pain. The
battering rams of doubt were undermining the very foundations of her faith
itself.

The devil never comes in single guise. He recruits his tempters from those
around us and offers his bribes to us in such a way that they appear as words
of hope whereas in reality they are a message of despair. Louis Martin
himself grew more and more disturbed as the days passed and there was no

G

word of any kind from the Bishop. Perhaps God did not desire the sacrifice of this his youngest child, but was going to leave her with him to be the light and glory of his old age. Those eyes, those lovely serene eyes that had once sparkled with inner laughter seemed dull and lifeless. Those cheeks that had glowed with health now looked pale and wan. That mouth that had always been ready to break into a smile was tightly drawn, its thin coldly set line looking like a defiant gesture at the merciless torment the fates had sent into his beloved child's life.

He took her by the hand for a walk she loved so well along the country lanes that surrounded the house. As they wandered along he told her of a new pilgrimage, a new spiritual adventure he was planning for them. They would visit the Holy Land together. They would stand on the sacred ground of Bethlehem and on the hallowed place known as Calvary. For a moment her face lit up. How near she would be to her beloved Lord if she trod the way that His feet had travelled? How deeply she might enter into His pain and suffering if she could kneel and pray in that lonely spot where He too had known the agony of desertion and denial and betrayal, Gethsemane.

The mocking voices of the tempters, the strident laughter of the evil ones, these had failed to force her into a renunciation of the way she had sought to follow for so long. The soft, persuasive tones of her beloved father's voice as he outlined his ideas for this sacred journey almost succeeded in winning her from her avowed purpose. Perhaps she had been wrong all the time. Perhaps she was meant to live her life out in the world and enjoy its day to day pleasures. Perhaps she was being selfish in seeking to leave her father to a life of loneliness and solitude as he reached the twilight of his days. A gentle breeze was caressing the branches of the leafless trees, a solitary bird song was echoing through the shadowed dusk of the winter afternoon. Suddenly, a soft and insistent voice spoke to her. She had no idea from where it came. It was very much akin to the inner voice that had guided her for so long. 'Lo, all the kingdoms of the earth I will give thee if thou wilt fall down and worship me.' No, No, No, the one word cleaved the air like the challenging note of the sanctuary bell. Denial and betrayal, was this all that the world was offering her in place of the abiding love that she knew awaited her in Carmel? Very quietly she told her father that she felt she must write to the Bishop and plead with him once more. Christmas had come and gone and the gateway to the cloister seemed to be closed to her forever.

Her uncle helped her to compose the letter that they posted to the Bishop of Bayeux. It was a simple letter, a final pleading with his Lordship to make his decision known to his obedient servant, and ending with the assurance that whatever the Bishop's decision may be she would accept it in all humility, in complete obedience as became a loyal daughter of the church. The waiting for a reply seemed interminable. Every second seemed to be a year and every day another long and desolate stretch of wasteland in the desert of despair. At last a message arrived from the Prioress of Carmel that the Bishop had left the final decision entirely to her judgement and that she had decided that Thérèse could enter Carmel on 9th April, 1888. Thérèse felt a trifle perturbed about the further delay for it was early January when she received the good news, but the Mother Prioress felt that it was wise to delay her entry until after the community had passed through the rigorous fasting and discipline of Lent, an ordeal that might prove too arduous for a new postulant who was only just over fifteen years of age.

On Sunday, 4th April, Louis Martin invited their relatives and one or two of their closest friends to the farewell party he had long planned to give when the day arrived before his daughter's admission to the convent. The table torches enhanced the polished wood of the dining table. The board was full and festive as became a meal that was to Thérèse the prelude to a wedding feast. Her steps were light as she walked from room to room saying goodbye to every shelf, every wall, every cupboard, every door in the place she had known and loved so deeply as home.

Her father accompanied her as she took her last walk round the garden where they had spent so many happy hours together. There were still one or two winter flowers tucked away in the nooks and crannies in the rockery and she plucked these to make of them her final offering at her own little shrine at the end of the shrubbery. A tearful kiss for Tom, her dog who had been such a welcome friend during the dark months she had passed through. There were tears and laughter, tales told of times long passed and hopes expressed for days that still lay awaiting them in the future.

> How full of anguish are these farewells! When one would wish to see oneself forgotten, the most loving words escape all around as though to make one feel the sacrifice of the separation all the more.

What a perfect felicity there is in these simple words that express perfectly Thérèse's feelings at this momentous day when a world would be lost to her in order that another world might be won. The family all walked with her to the convent chapel to take part in the Mass at which she was to offer herself to the novitiate.

As they knelt in prayer and thanksgiving awaiting the moment when Thérèse should kneel and seek her father's blessing before passing through the narrow door that would never open outwards for her again, the solemnity seemed to all the members of the congregation that morning to be overpowering. What a child she looked and how proudly she held up her head when the Mother Prioress opened the door leading from the sanctuary to the convent and beckoned her towards it. The serene affection on her face, a face haloed with her golden hair was remembered and talked of for many years after the event I am describing had taken place. Her own rapture was so intense that as she reached the door and knelt before her kneeling father for his benediction she felt that her heart was about to stop beating. Happiness, unalloyed joy, no not quite, for when the ceremony of her reception was over and she moved slowly through the open door she heard Father Delatroette, the spiritual superior of Carmel, say in a voice loud enough for all those nearby to hear, 'Well, my Reverend Mother, you can sing a Te Deum. As the delegate of the Bishop I present you this child of fifteen whose entry you have desired. I trust that she will not disappoint your hopes, but I remind you if it turns out otherwise you alone will bear the responsibility.'

Even the Reverend Mother was stunned into an amazed silence at the coldly calculated cruelty of these remarks. He had fought and he had lost; surely the vanquished could afford to be magnanimous on an occasion such as this. She had fought and she had won but her own heart trembled when she thought of the tasks that she knew lay ahead of her in nursing and nurturing this latest postulant into the life of sanctity that the Mother Prioress knew was her destiny.

Thérèse moved quietly out of sight and as the door closed on her she felt the prick of the first barb in the crown of thorns that was to be gradually placed upon her head. All or nothing, she was offering her all and nothing other than that mattered any more. I choose all, but did she realise as she recalled this phrase that all meant the loneliness of that deserted garden that lay close to a hill called Calvary?

Part Two

The Elected Silence

Elected silence sing to me
And beat upon my whorled ear,
Pipe me to pastures still and be
The music that I care to hear.

Shape nothing lips; be lovely dumb,
It is the shut, the curfew sent,
From there where all surrenders come
Which only make you eloquent.

And Poverty be thou the bride
And now the marriage feast begun,
And lily-coloured clothes provide
Your spouse not laboured at nor spun.

THE HABIT OF PERFECTION. *Gerard Manley Hopkins*

CHAPTER VI

The Cornerstones of Carmel

From time immemorial, man has sought for that something beyond, for that inner sensed reality that he feels is at the root of any meaning or purpose there may be in life. The New Testament is an ample witness to the significant role that awareness of God has played from the very outset in the Christian ethos. The fourth gospel opens with the strange and to some completely meaningless words, 'In the beginning was the Word, and the Word was with God and the Word was God,' and ends with a book of mystical and prophetic visions, the Revelation of St John the Divine. What is it that these men and women whom we meet all through the pages of the Christian story are seeking? What is the divine discontent that drives some of them to extremes of physical discipline that appears to us almost verging on madness, others to revel in orgies of sensuality that makes us question their sanity? An impulse for otherness, an appetite for sanctification, a desire for unity – or union with the beginning and end of existence in all its manifold manifestations.

As we are concerned here mainly with the Christian approach to mystical experience, and the impulse that drives men and women to seek to guide themselves away from the world to the quietness and seclusion of the cloister, let us narrow our approach in order to see this approach to reality in its historical perspective, in so far as it effects Thérèse Martin, henceforward to be known as Sister Thérèse of the Child Jesus and Holy Face.

There are those who claim that Christ Himself during the lost thirty years of His life lived among the Essenes, a Jewish sect who practised physical austerities and lived a carefully disciplined life to strive to discover for themselves Jehovah, and who sought to translate into terms of practical experience what the message of God was for the soul of man. They upheld the concept of a progressive revelation. They believed that the prophets of Israel were all part of a continuous unfolding of the mind and heart of God for mankind. They were the forerunners, the supporters of the Messianic tradition that saw in the sayings of the prophets the promise of the one who should come to restore Israel back to her true and noble purpose as the chosen people of God.

The basic ideas of this desert community has much in common with the mainsprings in the development of Christian mysticism and the concepts of Christian contemplation. Man was a threefold creature, a being of body, soul and spirit. His objective, in seeking for reality, was not to divide his

103

threefold nature but to strive to harmonise it into a perfect unity. The body, the soul and the spirit were all equally good in themselves. Evil, the breaking of the knowledge of man's union with God, had arisen from the misuse of the human will and had led in its turn to the abuse of man's freedom. If man sold himself in bonded slavery to the body, becoming by virtue of this state a creature encrusted in sensuality, he was denying his threefold nature, destroying his wholeness. If on the other hand he sought to deny the natural claims of the body and its appetites, he was in danger of forgetting that he had been made in the image of God, and would force himself into the false concept that the material world was an evil place, the realm of the devil and all his works, and thus deny it its true place in the plan of the Creator. Only by the subjection of the body under the restraint of a guided will that restored it back into its true relationship with the soul could he move into an awareness of spirit, and in so doing find the fulfilment of his deepest and most profound objectives.

Since Christ Himself established the pattern of solace through solitude and union through prayer and since His central mission was to lead men through death to life, then it becomes comparatively easy to understand why in the early days of the church many sought to find His way in the deep silences of the desert places, where, withdrawn from the world, having tasted to the full of its disillusionment they might by disciplined contemplation find the alpha and the omega, the beginning and the end of all human striving. Man may be, as the mystics throughout the ages have claimed, a spark of the divine flame; his human life may be, as Plato saw it, simply shadows on the walls of the cave of the flesh that imprisons him, but he is also a social animal and can only realise himself in a community.

St Benedict was one of the first men to recognise the true significance of this fact and so he endeavoured to persuade the hermits, the Desert Fathers as they have been called, to join in communal work and worship, and to bind themselves together under the Ancient Rule that forms the basic foundation of monastic life today. The rule itself, like all other things that man has devised for his guidance from the temporal to the eternal has been modified with the passage of time, but in its essence it still maintains that only by the exertion of the will to foster those things that man knows by common acceptance to be good can time be redeemed and our intimations of immortality be realised.

With that wisdom that has always been part of the philosophy of the Christian Church it has always been recognised that the ascent to Carmel is not the pathway that all must tread who seek perfection. Some are called to be scientists, some to be legislators, some to be parents, some to be philosophers . . . the few are summoned age by age to withdraw from the world, to stand apart from the orbit of ordinary experience and strive to keep the reservoirs of divine power full enough to meet the needs of struggling humanity. Thus we see that the monk and the nun are not alien creatures, they are part of the common life of the community and as such are playing a necessary and proper part in completing the perfect pattern of a balanced order. They are the leaven of life and without that leaven we all suffer from a sense of our inability to seek and know the truth, and find in and through it our individual fulfilment.

The religious does not retire from the world to escape from his responsibilities. By a voluntary effort of the will he seeks to prove to us that sanctity can be found scouring pots, that perfection can be realised scrubbing pans, and that the practice of prayer is an essential part of the life of the whole man. The tragedy is that our prejudice prevents us from seeing our perfect ability, and that our arrogance blinds us to the need each one of us has to live constantly in a state of humility. We may well be on the way to conquering space, but we have not yet learned the most essential lesson of all and that is how to live in perfect harmony one with another?

The late Eric Gill has probably, more clearly than any other modern writer, summarised the meaning of the spiritual life for each one of us in the closing passage of his *Autobiography*.

> And if I might attempt to state, in one paragraph the work which I have chiefly tried to do in my life it is this: to make a cell of good living in the chaos of our world. I hope above all things I have done something towards re-integrating bed and board, the small farm and the workshop, the home and the school, earth and heaven.

These words are in some ways a restatement by a layman for laymen of the life of the religious. They open up for each of us a doorway into Carmel. They summarise for us the underlying meaning of the discipline that forms the basic pattern of life in an enclosed order. Eric Gill himself was a member of the Third Order of St Dominic, a body of laymen and women who strive while living in the world to direct their lives under a modified form of the Ancient Rule that they too may know something of a peace both of solitude and a life of action rooted in the way of contemplation.

Let us pause for a few moments to take a closer look at the woman who was to have such a decisive influence on the monastic life for all time.

Teresa de Cepela y Ahymadas, better known as St Teresa of Avila, was born on 28th March 1515. She was a daughter of one of the upper-class families of the town, and from the earliest days of her childhood took a keen and lively interest in all that was going on in the world around her. The echo of the Crusades could still be heard in the market places and taverns of Spain, and the battles to cast out the Moorish invaders and infidels who had almost conquered the country were still burning topics of conversation in the business houses and drawing rooms of the city. At one period in her childhood she set out with her elder brother on a missionary journey, and although it did not take her very far from her home it set its stamp on the pattern that was to emerge as the underlying feature of her future life.

She was a strong-minded, disciplined and determined person, very feminine in appearance but distinctly masculine in outlook, and she was to reform the Carmelite order and establish for it the pattern that still persists as its central feature today. Her reading was extensive, her knowledge of the weaknesses and frailties of human nature terrifying, and her kindness and consideration for others unbounded. Teresa of Avila might well have claimed, as did Queen Elizabeth of England, that although she had the body of a woman she had the heart and mind of a man. In fact these two women who were so diametrically opposed in many ways had much in common when one studies the lives they lived in the world of action. The one, dominated all her life by a hatred of the Papacy, linked with political ambitions that made her name a byword in all the diplomatic circles in the courts of Europe, the other guided by an allegiance to the Papacy and a desire to see the Church militant reformed from within was a thorn in the flesh of many of the worldly and pompous ecclesiastics of her day.

The Convent of the Incarnation at Avila was not better but not worse than many of the religious houses of its day. Its discipline was lax, in fact some might even claim it was non-existent, its rule of life centred on the material well-being of its occupants, many of whom although they were clothed as nuns of the Carmelite order were little more than worldly-encrusted women who saw the convent cloisters and parlour as an easy background for the self-indulgent lives they lived. They ate meat regularly although this was forbidden in the discipline to which they had vowed obedience. They ignored the fast-days of the church when it suited their purpose. They entertained their male friends although the portals of the convent were supposed to be locked against any invasion of the male sex except their confessors and spiritual advisers. Their lives, although they were meant to be lived in poverty and austerity, were surrounded by pleasures and worldly luxury making them an easy target for the many criticisms that were being made against the religious houses of that time.

There were still the few who followed the ancient rule of St Benedict, seeking to dedicate themselves to work and worship. There were still the isolated hermits and anchorites who were striving in their personal lives to sanctify the meaning of holy poverty. In the main, however, the Catholic Church was at low-water mark, and many shook their heads and murmured that its days were surely numbered. The Spanish Inquisition, a wicked and formidable institution that had little in common with the Holy Office was always waiting to persecute, imprison, torture and execute those who too openly voiced their opinions about the growing corruption within the church, and few were bold enough or brave enough to dare to challenge the authority it had usurped from Rome.

It is difficult in some ways to understand why Teresa never married; not only was she attractive to men but many were very deeply attracted to her as was proved throughout her long and arduous life as the Reformer of Carmel. There was undoubtedly a touch of the spartan about her, a suggestion of intellectual arrogance that made her look a little askance at the pleasure-loving and at times rather effeminate young men who crossed her path in her late teens. Whatever the cause may have been, and even in her own life she does not give us any very clear indication on this point, we know that she entered the Convent of the Incarnation as a novice on All Souls Day 1536 when she was twenty-one, and became a fully professed nun a year later.

From the outset she was moved by a spirit of discontent, an inner rebellion against the life that was lived by so many of its inmates. Her sole objective was to know God, to love God and to seek in all things to do what she felt was His will for her as a woman dedicated to the religious calling. The nuns around her might view with a certain amount of trepidation the manner in which she imposed upon herself the basic discipline of the spiritual life. Her confessor and spiritual adviser might from time to time question the austere attitude she had towards her own vocation. The Mother Prioress might wonder who this wild bird was that seemed in some ways to be the cuckoo in the nest. In spite of these things or perhaps because of them, most of the people who came into contact with her had to give a grudging admiration for her courage and sincerity.

Teresa of Avila has given to us in her own writing, and what fresh and vigorous writings they are, her own account of the journey she took from the shadowed places in the valley of desolation to the illumined heights at the summit of Mount Carmel, and it was out of the fruits of her own experience that she was to formulate the rules that were to underlie her foundation of the reformed Carmelite Order. Her life of prayer was to open up to her realms of inspiration and experience that made her one of the greatest Christian mystics of all time, and was destined to give to her a reputation that even her severest critics have never dared to challenge. Her writings on the practical business of organising and running a convent were full of a down to earth common sense that is as pertinent today as it was in her own times.

Of one thing we are certain and that is that she had made a deep and profound study of the Spiritual Exercises of St Ignatius Loyola, and that she had applied these exercises, in a modified form perhaps, to the development and unfolding of her own interior life. These exercises, and they are still part of the basic training of the Jesuits of today, might fairly be summarised as a Christian form of Yoga leading men stage by stage to the dwelling place of the soul itself, and from there to a perfect and complete union with the will of God, that is by its very nature the mind and heart of love itself.

The word psychic is today looked upon by many as base coinage. Every newspaper has its tame astrologer, every magazine its popular fortune teller. Crystal gazers and clairvoyants abound everywhere. These things in themselves do not deny the reality of psychic phenomena, and just as the manufactured diamond cannot be used to dispute the sparkling radiance of the true stone no more can the camp followers of these strange, contradictory and bewildering cults be called upon as witnesses against the genuine manifestations of divine grace.

On August 15th, 1539, Teresa passed through a terrifying experience where she found herself in a state described at the time as the living death. The medical knowledge and skill of those days knew little or nothing about the 'fit' that possessed her, but from the descriptions we have of it, it appears to have been a cataleptic seizure of some kind. All those around her stiffened body pronounced her dead, in fact they were so sure they were surveying a corpse that when she eventually regained consciousness she found that she had the wax on her eyelids that was used in those days to close the eyes of the dead. Her own words as to how she felt when this frightening experience was over give a more graphic description of how she felt than any of mine can hope to do.

> My tongue was bitten to pieces. Nothing had passed my lips and because of this and of my great weakness my throat was choking me so that I even could not take water. All my bones seemed to be out of joint, and there was a terrible confusion in my head . . . I could move, I think, only one finger of my right hand. They used to move me on a sheet one taking one end and the other the other.

The effects of this seizure lasted until the following Easter, and for three years she lay in bed, in her cell, in the convent almost completely paralysed. There were moments when a sense of hopelessness, a feeling of utter despair possessed her, but with that volatile spirit that gave her an unknown inner strength she assures us that, 'when I began to get about on my hands and knees I praised God'.

We now move into what is undoubtedly the most dangerous period of her life to write about and certainly, in some ways, the most difficult to understand. Dangerous, because we are moving towards the fringe of the unknown, difficult because there are our personal barriers of prejudice and scepticism that seek all the while to betray us into cancelling her experiences out as either honest delusions or fraudulent impositions upon the credulity of others. Clairvoyance, the ability to see with the inner eyes, and clairaudience, the power to hear with the inner ear are both suspect territories in the twentieth century. They bordered on the fringes of witchcraft in the century of which I am writing and many a woman found herself on the ducking stool in gallows for claiming to possess these uncanny powers that many believed were a gift from the devil.

Teresa claims that during the formative years of her life's mission she was guided almost entirely by 'visions and voices' that directed her soul along the pathway it must tread in its heavenly pilgrimage. It must be stressed, however, that at each stage in the perilous journey she made herself completely subject to the guidance of her confessors and to the advice of her spiritual superiors, and that none of them found the slightest semblance of error in what her visions showed her or in what her voices directed her to undertake. Within the Convent of the Incarnation itself she had her enemies, those who saw her as a fake and a charlatan, but they based their charges mainly on the fact that she was challenging them to live their lives in closer accord with the rule of holy poverty than they were prepared to do, and in implicit obedience to the austerity that should have been the foundation stone of their spiritual lives.

The truth, when it was finally revealed to her, both staggered and startled her, for her mission, she was told, was to set about the complete reformation of the Carmelite Order.

As to how she was to accomplish this and how she was to achieve her ultimate goal of recreating the monastic life in accord with the primitive rule out of which it had developed and emerged was a task that had no easy solution. She was bound by obedience, she lived under authority, so that it was no simple thing to walk out of the Incarnation and found a convent of her own. For to do this she must have the permission of her immediate superiors, the blessing of the bishops in whose diocese she wished to carry on her activities, and letters patent from Rome authorising her to set up new religious houses under her reformed rule.

Poverty was to be the cornerstone. In seeking the service of God they must not rely on the rich patrons who gave much of their wealth to the already existing religious communities. Complete trust in God, an ardent realisation that He would provide the means for their subsistence, this was the second cornerstone of the new edifices that were to rise all over Spain to the glory of His name. A realisation that there was no fundamental division between work and worship, and that you could praise God while scouring pots and scrubbing pans was the third, and the fourth and in some ways the most important of all since the other three were there to guarantee its stability, a determination to make steady and gradual progress to the unfolding of the interior life.

Avila itself was more than doubtful of the wisdom of what it saw as a foolhardy project inspired largely by a cranky woman who claimed to have special revelations from God. Her superiors, while being forced by Teresa's obvious sincerity to recognise the honesty of her aims were very dubious as to what might be the consequences once she had commenced to put these aims into action. The bishops, in spite of the fact that they were forced to see that her objective was closely akin to the monastic ideals of the primitive church wondered whether it was a wise course to follow in the sixteenth century. While the Papacy, with the ability for compromise when it came to matters of this kind, was content to hold a watching brief leaving any immediate decisions to its underlings.

Like Jeanne D'Arc who had been such a thorn in the flesh of both the English and the French, and about whom the ecclesiastical authorities of her day had been equally divided, Teresa of Avila knew that her visions were true, and that what her voices bade her do must be done in spite of any obstacles that might be put in her path, and that it was as a penniless supplicant that she must take up her staff and make those long, tedious and difficult journeys, the results of which were to make her a legend even in her own lifetime. The Discalced Carmelites, the barefooted ones, must live in separate cells, their monasteries must be small, each community not exceeding thirteen in number, they must live completely enclosed, cut off from the world of their fellow men, and their lives must be dedicated wholly to the salvation of souls through prayer.

This was a revolution that even the Catholic Church itself in those days had not bargained for, but this straight speaking, hard-hitting, undefeatable optimist knew that in the end her way must prove victorious. Almost as soon as she had one house established she set out to found another, and very soon the men as well as the women were all seeking to follow in the footsteps of this living saint who was bringing a spiritual renaissance to Spain that was to spread very rapidly all over Europe.

St Teresa of Avila and her followers were to become the ambassadors of Christ, and were to challenge the Catholic Church from within to reforms that far outreached those demanded by Wycliffe or sought for by Luther and his followers. To the Discalced Carmelites it was a renewed springtime of of the Faith, and the Holy Face of Christ Himself seemed to be smiling serenely upon all their endeavours.

Carmel was to be a place of silence, a house of solitude, a mansion of prayer. Its occupants were to live and work and pray in their separate cells only meeting once a day for corporal worship. The commonest and most menial tasks must be acts of worship, washing up pots, cooking meals, scrubbing the floors must become just as much an act of worship as the offering of the Divine Sacrifice each morning in the monastery chapel. The routine initiated by Teresa in the sixteenth century was the same in its essential details as the routine laid down and carried out in Carmelite houses all over the world at the present time. A strict discipline in the simplest things was demanded since God is glorified by order.

The pattern of the day rotated around the singing of the divine office, the book of the hours, and of the oldest forms of worship in the church. Rising at five in the morning the brethren would recite Lauds in chapel, then retire to their cells for an hour of mental prayer. Between six and ten o'clock Prime and Terce would be said and the household duties fulfilled for the day. Mass would be said during this time and their first meal taken, a cup of water and two ounces of dry bread. Work in their cells until noon and then a frugal meal before an hour's communal recreation. Work again until Vespers at four-thirty in the afternoon. An hour of mental prayer followed by a light collation for supper. Compline at seven-forty in the evening, spiritual reading for an hour afterwards, and examination of conscience and then retire for the night. Most of the day was to be spent in silence and solitude and every action was controlled and disciplined in exact obedience to the Mother Prioress who was for them their guide and mentor through life until death claimed them for its own. A wasted life some will say, a useless life others will murmur, but what man has climbed mountains without a strict discipline of body and mind, and who shall ascend the hill of the Lord without perfect control of body, mind and spirit?

It is well worth our while at this point to consider in detail what this great saint of Avila meant by mental prayer, as in this alone shall we discover a clue to the meaning and purpose of the Carmelite way of life. She has given us a very clear exposition of its meaning and practice in her *The Way of Perfection*, and some account of its trials and tribulations in *The Interior Castle*.

Prayer for most of us is a habit forced on us against our will at school and completely abandoned by us in our later years. Even if we belong to that minority who call themselves practising Christians it is largely a stale repetition of parrot phrases that are mumbled out from memory and whose meaning is almost completely ignored or forgotten. We are practical people, we boast of our down to earth good sense and are content to let the priests and parsons get down on their knees while we stand upright on our own sturdy legs taking part in the scrum and scramble of the market place. We go to church three times in our lives. The first time when we are taken to be christened and have no say in the matter; the second when we get married and seek to endow our union with the seal of middle-class respectability; and the third when we are buried and are completely oblivious of the fact that we are there at all.

If this seems too callous or too cynical a summary of our spiritual aspirations we shall do well to remind ourselves that the vast majority of folk at the time of which I am writing were no better and no worse than we are today. The church controlled the state and the state enforced the Catholic faith on its inhabitants. Attendance at Mass was obligatory, as it still is today, but in those days failure to attend could give rise to your having to face the Inquisition and find yourself chalked with heresy. A stake and burning faggots were not a pleasant way of ending your life, so in the main you conformed to what was demanded of you even if at times you found yourself wondering what it was all about. What the Catholic Reformation sought to achieve through the work of people like Teresa of Avila and their like was to bring a new vision, a sense of literacy, a knowledge of personal responsibility into the lives of the individuals who made up the lay community and the high esteem in which the Pope and the Church are held today owes a great deal to these pioneers who kept the flame of truth alight when it was being threatened on every side with extinction.

Teresa saw that through prayer the waters are released that nourish the soul and bring it to its maturity. The soul to her was God's garden, and it must be nourished regularly and carefully if it was to come to its full flowering and fruition. Allison Peers, in his excellent short biography of St Teresa, *Mother of Carmel*[1] gives us a perfect description of just how the saint viewed this aspect of the soul's needs.

> How is a garden watered? There seemed to be to Teresa four ways. First, the water could be taken from a well – a laborious proceeding which later she often witnessed in her own convents. Secondly – a variant of this method – by water wheel and buckets, when the water is drawn by a windlass. Thirdly, by means of a brook which waters the ground much better for it saturates it more thoroughly and there is less need to water it often. Fourthly, by heavy rain when the Lord waters it with no labour of ours, a way incomparably better than any of those which I have described.[1]

[1]S.C.M. 1945

There is a homeliness, a simplicity and a directness in these similes that shows us why this woman had such a wide appeal to the people of her own day and why she still draws women to her in the Carmelite convents of our own time.

In this woman's nature there seemed to be something of the toughness, the grimness, the hardness of the rocky crags that had formed a natural fortress of Avila, the place of her birth. Life was never an easy business for the ordinary folk who had to labour from dawn till dusk in order to wrest a meagre livelihood from the almost barren soil of that part of Spain. Water was a necessity without which nothing that was planted could come to fruition. How she had revelled, as a young girl, in the shimmering green of the grass splattered hillsides after a burst of summer rain. What delights she had found in the formal gardens that surrounded her home as she had walked among their riots of colour while the leaves still had the crystal splendour of dawn-times dew upon them. Another thought, another image passing through her mind. The look of gratitude she had seen on the peasants' faces as they had watched Spring showers nurturing the cracking soil of the parched plains. Was there not a note of danger too? The kindly rain could so easily turn into a blustering storm and what had at one moment seemed to be full of creative promise could at the next appear as a raging tyrant destroying all that fell across its path.

This woman, this strange, bewildering, frightening and fascinating creature who had known in her cataleptic state what it was to die into life, who had seen so clearly in her visions the way she must travel, and had heard so clearly in her voices of the pathway the soul must take if it was to find the fulfilment of its most sublime journey of all, she knew that she must lead her followers gently, persuasively but ardently on to the road to perfection that she herself was treading. The rapture she was to know still lay ahead of her, the heavenly marriage she was to participate in and that was to be the consummation of her own spiritual travail had not yet called her to its feast. She thought of the trust, the affection and the servitude that those who had enrolled in her Discalced Order had always shown to her, and she knew that she must return that trust with confidence, that affection with love, that servitude with freedom. It was in this mood, with these ideals in mind that she set out to outline for her immediate followers and for all those who would come after and who would wish to follow in her way, the simple pattern of mental prayer.

Prayer for her, as for all the true mystics was never an asking but always a giving. It was an emptying of self in order that other than self might flood into one's own being. It was a positive movement, taken by easy stages towards complete abandonment of divine providence. It seems essential to

H 113

enlarge this last statement a little further, otherwise it will only seem a meaningless string of words that has no application at all to the lives of the ordinary men and women in the commonplace world most of us inhabit. Since her basic faith, and it is fundamental to all true Christian thinking no matter what creed you adhere to or to which denomination you belong, is that God is by His very nature All Good, it must be obvious that out of God there can come no evil. As God created man to be His companion, making him in the image of His own eternity, that is in a state of perfect freedom not bounden in by the relatives of time, then God's will for man is that he too shall share in and know perfect goodness. Evil is born of time, it is man's surrender to something that he knows is a betrayal of his true potential, a choice of the lesser when he knows the greater is demanded from him, and so man must move outside the imprisonment of time, beyond the relatives between which his ego is constantly swinging if he is to find the joy of knowing and loving and serving God. Only abandonment, the loss of self and the finding of selflessness can bring to him any true inner satisfaction, and it is the pursuit of this satisfaction that has always been the goal of the mystics from the very dawn of history.

The Hindu strives through a series of rebirths into a physical environment to find himself finally enfolded in the bosom of Brahma. The Parsee's ardent desire is to be burnt up in the consuming flame of love itself. The Muslim looks to the prophet to lead him to that paradise of perfect contentment that has always eluded him in ordinary life. The Christian seeks for perfect fellowship in that perfection he can only call by one name – divine love. The roads may be many but the ultimate objective the same. It seems highly probable that some of the early Christian missionaries had studied the wisdom of the east, and out of these studies had emerged the Spiritual Exercises of Ignatius Loyola that as I have already pointed out played such a prominent part in the inner development of Teresa of Avila's own spiritual unfolding, and it was out of this that she built up for those who sought her way that pattern of prayer that she has made in some ways peculiarly her own.

The first movement must be towards stillness. 'Be still and know that I am God' is cardinal to her whole method of personal transfiguration. One must hold in mind consciously the idea towards which one is moving. The beginner will have had no vision. There is no mystical experience to spur him on. There is no feeling of emotional exhaltation to hold him firm in the way. The senses must be controlled, the emotions must be held in check, the thoughts must be preserved from endless distractions, 'which', as Teresa herself tells us, 'will be a great labour because they have been accustomed to a life of distractions'. All the postulant may find at this stage in the journey is dryness, aridity, and if they are not very careful they may fall easy victims to a sense of despair. The all important thing for the beginner to remember is that it is not his will that he is seeking, but that another will than his may be done. Whatever happens, no matter how barren the soil may seem the thing to remember is that God is watering the soil. 'Even', Teresa warns us, 'if this aridity should persist our whole lives long we must persevere in prayer and never let Christ fall beneath the Cross.'

We now move to the second stage, commonly known in mystical theology as the prayer of quiet. The soul, realising through its experience of the first steps it has taken, knows that of itself, no matter how ardent its prayer in stillness may be it cannot find the totality it is seeking. The senses are held in check, the emotions are under control, the mind has been stilled, and the will, the human will that has been used to carry out this tough and arduous discipline, must now allow itself to become the prisoner of the will of God. Now, no matter how often one feels in doubt or on the verge of despair the realisation that God is at work must be the dominant thought. He has placed in the soul a tiny spark from His great fire, and this must be neither quenched by useless distractions, nor must the individual who has known this experience if he feels the spark is dying try to rekindle it by his own efforts.

Once the postulant has mastered the first two stages on the way to perfection she is ready to move into the depths of interior prayer, the prayer of abandonment itself. It is at this stage that Teresa tells us, 'God may be said to be the gardener Himself, for it is He who does everything, we who do nothing'. To some people this may seem very closely akin to the popular conception of Nirvanah, . . . nothingness, negation. It is not so however. It is a deep and profound flowing of the inner being into a stream of spiritual consciousness, an unfolding of the innate potential that exists in every human being, but to which so few men and women pay any real attention. When this state is reached and perfected it means that the ordinary faculties of memory, understanding and will are no longer concerned with the transient incidents and events of the material and temporal world, but are striving to become completely united with God. Here is a selflessness that perfect condition of surrender that is the proper prelude to the last stage of all, the prayer of reconciliation.

Ecstasy, rapture, a swooning into the arms of divine love; all these words seem to her to be empty phrases when she is striving to share with us the innermost experience of her own soul. The body feels weak, the tongue is powerless to utter any words, nothing at all is apprehended with the senses. Perhaps the only phrase that hints at it is that of Plotinus who writes of it as 'the flight of the alone to the Alone'. It is generally an experience of very short duration but while it lasts one feels that the self is being burnt up, the dross in one's nature is being consumed and purified in the flame of perfected love. There is a certainty, an assurance of the being of God that henceforth nothing can destroy. One may have to travel over stony paths, one may be destined to spend years in the desert wastes of aridity, one may sink back into a temporary imprisonment of the senses once more, but, ' . . . the soul feels close to God and there abides in it such a strength that it cannot do other than believe'.

The fundamental point that must be borne in mind all the time is that the treading of the way to perfection, the discipline of mental prayer, the embodiment in one's own nature of joyful fulfilment is not an end in itself, it is only the means that the cloistered postulant must use as she seeks the final thrust of the spear of love that brings to her the consummation she seeks in spiritual marriage.

I am well aware that the experiences and writings of St Teresa of Avila have been looked upon by some modern sceptics as arising from a series of neurotic states, and explained away as being simply a rationalisation of her own repressions. Some have even sought to dismiss her life and work as a concrete example of perverted sexuality. The fact that she uses the language of the loved one seeking her beloved spouse, and that she turns to the similes of the consummation of physical love in marriage when she is trying to convey to us what she had known and felt in the deepest reaches of her soul has given her enemies ample ammunition for their scurrilous attacks upon her sincerity and sanity.

What they either fail to, or refuse to face up to, is that here was one of the most practical women of her time, whose writings have given to her a justly deserved immortality, and whose political acumen and statesmanlike way of recreating and revolutionising the Carmelite Order prove her to have been well aware of the accusations that might be made against herself, her work and her Order by the rationalists, cynics, and sceptics centuries after her death.

There were two essentials for every human being who wishes to find true and complete fulfilment, work and worship. The first, work, was an incomplete thing in itself and this is ably witnessed to by the fact that man the workman strives to become man the craftsman, thus moving creatively into an awareness of his true nature. Here we see work moving inwards until it verges on worship, and worship 'redeeming time' that it might take to itself the vesture of eternity. It is equally dangerous to make worship an end in itself, for this will only lead to a false quietism that is within itself a denial of the natural duty of the whole man. All men and women are seeking God, even when they seek to deny Him, but there will always be the few to whom this quest is the ultimate adventure of the human soul, and it is these who will seek the surrender and discipline of the religious orders.

Another of the radical changes that she brought about when she established the foundations of the Discalced Carmelites was in her insistence that the communities must be small in number. In fact she laid down that no community should exceed thirteen members, for she knew that a good Prioress must take a personal interest in the direction of each soul placed under her care, and that this was a practical impossibility once a community became too large for her to be able to devote the necessary time to each postulant. The life and work of this great woman of the sixteenth century was like a shaft of light in a darkened room, and I have felt it necessary to deal with her outlook and her teachings in some detail in order that we can get as complete an understanding as possible of the life of Thérèse Martin once she had entered the cloister at Lisieux.

In 1838 a small group of Carmelite nuns led by Mother Geneviève and Mother Anne established themselves in a small house at Lisieux where they hoped to establish a monastery of their order. Like their famous founder, St Teresa of Avila, they arrived with little money and few possessions. Poverty was the symbol of the divine way for them, and prayer was the means by which they sought to know and fulfil the will of God. The house that they found was old and weather-beaten and for years they lived on the verge of starvation, and this is not an overstatement even when one has taken into account the sparse diet that is the daily sustenance of every member of their Order. Many looked at them askance, grumbling among themselves about these begging nuns that meant a drain of the frugal resources of the town and its inhabitants. It is true that the devout catholics of the town saw them for what they claimed to be, a community of contemplatives offering themselves and their lives in the service of their fellows.

Gradually they furnished their chapel, built their cloister, planted and tended their garden, all these things being carried out against the disciplined pattern of the singing of the Divine Office and the keeping of the Ancient Rule. Daily they offered up the sacrifice of the Mass for the wellbeing of mankind. Hourly they offered up prayers for the salvation of souls in every corner of the world. Their objective, not an easy one to uphold and certainly not an easy one to fulfil, was to become a living fountain of love for the re-making of men and the healing of nations. Unity through the universality of truth, sanctification through a life of sacrifice, atonement through the following of the pathway of poverty and obedience, these were their aims.

It was to this community that Thérèse Martin offered herself as a novice on the Feast of the Annunciation, 9th April, 1888, fifty years after the community had first taken up residence in the red-bricked house that was to become the Carmel at Lisieux.

CHAPTER VII

Entertaining Angels Unawares

A convent is neither a rest home for spiritual invalids nor a place where the world-weary can find escape and respite from the burdens and responsibilities of day to day living in the ordinary world. It is within its enclosed walls a microcosm of the world outside, with all its weaknesses, all its failings, all its difficulties and all its shortcomings magnified a hundredfold. The taking of the veil and habit is not in itself the fulfilling of the vow of poverty. The acceptance of a disciplined way of living is in itself no guarantee of chastity. The following in implicit obedience of the letter of the rule of the order may well be merely the fulfilling of the letter of the law and no justification at all for suggesting that one is living in perfect obedience.

The outward forms will each in turn call for an inner sanctification, and the external conflicts arising from the clashing of wills can only be resolved by a willing renunciation of personal pride and a complete abnegation of oneself to the overriding authority of the Mother Prioress under whom one must live in confidence and trust.

It seems a wise course at this point to take a closer look at the two contestants who were to make of this hallowed place in Lisieux a battleground of wits during the nine years in which Thérèse Martin was to live among the community of dedicated women whose avowed objective was the hourly adoration of God and the daily service in prayer of their fellow men and women.

From the day of her entry into the convent, 9th April, 1888, to the day of her death, 30th September, 1897, this simple and devout woman whose sole objective in life was to perfect herself in the ways and discipline of Carmel was to find herself the centre of a constant battle between the Mother Prioress and her own sister, Pauline.

Mother Marie de Gonzague saw herself as called upon to lead to perfection the simple soul that had been placed under her care, while Sister Agnes of Jesus felt she was duty bound to fulfil the wishes of her own mother as she lay on her deathbed, and see that all that could be done was done to ensure that Thérèse's name would be engraved in letters of gold on the scrolls of heaven. The difficulty that faces us here is that with the passage of time and the evidence at our disposal it is extremely difficult to get a rounded and unbiased picture of either of these two contestants in this heavenly journey.

The Prioress herself, Mother Marie, has been much maligned by most of

119

those who have written of the saint since her death and canonisation. She has been portrayed for us as a self-seeking, selfish, arrogant aristocrat, whose personal life in religion was an open disgrace to the order she had enrolled in and to her own special place as Prioress for so many years of Thérèse Martin's life in the cloister. The facts, when they are examined carefully and impartially do little to support this distorted image that her detractors have tried to reflect for us on the screen of time.

She had been born of the decaying remnants of an aristocratic family so that both by birth and breeding she had little in common with the other members of the community that she joined at Lisieux at the age of eighteen.

There were moments when she undoubtedly felt that God had created a special place and offered a different dispensation to those of noble birth. The one thing that must be recognised, however, is that she felt the call of the cloister, and that Mother Geneviève, who was the Prioress at the time she entered the Carmelite Order, was convinced that she had the correct disposition and the right attitude to test out her vocation. It is true that at the age of nineteen she appears to have attempted to run away from the convent, and was discovered by the search party that had been sent to look for her hiding in a woodshed, and that her act of disobedience was put down to a fit of jealousy. It is true that she had a cat that she appears at times to have considered more important than the human beings placed under her care, and that once when it was missing she demanded that the nuns should break the vow of silence and go all round the garden calling out its name to see if they could find her precious pet that appeared to have got lost. There were odd occasions when it caught a bird and when she insisted on the cook roasting this tasty morsel for the cat's dinner.

The nuns, as part of their work were set to embroider the family coat of arms on sheets, table cloths and pillow cases for the use of her sister, and at one time she allowed this sister to have a large loan from the convent's funds, the loan being repaid with interest after the sister's death. Even when we take all these misdemeanours together they add up to little more than the mistakes and misjudgements that any human being might make, and haloes are not handed out with habits when one dedicates oneself to the life of religion.

Very little has been made of the positive side to her nature, but if we look at this coldly and impartially we shall find that the scales of justice are very heavily weighted in her favour. While Thérèse Martin was still a child at school this woman sensed that there was some extraordinary quality in her and that she was destined for a life that would be full of meaning and purpose for all who came under her influence. She disagreed with her own Superior's attitude towards the girl's vocation. She brought pressure to bear upon the Bishop to sanction her entry into the convent at the age of fifteen. She bore the frowns of disfavour that were only too obvious on the day of the girl's entry as a novice, and if at times she seems to have been harsh and unkind in her treatment of the nun placed under her care it was because she had seen a potentiality for sanctity more clearly than many of those who were in daily contact with her in the cloister. As she lay dying she turned to the nuns grouped around her bed and almost her final words were, 'I have often offended God. I have sinned more than anyone in the Community, and I should not hope to be saved if I had not my little Thérèse to intercede for me. I feel I shall owe my salvation to her.'

Thérèse herself is the finest witness we can find to plead for understanding and tolerance for the Mother Prioress. 'I thank God for having provided me with such a sound and valuable training. It was a priceless grace.' And in a letter to Mother Gonzague she writes:

> God has given her a deep knowledge of souls and all their wretchedness. She understands everything. Nothing is hidden from her.

In another letter to her sister Céline, Thérèse says,

> In the exile of our life the maternal hand of our Beloved Mother knows so well how to lead and comfort us.

Mother Gonzague may have been at times an unkind woman, she may have been too much of this world to fulfil in every detail the demands of the cloistered life, her own family may have played too large a part in her personal thoughts and ambitions, and yet in spite of these things she had much more in common with the Founder of Carmel than many of her detractors realise. The great Teresa of Avila herself had had many detractors in her own lifetime. There are always those who are ready to magnify our faults and minimise our virtues and it could not have been either an easy or an enviable task for the Mother Prioress to stand up to the eagle eye and whispering tongue of Sister Agnes, who was on the lookout for and ready to pounce like a vulture on the least of her failings.

Sister Agnes of Jesus, Thérèse's sister, was in some ways a cold, hard and calculating woman. She was so obsessed by the idea of Thérèse's destiny that at times she exaggerated trivial incidents in the day to day life in Carmel to present an almost slanderous portrait of the Mother Prioress to the outside world. In some ways, it would almost appear to have been a mistake to allow the three sisters, Pauline, Marie and Céline to all enter the same convent as the one in which Thérèse was living, and I think the fact that they were all living under the same roof for so many years inadvertently did a great deal to detract from the greatness of Thérèse's own life, distorting the image of her into that of a little child instead of projecting it into the great and noble saint I am convinced she was when we view her in the right perspective.

It is true that Thérèse of the Child Jesus and Holy Face looked upon the pathway she was to tread to perfection as the Way of Spiritual Childhood, but had not the One she was seeking to find and to serve warned His followers that 'unless ye become as a little child ye cannot enter the Kingdom I have prepared for you,' and is it not true to emphasise that there is a deep and fundamental difference between 'childishness' and 'childlikeness'? The one is completely alien to the mind and heart of Christ, the other is in perfect harmony with the challenge He has offered to all who would seek to follow in His footsteps.

Let us look a little more closely into the way in which Thérèse lived the whole of the ten years she spent in the convent. Every act she performed must reflect and radiate complete humility. Every feeling she experienced must be purged and sanctified in order that it might prove a worthy offering to her Divine Master. Every word that passed her lips must be filled with truth and charity. Every thought that entered her mind must be worthy of the bride of the Heavenly Bridegroom that she was striving to become. It is a comparatively simple thing to be heroic in the face of tremendous odds. It is the hourly acts of heroism, unheralded and unsung that are the most difficult of all to accomplish. Anyone who is so keyed up to their task can die a martyr's death on the mission field. It is the few, the very rare few, who can accept willingly and without any moans of self-pity the more difficult challenge of a daily martyrdom in the cause of duty. Most of us in times of grave crisis can rise to our full nobility on such an occasion, but few of us are able to meet every minor crisis in our daily life with that same nobility of spirit. And yet, it was just these things that the splendid soul did every day of her earthly life.

In humility, in abiding patience, in simple obedience, she sought to express the letter and spirit of the vows she had taken, living out an interior life in such complete obscurity that after her death one of the nuns who had lived with her day by day said that there was nothing much anyone could say about Sister Thérèse for she certainly seemed to have done very little that was worthy of recording in the annals of Carmel.

I think that the main trouble was that the majority of the nuns around her, and I am not stating this in any derogatory way, were seeking to move inward all the time, to perfect themselves in spite of the world. Thérèse on the other hand was always striving to move outwards, the world was her parish and the saving of the souls of others was far more important to her than her own salvation. She was a dedicated person who was to dream of and hope for and pray for a reunited Christendom. The reunion of a church divided was an unheard of objective in the year of which I am writing. The Catholics were the salt of the earth, and those outside the fold of Rome were the salt that had lost its savour. To Thérèse, unlettered as she was in philosophy, untutored as she was in moral theology, unschooled as she was in historical development, the words 'and they shall be as one', were an inspiration and a challenge throughout her all too short life. 'I will spend my heaven doing good on earth,' was her battlecry. 'On earth,' notice, not merely among the faithful, not only for those who considered themselves already numbered among the elect, but on earth for all people who needed prayer and love and understanding.

The more we examine the records of the life she lived in the convent the more we realise why the life of this nun seemed to be lacking in anything that singled her out as being in any way to or greater than, any of the other nuns in her day to day existence among them. She performed no miracles, there were no voices to urge her on to the heights of spirituality, no visions to speed her feet along the pathway to perfection. The outward signs, that one at times associates with a deepening life of sanctification were all lacking no stigmata, no ecstasy, no violent penances, no overflowing of supernatural grace.

She was to all those who lived with her a very ordinary woman, but a few of them soon started to realise that she did the ordinary things of life in a most extraordinary way. The possibility of perfectability was an ever-present reality with her, and she enshrined in the most commonplace events of her day to day living an element of what I can only call, for want of a better word, the Holy. The one thing that shone out above all others, that was a self-evident fact to all who came into contact with her, was the intensity of her love of God. She knew of no way to perfection except by love, and as though to be kept in an hourly awareness of this in the night-time as well as through the daylight hours she scratched on the walls of her cell the words, 'Jesus is my only love'.

So complete was her adherence to this lofty ideal that towards the close of her life she was able to say, quite humbly, 'I don't believe that I have ever spent three minutes without thinking of God. It is natural to think of the One one loves, but the only thing that can really be called love is the complete sacrifice of oneself.'

Words, you may say, delightfully phrased, charmingly spoken, admirably written, but what basis had they in the hard realities of daily living? The answer is that every moment was for Thérèse Martin a moment that opened up the opportunity for sacrifice; every hour presented her with ample opportunities for self-abnegation; every day demanded from her an unreserved acceptance of suffering born of misunderstanding about what she was doing and fault finding about what she did.

Pause for a moment and try to realise how difficult it is for any of us to spend one hour without thinking ill of our fellows, without bursting out indignantly in self-justification when we are misjudged, without lying about some insignificant incident or event that does not appear to us to be very important anyway. Sit down, away from the blare of the radio and the glare of the television screen, and at the end of the day try to measure up your own life for the past twenty-four hours against the stringent and transparent truths of the Sermon on the Mount. We are all failures when we take these things as the measure of our days, but this nun, this simple girl, living in cloistered solitude did exactly these things, and what is more succeeded in becoming the embodiment of perfect love in her own lifetime.

Her Testament, her Gospel of Love was in what she called in her own autobiography the New Commandment, and the whole of the teachings of Christ were crystallised for her in the simple phrase 'Your love for one another is to be like the love I have borne you'.

Three years after she entered the Carmel at Lisieux an epidemic of influenza swept the convent. Thérèse herself only suffered from a mild attack but three nuns died and most of the others were gravely ill as the disease claimed one after another as a victim. The whole burden of nursing the community fell upon Thérèse and two other lay sisters. With a matter-of-factness, far greater than her years – she was only nineteen at the time – she supervised the nursing for twenty-four hours each day. Her patience was inexhaustible, her sense of humour a source of comfort and consolation to all those who were stricken down, and her simple and yet profound faith was like a light in a dark place to the dying.

In fact, her daily heroism, in the face of many difficulties was so great that she at last won over the admiration and confidence of the Superior, Father Delatroette, whom it will be recalled had persistently opposed her admission to the cloister at the tender age of fifteen. The quiet determination to serve her ailing sisters, the refusal to panic when faced with a crisis, the serenity with which she faced the fact of death itself, these things unspectacular and commonplace as they may seem were nevertheless the stepping stones she was to tread upon as she mounted the stairway of grace.

What can be more trying to any of us than a complaining and cantankerous invalid? One of the old nuns was just such a person, and the duty fell to Thérèse to look after her in the closing years of her life. Because of her age and her infirmities the rule was relaxed a little for the ageing sister, and she was allowed to leave recreation to go to the refectory for ten minutes before the bell rang in order that she could be in her place in time. Grasping the invalid's girdle Thérèse would commence to lead her on the hazardous journey to the refectory. If she pulled the girdle ever so gently to show that she was leading the way she would be reproved for going too fast. If she let the girdle slacken a little after this reproof she would be scolded for going too slow. At every step the invalid grumbled that Thérèse was letting go of her and that she was going to fall.

Grumbles constantly poured from her peevish lips reminding her helper that she was too young to really take proper care of her. Settling her in her chair presented endless problems as the ageing woman was determined to find fault with everything. 'Don't rush me or I shall fall. Don't hold me too hard or I shall be in pain. Don't roll up my sleeves like that you are pinching my arms.' On and on the words of complaint poured out.

Gently, reverently and patiently Thérèse listened to them all, trying all the while to do whatever she could to make things easier for the petulant invalid. This to her was the challenge and demand of love that she should serve all who needed her help without question and without complaint, apologising for ills she had not inflicted, giving understanding when she herself was all the while being misjudged and misunderstood. Trivial, I can hear you saying, yes, but how would you or I face up to a situation such as this?

If any nun were old and feckless, filling every hour with grumbles and complaints until she became the one that all the others in the community avoided, Thérèse would be at her side as much as possible. She would listen to her endless stream of grouses then try to understand why the ageing sister was like this, and what it was that was lacking in her spiritual life to make her so difficult to understand. If a lay sister felt neglected and alone because she was lower than the rest of the community in her mental ability she would find in Thérèse Martin an endless source of ready companionship and compassion. The young novices loved her because she gave so freely of her own love to them. The weak and the ailing found in her one who gave a healing understanding to their troubled bodies and minds. The aged and infirm saw her as a beam of light in the surrounding darkness that seemed to be closing in on them. With a gentleness that endeared her to all, a tenderness that won her a place in everyone's affections, a sympathy that poured itself out in ceaseless compassion, this quiet little soul moved every minute of every hour of every day in the shadow of the Cross.

The Mother Prioress seemed deliberately to single her out for a never ending stream of complaints and reproaches. 'Don't fuss round the novices so much or they will never harden up enough to stand up to the strict austerities of Carmel.' 'Why are you always fussing round the older nuns, have you nothing better to do with your time than waste it?' 'Are you so lacking in understanding the meaning of the vows you have taken that you waste your afternoons walking and playing in the garden?' This last rebuke was uttered when Thérèse Martin's back was aching to breaking point through weeding the flower beds for hours on end. She accepted every charge made against her without a word of protest or self-justification. Humility to her was a readiness to be misjudged without attempting by a word or a gesture to do anything in her own self-defence. Her vow of obedience to her Superior was a total one providing she was asked to do nothing that offended her conscience.

Mother Gonzague often found herself ashamed at the way she had treated the self-effacing postulant and astounded at the complete self-abnegation of the girl in every situation. She knew that she herself was an arrogant, restless soul, that her following of the religious life was proving to be a hard task-master. There was too much worldliness, too much pride, too much sense of family in her, and these things often overshadowed her running of the community that had elected her to be Prioress. We must not, however, be misled by the cruel and in some ways unjust statements that have been made against her. Although she may have been no saint herself, not even a saint in the making, she saw the inherent sanctity in this simple girl who had been placed in her charge, and realised how important it was to discipline her life in such a way that not a single flaw should mar the wonderful life that was unfolding before her.

Thérèse Martin was so ordinary, everything she did seemed so common-place. Thérèse Martin was so insignificant and there was nothing spectacular in any way about her daily life in the convent. Thérèse Martin was so humble that she appeared to most of those who knew her to be a bit of a simpleton. These are the things her critics have written about her, and it is a very easy matter to justify the contempt in which some of them have held her.

Where was the strength, the over-riding power that had enabled the Founder of her order to face the Inquisition without flinching? Where was the fortitude that had led Joan of Arc to the burning faggots and beyond them to glory in her determination to follow the inner voice of God that had all through her life directed her soul? Where was the uninhibited purpose that had seemed like a golden halo surrounding the head of Francis of Assisi even while he still lived and laboured among his fellows? The strength, the power and the purpose were there, hidden under the veil of simplicity that proved to be the perfect disguise for her daily self-purification.

Love, the perfect love she sought, could only find itself in the service of others. A sense of failure, a feeling of futility, a gnawing doubt as to her own sufficiency, these were the factors that constantly spurred her on. Most of our lives are within themselves a betrayal of the love we strive to reach out for that through it we may discover a way of fulfilment. Our love is often perverted into possessiveness under the fierce strain of physical passion. Our service of others is often desecrated into a selfish desire for adulation. To give and give again without counting the cost to ourselves. To labour without thinking of any reward except that which comes from an inner serenity. To struggle and fight against evil without passing hasty judgements about the wrongdoer. This is her challenge to us, and how badly we measure up to the high standards that she set for us in her own life and character.

One of the accepted practices of the Carmelites is that they shall subject themselves constantly to physical mortification. The wearing of chains to restrain the desires of the flesh, self-flagellation with knotted thongs to keep the body in subjection to the will, rigorous fasting to curb the physical appetite; all these things were the means applied to a spiritual end – self abasement.

During her first few months as a postulant Thérèse wore a spiked cross next to her skin, but found the pain it caused when it pierced her flesh distracted her from a true following of the way of life she had chosen. 'God will mortify me in His own way if I strive to discover His will for me,' was her constant thought. The wearing of chains, the whipping of the body, the donning of a hair shirt, even in the refined atmosphere of a convent can easily deteriorate into exhibitionism. The fakir on his bed of nails can easily become a sideshow at a fairground and the walled-up anchorite is at times nothing more or less than a spectacle to satisfy the avaricious spiritual sight-seer. These things may be good, but they are not good in themselves – it is their final end that is their ultimate justification.

'I will spend my heaven doing good on earth.' 'I desire to show to all who seek the love of God in their own lives the little way of spiritual child-hood'; these were the signposts that directed Thérèse Martin throughout the nine years of her sojourn in Carmel. Her own salvation would only be discovered if she could open up to others a way in which they too could save their souls, and so to her mortification became something we all can do in exactly the same way as she.

When a voice is raised in anger against us we must learn to submit in silence to its biting and unjustified abuse. When our words are misunder-stood, our actions misjudged, we must strive to accept the undeserved rebuke in silence. When selfish love and possessive friendship seeks to destroy us to satisfy its own misguided ends we must give a greater love, a fuller friendship in order that we may win others back to the way of peace and tranquillity. When a child is born blind, when one we love deeply becomes a hopeless alcoholic, or a friend whom we cherish contracts a fatal disease, we must devote ourselves to an unstinted service that through us they may learn to see the will of God being made manifest. 'Until ye become as a little child', a hard, terrifying and difficult saying since it implies a complete and simple trust in love of which few of us are capable.

It would be foolish to assume that because she had voluntarily shut herself away from the world that she had also cut herself adrift from all that was going on outside the walls of her convent cell. All of us know that when our friends are thousands of miles away, or if we are out of touch with those who mean so much in our personal lives the pain and agony of wondering where they are, what is happening to them and whether in their loneliness and isolation they need our help and sympathy and understanding.

The Little Way has within it all the torment, all the turmoil that beset the life of John Newman and led him to write:

> Guide Thou my feet, I do not ask to see
> The distant shore, one step enough for me.

As though the struggles going on within the confines of Carmel were not sufficient to test Thérèse's strength and to discipline her into her vocation, disturbing news from the outside world was destined in her early years in the enclosure to add to her burden.

Louis Martin had always found it difficult to adjust himself to the changing facets of life. Placidity and solitude had been the things he had sought; restlessness and the constant demands of social changes were the things he had found awaiting him at every turn in life's pilgrimage. The vocation he longed for but could not fulfil; the marriage that had certainly not been of his own seeking but that he had accepted as part of God's pattern for his personal fulfilment; the deaths of some of his children in infancy, the loss of a wife upon whom he had come to lean for so much; each of these things had left its mark upon his indrawn and sensitive nature.

Zélie had been his anchorage, and after her death first Marie, then Pauline, then Céline had taken her place. Two of these were already in the cloister and a third was longing to join them. Thérèse, his little queen, the Benjamin of the family, had become so much part of his need for his desire to live in an atmosphere of affection that her decision to take the veil had dealt him a very hard blow. Léonie, the wayward one who had tested her vocation twice and each time returned home sick at heart and disappointed at her failure, had come to a final decision to try once more to enter the religious life and had joined the Convent of the Visitation at Le Mans.

His world seemed to be contracting all the while, and Louis Martin found himself creeping away more and more to the velvet shadowed peace of the Belvedere and his beloved books of spiritual readings. He had always had a touch of the fanatic about him and in his attempt to rediscover the silence of a monk's cell his mind was gradually snapping. All his life he had been tortured by his own inadequacy and now he was finding his imagined failure to be too much for him to cope with.

The peace of the home was slipping away, creeping with Louis Martin into the dark places where he himself was wandering in the last lingering twilight of sanity. Long fits of melancholia would take possession of him. A deepening sense of despair would hold him imprisoned in an agony of uncertainty. Had he failed God? Why had Zélie been taken away from him when they might have had so many more years together? Was it right that all his daughters should seek the consolation of the cloister? Questions, questions, questions, but seldom any answers. Had God also deserted him? Was this, the final loneliness, a sign of a soul that had already surrendered itself to damnation?

Louis Martin would shut himself in his room for days on end, sometimes not even emerging from his solitude to share the meal that Céline had prepared for them. There would be days when he would leave the house almost before dawn and not return until long after darkness. There would be periods of complete lucidity when the old Louis Martin would joke and laugh with Céline, but these times were becoming more and more infrequent. Fortunately when the day came for Thérèse to take her solemn vows and be clothed in the full habit of the Order he was in one of his good periods and was able to be present and lead her to the altar for the ceremony. His tired eyes filled with tears as he looked upon this child-woman, clad all in white with the bridal wreath of roses upon her golden hair. She looked like a very young girl and many of those present shed a tear themselves as the golden ringlets were shorn, the habit adjusted and the door of the enclosure shut on her for ever.

Thérèse herself found it difficult to face the ordeal of seeing her beloved father looking so frail and weak and old, but with that fortitude that was becoming basic to her character accepted this new form of strain and suffering as part of the mortification she must suffer if she was to prove herself to be a worthy victim of divine love.

A few weeks later Louis Martin left the house one morning but had not returned as the old clock on the wall struck the twelve strokes of midnight.

Céline sat up with one eye on the door and the other on the clock. Dawn broke and there was still no sign of the wanderer. Her uncle Guérin joined in the vigil and when there was no sign of Louis by the second evening search parties were sent out to try and find him. He was discovered many miles away, his mind had gone and when they spoke to him the only answers they got were the incoherent ramblings of a man on the fringe of insanity.

After discussing the situation with Isidore Guérin and his wife, and seeking the advice of Pauline and Marie whom she visited in the parlour at the convent, Céline decided that her father must be placed for a time in an asylum in Caen. It was a sad, docile and pathetic figure who found himself incarcerated among fellow sufferers from mental instability. The tragedy was all the more pathetic in that Louis Martin returned to his childlike faith and trust in God without fully comprehending its meaning or its significance. The home was sold and Céline went to live for the time being with the Guérins. She already decided that she too would join Marie, Pauline and Thérèse at Carmel, but felt that it was incumbent on her not to take this step while her father needed her in any way.

To Thérèse the news of the sale of Les Buissonnets was another heavy blow. The garden that she had loved so dearly and where she had built her simple shrine in honour of Our Lady. The peaceful dining room, where in the evenings in a past that now seemed completely dead her father had sang to them the old folk songs of Normandy and the lovely hymns of the church. The Belvedere, a place of recollection and refuge where at times he had read to her the simple stories of the lives of the saints. The sternness of Marie, the gentle guidance of Pauline, the happy companionship of Céline, the boisterous waywardness of Léonie, all these things seemed like a bitterness of the tongue, a slowly corroding pain that was searing the soul itself.

'I choose all,' little had she realised when in a childish moment of ecstasy she had uttered these words for the first time their full import and meaning. God had seemed to give her so much and now He seemed to be taking it all away. Her father living in the frightening atmosphere of a nineteenth century asylum, the familiar paths in the garden and floors of the rooms she had cherished so dearly being walked upon by strange feet. Marie and Pauline living so near to her but by the very discipline she was imposing upon herself having to be pushed further and further away. Sisterly affection had no place in the life she had chosen for herself, and in some ways the fact that they were all in the same enclosure made her cross a little heavier to bear. It was not Thérèse's own wish that they should all be together in this way, for in her early months as a novice she had offered herself and hoped for missionary service in one of the Carmelite Houses in India. This was not to be since the Mother Prioress felt she had a special obligation to this sanctified soul that had been placed under her care.

'If it be possible let this cup . . .', no, no, no, she must push this thought aside, it was a temptation and might even become a betrayal. Thérèse Martin had asked to be only one thing, a suffering servant, and as she sat in her tiny cell pondering upon the tragedy that had cast its deepening shadows across the closing years of her own father's life she knew that she must accept this as part of the purgation that can only come through suffering. Her thoughts turned to Céline, and she found herself wondering what she could do to send some words of comfort since so much of the burden of looking after the ailing father had fallen upon her shoulders.

As she knelt in prayer, struggling to find that inner stillness in which the soul alone can find a lasting peace, she felt an inner prompting, an urgency that seemed almost like an external messenger directing her to copy out and send to her sister a portion of the fifty-third chapter of Isaiah. The tears rolled down her cheeks as she penned the words for every phrase, every sentence seemed in some strange way to apply to her own father.

> For he shall grow up as a tender plant before him, and as a root out of a dry ground. He hath no form nor comeliness and when we have seen him there is no beauty that we should desire him.

She herself found a deepening sense of consolation in these words. The father they had loved and cherished, the one who had in all things striven to serve God, the beloved parent who had struggled against his own wishes to offer each of his daughters to a life of prayer and solitude. Why had this terrible malady affected him? Where could the goodness of God be seen in the sacrifice He had demanded from this imbecile, whose babblings were most of the time as incoherent as the first mutterings of an infant striving to master the art of speech?

Like a shaft of light piercing the darkness of her cell the answer came to her. God Himself was in charge of and taking care of her father's soul and in this knowledge and assurance he himself was at peace. It was her duty, her obligation to take upon herself the intensity of his suffering as the way of the Cross for her was a willingness to accept the full burden of another's pain. The One she loved more than all others had had to stand at the foot of a cross and watch her only son die the death of a common malefactor. Those who followed after Him had been stoned, crucified, torn to pieces by wild beasts because they refused to betray His love and surrender their loyalty to the demands of power-lusting conquerors. The Cross, the perpetual enigma to which no man had yet found the complete answer, but in and through which all who gave an unstinted allegiance had found inner sources of strength, power and peace that nothing external could disturb or destroy. 'I choose all', each hour, each day, each week, the meaning became clearer to her; self-abnegation was the royal road upon which she had set her feet, the old Adam must die that the New Man might be created within her. Only in this could she discover the purification that would make her own sacrifice a worthy offering to her celestial Spouse.

By the spring of 1892 Louis Martin, after several strokes had become partially paralysed and almost completely bedridden. Céline, whose devotion to her father was of an outstanding quality, pleaded with her uncle to let them have him back at Lisieux as there was now no fear of his wandering away and his malady was not dangerous in any way to those around him. With Léonie she rented a small house opposite where the Guérins lived and installed the invalid there, taking upon herself the full duties of nursing him.

On fine days he was occasionally able to go with her for a short walk, and there were even times when he was strong enough to pay a visit to his daughters in the parlour at Carmel. These visits were a source of constant pain to Marie, Pauline and Thérèse, for this tired, stuttering old man seemed to bear no resemblance at all to the father they had all loved so dearly. The months drifted on and gradually the paralysis took a deeper hold over him until the time came when he lay semi-conscious and helpless, moving into the last months of his life on earth that were in every way a living death. By the summer, it was as obvious to the doctor as it was to his relatives and friends that he was very near his death-agony. The eyes grew lifeless, the pulse slowed down, the breathing became weaker as day succeeded day. On 29th July, 1894, Louis Martin was given the last rites of the church and the next day he passed away very peacefully, simply seeming to those who watched by his bedside to fall into a deeper and deeper sleep from which he awakened no more.

Céline, who was sitting by his bedside on the evening before his death was sure that for a few moments he regained the lucidity of mind that he had known in his prime. As she quietly prayed aloud calling on the Holy Family to ease his sufferings the old man's eyes opened and he gazed across at her and slowly moved his lips. The old light was in the darkened eyes, the familiar smile crossed the bloodless lips, there was even a gesture of benediction in the moving hands that lay on top of the counterpane. A deep sigh and then a relapse into unconsciousness to await the final summons that came to Louis Martin on the following day.

Louis Martin's life was in many ways a bewildering and complex example of defeated objectives and inner contradictions. Slightly arrogant, a stern disciplinarian, a disappointed religious, and an escapist recluse; a man of kindly ways and generous habits; a loyal servant of the church; we can see him as a perfect father even if in some ways a difficult and trying man to live with. The danger in trying to rediscover and recreate him lies in the simple fact that what we know about his life has been carefully pruned, so that all we see on the surface is what his daughters wished us to see. It is from their words alone that we get most of the information about him, and even his biographers have shown a strange lack of balance that makes you feel when you read their testimony to him that you are reading a legend that has been made out of a life, and never get quite near enough to the life itself to see the central character in his right perspective.

Mother Gonzague sat looking out of the small window of her cell at the strange half-light that was casting fantastic shadows across the convent garden. It gave to the place an unearthly, an almost eerie look as it spread across the lawns and flower beds, those pinks and purples and turquoise tints that are familiar to all who have seen a Normandy twilight in early spring or late autumn. The peace of it all overwhelmed her, seeming to give an added sense of tragedy to the turmoil in her own heart. The nuns thought of her as cold and impersonal. Some of them hinted that she was not at all suitable for her position as Mother Prioress of Carmel. Sister Agnes of Jesus was often openly antagonistic to her ideas and outlook on the running of the community. 'The Wolf', that was what they called her behind her back, a snarling animal always ready to spring out on them unawares.

She thought of her sister and the children and the never-ceasing demands they always seemed to be making upon her. She stroked the purring cat that had leapt on to her lap and knew that the love for this creature, good as it might be in others, was a corrupt and possessive thing in her own life. In some ways she had so much in common with the Visionary of Avila while in others she was the complete negation of all that the Foundress of the Order had stood for. The burden of loneliness lay very heavily upon her stricken heart. Affection, how much every human being needed it, and how deeply she felt that need in the agony that seemed to be almost breaking her heart.

Was she as callous as some of the novices thought her to be? Was she as cold and imperious as some of the older nuns suggested she was? If only she could explain to someone what lay behind her actions that were so often misunderstood. It was out of her knowledge of her own imperfections that she realised how essential it was to demand perfection from others. It was because she herself found it so easy to betray the Rule that should direct every moment of her life that she applied that same Rule so rigorously to those who had been placed through the grace of God in her care. If she could help in the moulding of one of the sisters so that that one became a worthy offering to God then perhaps she too would enjoy the redemptive power that would pulse through that sister's soul.

Thérèse Martin, Sister Thérèse of the Child Jesus and Holy Face, what a strange and in some ways bewildering creature she was. Her simplicity had that pristine quality that belongs to a perfectly cut diamond. Her reverence had that nobility of purpose that cast a radiant splendour on everything she did. Her veil was covered with neat darns, her habit extensively patched and the leather soles of her sandals a mass of mends, all these things a living witness to the strict manner in which she upheld her vow of poverty. Her lamp was always kept as low as possible giving her hardly enough light in which to carry out her duties of spiritual reading, her platter was scrubbed clean of every morsel of food with a tiny crust of bread at the end of the daily meal exemplifying to perfection her respect for the property of the community and the need to guard at all times against waste. A letter she was writing would stop at the middle of a word, a book she was reading would be laid down before she had finished the sentence, the poem she was reciting in recreation would stop before she had reached the end of the verse, and all these things as a daily tribute to her vow of obedience. The Little Way, so she herself had called it, but the Mother Prioress knew it was the hidden way by which a soul was purged and purified that it might put upon itself the habit of perfection.

Her thoughts moved back in time to the first time she had seen the child in the convent parlour. The luminous look in those clear blue eyes, the unfaltering way in which she had said she wanted to become a nun, the serenity that enfolded her in an aura of sanctity, these things had called up all that was finest in the Mother Prioress, and she had felt at their first meeting that a deep and lively and unspoken bond existed between them. And now this child of Lisieux was growing into a woman.

Sister Agnes made it obvious that she thought she was too hard with her sister and the Mother Prioress could not explain that the apparent hardness was the only way in which she felt she could help to develop and train this sanctified being placed in her care. The higher the aspirations of a soul the greater the need of a strict and unreserved discipline from her Superior. Inner mortification was much more important than external discipline. The words that fell from her lips as she criticised or issued an order to this aspirant for heaven were often cold and imperious, but the feeling in her heart as she uttered them was one of kindness and generosity. Those of us who linger in the valley may be given the right to spur those on who are struggling to the mountain top. Our words of encouragement may sound callous and indifferent to those who hear them but the aspiring pilgrims know that they are just the phrases needed to strengthen them of the final and more tortuous stages on the journey. Thérèse Martin loved her and in that love she herself found comfort and consolation.

Mother Gonzague had often witnessed the ecstatic radiance that glowed in her eyes like a golden aureole as Sister Thérèse received the Sacred Element in her mouth at Mass. She had heard from the novices how on one occasion when Thérèse had found a crumb on the paten after communion she had made them all kneel down in adoration until the priest she had sent one of them for had partaken of the hallowed morsel that was verily the body and blood of her beloved Saviour.

Another day she had been told how the nun had knelt in adoration before the tabernacle and had then risen silently to her feet and tapped lightly on its door whispering words of love and affection to the Christ Child who for her was enshrined in that sacred chamber. The nuns who had told her this said they had never seen such an unearthly look on any person's face before as they had seen on the face of Sister Thérèse that morning. She had spoken quietly and gently to her Lord, and all who were present when this happened were sure that He had replied to her and that His words had opened up a wondrous vision to her tear-filled eyes.

In spite of these things – or was it because of them – Mother Gonzague could not find the answer to the question why Thérèse Martin was tormented with scruples, imprisoned in an aridity that was often the price one had to pay for the special graces that were part of the process of purification. 'Unless a seed die and fall to the ground and wither', hard words these but filled with a lively meaning for those rarified creatures whom God had set aside for His special favours.

What a contradiction Thérèse Martin's life presented when you viewed it coldly and impartially from its outward manifestation. She weeded the garden, she worked in the laundry, she helped in the refectory, she cleaned the sacristy, menial tasks, leaving little or nothing behind them as a witness to her labours. Her sister Marie wrote interesting commentaries on her spiritual reading. Her sister Pauline was clever with needles and brushes, and her embroidery and painting were an outstanding testimony to her creative ability that would remain long after her body had been cast down into the quiet earth of the convent graveyard. What would Thérèse leave behind her when she too went to the final resting? The golden curls they had cut off her head when she was shorn of them in the chapel at her clothing. A tattered habit that most nuns would have discarded years ago. The knotted thong with which she whipped herself regularly according to the rule of Carmel. The well-thumbed copy of *The Imitation of Christ* that had been her constant companion. It is true one nun would recall constant acts of unsolicited

135

kindness, that another would remember words of encouragement and consolation that had meant so much to her in an hour of need; but acts of kindness were the corporeal works of mercy incumbent upon all followers of Christ, and words of kindness were a debt we all owe to those travelling life's highway alongside us in our daily endeavours.

In September 1894, two months after the death of her father, Céline Martin entered the Carmel at Lisieux as a novice. There were now four members of the family in the same enclosure, Marie, Pauline, Thérèse and Céline. In some ways it seems very strange that they had all been allowed to enter the same convent and it is obvious when we read of all that occurred within its walls that the three sisters, Pauline, Marie and Céline formed a small clique who felt that they were destined to aid in fulfilling their mother's hopes that one member of the family would be raised to the altar of the church. There are some, and they are in the majority, who see in this event the hand of God mysteriously at work furthering His own purpose in the nursing and nurturing of the youngest member of the family, Thérèse. There are others, and I must confess that I number myself among them, who see that the hand of God moulded Thérèse to His own Glory in spite of the other members of the family who had joined the community.

Thérèse herself was the first to realise the inherent danger in this situation, and she appears to have assiduously avoided turning to her sisters for help or advice, and in fact from all the evidence I have studied she appears to have cut herself adrift from them as much as possible. Had not the Foundress of the Order warned her followers against the danger of 'inordinate affections', and was it not part of the duty of every nun to lose her own identity and seek to identify herself completely with the inner life and purpose of the community of which she had become a voluntary member?

Thérèse was only too well aware of the transience of earthly ties and the frailty of human affections. These things were the shadows that God cast across the world in which the majority of us seek to find a refuge from His demanding radiance. To love another human being is a good thing in so far as it leads us into a deeper understanding and a more profound love for all mankind. The ties of family affection can be either the golden cords that bind us ever closer to that love whose service is perfect freedom, or the iron fetters that imprison us in a possessive selfishness that slowly corrupts and corrodes the soul.

The first demand that the call to the religious life makes upon those who answer it in the way Thérèse Martin did is that we shall forsake the ways of earth and seek above all things the pathway to heaven. 'Unless a man shall leave his father and mother, sisters and brothers, wife and children and follow me he shall not be worthy of my calling.' The men and women who listen to, hear and answer this challenge are the ones who seek the hermit's cell or the discipline of the cloister. They are the dedicated ones whose daily life is to be constantly spent in striving through grace to remake themselves until they are seen as being in the image of God's eternity. Thérèse Martin belonged to this gallant company and she knew that to love her sisters who had done so much to help her in the years that followed her mother's death was a natural thing, and as such had nothing of the quality of heroic virtue in it. Her love must not contract itself in such a way as to betray her into the false security of earthly affection, but must expand all the time so that she might move into the fullness and joy of heavenly love that alone could bring an enduring satisfaction to the hungry soul.

She loved Marie, she loved Pauline, she loved Céline, this was an easy thing to do demanding little from her as it was inherent in her nature. What she had to do was love the murderer, the criminal, the spoiled priest, the black people and the white people for whom she prayed so zealously every day. Her vows of poverty, chastity and obedience were not and never could be an end in themselves. If they were allowed to become this they would stultify her. These things, good as they were had no native goodness in them, they were means and the end was to seek a widening, a deepening, an enriching of love in such a way that she could honestly say in the quietness and solitude of the confessional that she was moving constantly towards an all embracing love for all living creatures. Filial love, sisterly love, communal love in the cloister, these were the stepping stones over which we must tread if we were to find that absolute love that had manifested itself for millions of people throughout the ages on a desolate hill known as Calvary. While we experenced a need for human understanding we were falling short of that completeness which is ours in the complete understanding of God.

It is only when we get behind the simple phrases in which Sister Thérèse clothed her message for all humanity, Catholic and non-Catholic alike, that we discover that the little way was a lonely way, a hidden way that leads us, if we are courageous enough to follow it to the portals of paradise.

It was about this time, soon after Céline had entered Carmel, that Thérèse was allotted the task of helping the novices to understand the meaning of the religious life to which they had dedicated themselves. With an assurance that staggers us unless we have grasped the depth and intensity of her own spiritual vocation, she proved herself to be just the person they needed to help and guide them in what were the formative and in some ways the most critical months of their lives in religion. Once again it was the ordinary, and seen on one level the triviality, of her teaching that gave them the assurance and confidence they needed.

Sister Thérèse proved herself to be the strictest and yet at the same time the kindest of teachers. If a novice attempted to rush through her prayers she would be asked very quietly, 'Haven't you got time to talk slowly to Jesus?' Should a novice fail to do the task she had been set to the best of her ability she would find herself facing the question, 'Is that the best you can offer to Jesus? Can you only do so little for Him when He did so much for you?' Let a novice break one of the rules of the community and she would be sternly reminded that she had entered the convent to practise obedience and if she could not do this surely she would be better to return to the outer world she was seeking to leave behind.

Thérèse knew that to assist in the unfolding of the hidden flower within the soul called for endless patience, unceasing kindness and an unstinted understanding. The little mistake, if left uncorrected, could become a major error. The apparently trivial giving way to a minor temptation could lead to a danger zone in which one might prove easy prey to the devil. For her trivialities did not exist, as every thought, every feeling and every action must be a witness to the depth and sincerity of one's calling.

Her greatness of soul manifested itself in the way in which she proved the significance of the most insignificant word or action in one's life. To spill crumbs without picking them up and eating them was waste. To fail to adjust one's veil properly was being untidy. To leave specks of dust in the corner of one's cell was carelessness. Only as we learnt to master these faults, unimportant though they might be in themselves, could we overcome the graver difficulties that lay ahead. The amazing thing is that there was nothing of a nagging, or carping, or killjoy attitude in her dealings with the novices. She was gay and buoyant and full of zest. Life was a happy thing and a life dedicated completely to God was the happiest thing of all.

Thérèse often thought during the hours she spent with the novices of the darkness that had enshrouded her the day before she herself had taken her final vows and become a fully professed member of the community. All the happiness she had enjoyed during her novitiate had left her. Suddenly, without a warning of any kind she found herself wondering if she had made a mistake in seeking to become a Carmelite. Her hopes seemed dead and her desire to remain in the cloister had deserted her. No one can possibly imagine the torture that convulsed her in an increasing agony of doubt as the hours passed by. She must leave the cloister and go back to the world, but what had the world got to offer her? She must forget her one-time desire to be a religious and once more return to the person she had been before she had entered the cloister, but in her heart she knew that that person no longer

existed, and in any case the one desire that had been part of that person's life
was to arrive at the point where she was now standing.

When she had spoken to the novice mistress of her fears Sister Marie had
laughed at her, not unkindly but in an honest attempt to bring her face to
face with the element of the ridiculous that seemed to run through the whole
experience. Other novices had often experienced at this stage a desire to go
back, to return to their ordinary lives, some of them in fact had done so.
Not Thérèse Martin whose calling had been so crystal clear that from the age
of four she had longed for the day that she was now so rapidly approaching.

As soon as Sister Marie had realised that she could not help the pitiable
suppliant who had come to her for comfort and strength she sent her to see
Mother Gonzague. The Prioress was just the right person to handle this
delicate and difficult situation. She spoke quietly and firmly of how temptation always assails us when we are on the verge of winning a spiritual victory.
She reminded the girl that only those who are tested and tried through the
twin fires of doubt and despondency are truly worthy of their calling. The
kindness and firmness of the Prioress's attitude completely reassured the
troubled girl, and she herself has told us how when she left the Prioress's
room her heart was 'filled with heavenly joy'.

> I longed that every sinner on earth might be converted, all captive souls in
> Purgatory set free, and in my heart I bore this letter containing what I desired for
> myself: 'O Jesus, my Divine Spouse, grant that my baptismal robe may never be
> sullied. Take me from this world rather than allow me to stain my soul by com-
> mitting the least wilful fault. May I never seek or find aught but Thee alone. May
> all creatures be as nothing to me and I am nothing to them. May no earthly thing
> disturb my peace. Oh Jesus I ask for peace. Peace and above all love. Love without
> limit. I ask for Thy sake that I may die a martyr.'

Limitless love, that was what she tried to teach each of them to strive
after in their daily lives. She had an innate capacity to make it sound so easy
for them to accomplish this conquest over themselves. If you find that one of
the nuns irritates you, seek her out, become her friend, let her look upon you
as the one person who has brought a ray of love into her life. If a member
of the community appears to treat you unkindly, go out of your way to do
the things that you know will give her pleasure, but do them for the sake
of love and not because you hope they will change her attitude towards
yourself. If there is something you dislike doing then go and do it because
by this means you will learn to overcome it. How simple her words are.
How easy she makes it all sound. The more we think about her advice the
more we recognise that a spiritual genius is trying to open up the way to
heaven to very ordinary people like ourselves.

Gentleness and affection, kindliness and understanding, trust and diligence, these were the things she used in dealing with all the novices who came under her care, and after her death, many of them who had lived for some years with her in Carmel all testified to the life Thérèse had lived among them as being one of complete charity.

The year was 1895. Thérèse Martin was twenty-two years of age, had been in Carmel at Lisieux for seven years, and outside the four walls of the enclosure little was known about her. If she had died at this time it is very doubtful if her death would have made very little impact either in the convent itself or in the outside world. A few of the older people at Alençon had they heard the news might have remembered the golden haired little child whom some of the less charitable ones had said was 'too pretty by half'. Her relatives at Lisieux and her sisters in the convent would have felt a sense of loss and a personal sadness at her passing, and Pauline would probably have maintained that the nuns had lived in daily contact with a saint in the making. Mother Gonzague would have found it very difficult to write much about her in the biographical memorial that was always written in Carmelite Houses in France and circulated to the other houses in the country. A simple, pious little soul, a charming and devoted nun, one of those almost too good to be true characters – all these things might have been said but basically she would have been seen as a nonentity. No one knew very much about her interior life and she had said little or nothing to her fellow nuns about her mystical experiences.

It is true that the novices who had come under her guidance and influence had found her a wise, gentle and kindly teacher who not only told them what they should do and how they should do it, but who set them a perfect example herself of the contemplative's way of life. There were several priests training to be missionaries who had sought her advice and who treasured the letters in which she had outlined the basic principles of what she called her 'Little Way of Spiritual Childhood'. The priests who visited the convent itself were all impressed by her charm and her obvious piety. Her confessors and spiritual advisers sometimes felt she was a little too strict with herself and worried far too much over trifles. Perfection was a pleasant enough sounding word and obviously represented something that every Christian soul must seek to achieve, but applying it to such menial tasks as weeding the garden, scrubbing the blankets in the laundry, darning one's habit, and seeing these things as gifts one must offer to God as an expression of one's love of Him, well it all seemed to be taking things a little too far. Many clerics have a great deal more in common with the laity than ordinary people realise and probably share with them that oldest prayer of all 'God make me good – but not yet'.

Most of us who have made any kind of study at all of the great saints and mystics expect to find extraordinary things happening in their lives that sets them apart from the common herd. As we know, St Francis of Assisi was reputed by his followers to have the stigmata. The great St Teresa of Avila was said to have levitated while kneeling in prayer when she reached a complete state of ecstasy. Juliana of Norwich was acclaimed to be constantly plagued with voices and visions, some of a heavenly nature, others being of a more doubtful origin. Madame Blavatsky, the founder of the Theosophical Society claimed to possess clairvoyant and clairaudient powers, and to be able to travel astrally from her flat in London to the hidden places where the Masters of Wisdom resided in Tibet.

I admit that one needs to take these claims not simply with a pinch but with a pound of salt, but once we have sifted the true from the false there remains a residue of attested evidence that even the cynic and sceptic will find difficult to explain away.

On 9th June, 1895, Sister Thérèse of the Child Jesus and Holy Face had a strange mystical experience that she herself simply spoke of as being pierced by the dart of Divine Love. We know that her famous predecessor of Avila had herself passed through stages of ecstasy and rapture accompanied by fierce and intense feelings of being wounded through the heart by a sharp instrument like a javelin, and that this had been the prelude to what the saint of Avila had claimed was a spiritual marriage to Christ himself.

I am convinced after carefully studying the very scant evidence available on the subject that St Thérèse of Lisieux passed through a similar experience. All we know is that she was fit and well when the incident occurred and we are also certain of one fact and that is that she never suffered from hallucinations. She was too much the sound sturdy Norman for that. As she knelt in prayer on the morning in question a shaft of light seemed to engulf her until eventually she felt herself to be wrapped in a sheet of flame.

Those around her realised that she was in a state of complete ecstasy, a state in which she seemed to be almost independent of the body and the senses. There was a stillness, a rigidity about the kneeling figure that appeared to send out an aura of enraptured sanctity. And then it happened, a dart, like a long thin pointed javelin rushed through the air towards her and pierced her right through to the heart. The nun said very little about this profound mystical experience herself but its effect upon her was so marked that it made a clearly defined impact on the few years of life that remained to her.

Her own words, written under the vow of obedience in which she describes this startling incident are as follows.

I was commencing in the choir the Way of the Cross, when I suddenly felt myself wounded with a dart of fire so ardent that I thought I would die. I know not how to explain the transport; no comparison could make known the intensity of that flame. It seemed to me that an invisible power plunged me wholly in fire. Oh what fire, what sweetness!

When later Thérèse was closely questioned about all this by her sister Pauline, who at that time had been elected Mother Agnes, Prioress of the Carmel at Lisieux, she admitted that this was the culmination of a series of like experiences, but that the earlier ones she had experienced in private were of a minor order when compared to the trial by fire and steel she had undergone in the convent chapel. 'My Mother,' she stated,

> I have had transports of love several times, once in particular during the novitiate when I remained for a whole week far away from this world. I cannot explain it. I acted, so it seemed to me with a body not my own. For me there seemed to be a veil thrown over every earthly thing. But I was not burned by a real flame. I could endure those delights without expectation of seeing my hands riven asunder by their force. Whereas on the day of which I now speak, a minute, a second more and my soul must have parted from my body. Alas, I found myself returned to earth and aridity returned immediately to my soul.

These words and the experiences they relate to call for a little more detailed examination than a mere cursory reading on the nun's simple but explicit phrases. For they lift her from the mundane level on which many had placed her up to this point in time in her spiritual career into perfect alignment with the greatest mystics and saints of the church.

The experience of that spiritual marriage of 9th June has within it all the elements that writers of mystical states know as the Dark Night of the Soul. Dark because once the creature has known the timeless rapture and glimpsed the frontiers of eternity it can never find any satisfaction in the future things, happenings and events of this world. The piercing of the heart, the wound of love that comes to each of them creates a transport and yet at the same time a feeling of aloneness, sadness, and disappointment. Every moment of life is as a fragment of dust after this great event has claimed their soul for its own.

All they strive to achieve, all they seek to accomplish will taste as bitter as gall in their mouths. Prayer will seem empty, meditation meaningless. They have been drained dry of everything except the desire for God, and the very God they love so deeply and strive after so ardently seems to have turned His face away from them. Like St Paul they cry in a continuous inward agony, 'Who shall deliver me from the body of this death'.

The Little Way has been transformed into the mighty road of mystical abandonment. The words, spoken in childhood, 'I choose all', have come to their fruition, the nun of Lisieux has looked on the face of her Beloved Bridegroom and the nuptials have begun that will declare her to be His Espoused for all eternity.

CHAPTER VIII

A Grain of Wheat

The year 1895 was to prove itself to be a crucial period in Thérèse Martin's spiritual unfolding. It marks a point of departure. In the preceding years all her energies had centred upon the acceptance of every area in daily living as an opportunity to discover for herself and to interpret in her own special way the will of God. The acceptance of the burdens and responsibilities of living, an awakening into and a fulfilment of the meaning that every passing day opened up to her had been her constant objective. It might well have been written of her as Edith Sitwell wrote in *The Canticle of the Rose*:

> From my little span
> I cry of Christ, Who is the ultimate Fire
> Who will burn away the cold in the heart of Man . . .

So much for the past. What of the future, the all too few years that lay ahead of her? The new theme that emerges, and it is a triumphant theme in every sense of the phrase, was to be the complete acceptance of death as something that God willed for her and therefore that she must in a similar way will for herself. This was not simply resignation, that is a negative outlook upon the inevitable, it was a positive realisation within her own soul that death was the only true gateway to life.

It is well worth while pausing here to look very closely into the appearance and character of Thérèse Martin. Fortunately we are able to do this since the Carmel at Lisieux has allowed the authentic photographs of the saint to be published in order that everyone who is interested in her can see exactly what she looked like. Probably one of the most unfortunate things that ever happened to her was allowing the idealised paintings and drawings made by her sister Céline to be printed and circulated as though they were true impressions of the saint herself. All we see in these is a highly imaginative and very unsuccessful attempt to befool the public into thinking that they are looking at something that bears the seal of authenticity when it actually disguises her authentic looks from us.

Some of the severest critics of the saint have based their attacks upon the fact that Céline was not only allowed to possess a camera in Carmel but was allowed to carry on her hobby as an amateur photographer. They feel it is against the spirit and principle of the simple life without possessions that they interpret as the correct rendering of the rule of the Carmelite Order. They are wrong in making this approach for at the time of which I am writing the individual Mother Prioress of every Carmel in France was allowed a great deal of latitude in her interpretation as to how the rule should be applied in her own community.

In any case every aspirant to the taking of the veil was expected to offer her ability and talents as a contribution to the wellbeing of the whole community, and Mother Agnes, Céline's sister, who gave her permission to have the camera and use it in the convent itself probably felt that it was a useful asset in helping to build up the community's archives. We must also remember that it was the same Mother Agnes who allowed the paintings and drawings to be presented as though they were lifelike portraits of the saint, and later, when actual photographs were selected from the community's collection, insisted on these being retouched before they were reproduced for general circulation. Vanity is not only the prerogative of the society beauty, it may even slip in unawares into the quietness of the cloister.

The actual photographs present to us a very clear picture of the saint during the twenty-four years of her earthly life. First of all we see her as a happy and attractive child with a glint of mischief in her sparkling eyes. Next she is presented as a novice, a tall, round faced, rather impassive girl, but in the eyes one can clearly see the deep intent and purpose that was becoming her dominant characteristic. The photographs of her as a professed nun give us a clear insight into every facet of her character. Here one sees complete serenity, unstinted devotion and an agony of suffering that has an element of terror in it.

The most interesting contrast to be found in this amazing collection are between the two photographs of her, one taken in the cloister as she lay on her sick bed and the other immediately after her death in the infirmary of the convent. The first of them portrays the face of a woman who has aged before her time. It is marked with intense pain, and the half-closed eyes capture for us some element of the extent of her agony. We might well call it the Gethsemane portrait taken the day before Golgotha. The second one reflects all the loveliness of a young girl. It has a serenity and radiance that immediately suggest to us the depth of her devotion to Christ and her seeking and finding the way to personal sanctification. I have sat and looked at this photograph many a time, sometimes for quite long periods, and in its sheer quality of heavenly beauty I have found myself saying, 'I know that I am looking on the face of a saint.'

And what of her personality, her character, as seen in the eyes of her contemporaries? The novices whom she helped so much and to whom she was so deeply devoted spoke with one voice of her justice, her love and her complete detachment from worldly things. The nuns who lived with her day by day and saw her passing through every phase of her spiritual unfolding were all unanimous in stating that she had the quality of heroic virtue, and that this could be seen in the willingness with which she accepted everything that came to her. If she was misjudged by one of the sisters she never tried to justify herself. If her wishes or words were misinterpreted she never spoke an ill word against the offender. If there were those in the community who felt that it was unwise to have four members of the same family in the same convent Thérèse went out of her way to disarm these critics by disassociating herself from her sisters as much as possible, and it must be very clearly emphasised here that at the time when Pauline, Sister Agnes, was elected to the office of Prioress she showed no preference for Thérèse in any way.

The one person who, more than any other, had a very clear idea of her sanctity, Mother Gonzague, has left behind her a very clear picture of her opinions of this nun who had been in her care. Writing on the back of a photograph of Thérèse which she was sending to the Carmel at Tours (now unfortunately it has been lost) the Mother Prioress says:

> The jewel of Carmel, its dear Benjamin. She has the office of painter in which she excels without having had any lessons other than observing the Reverend Mother, her beloved sister, at work. Mature and strong, with the air of a child and with a sound of voice and manner of expression that veils the wisdom and perfection of a woman of fifty. A soul which is always calm and in complete possession of herself at all times. A completely innocent saint, who needs no repentance to appear before God but whose head is always full of mischief. Mystic, comic, she can make you weep with devotion and just as easily die with laughter at recreation.

These are the words, let us remember, of a woman who has been said to be vain and worldly, lacking in sympathy, and if anything tending in all things to be a little harsh in her judgements. A visiting nun from another convent who met Thérèse in the parlour said this of her: 'How charming that child is. She appears to be more of heaven than of earth. There is something so pure and so honest about her that just seeing her makes you feel peaceful.'

Such are the comments of two people who knew her during her lifetime; the one from an intimate and daily association with her from the day she entered the portals of the convent as a novice to the day when she was carried out in her coffin to be buried in the sacred spot set aside for the use of the community in the nearby cemetery, the other a visitor who had only met her casually, yet who even at such a short meeting formed a very clear and defined picture of her nature and personality.

Another feature that emerges very distinctly in this year that I have defined as the move from looking earthwards to that of gazing heavenwards was that Thérèse herself appears to have had a very clear concept of her ultimate vocation when she had perfected herself in sanctity. The grave was not for her, the corridors of heaven would not offer to her sufficient opportunities to express that perfect love to which she had dedicated her life and for which she had consecrated her death. Heaven would never hold this warring spirit that sought to fight the devil's legions in every part of the earth. She would come back, how often she made that promise; she would return to walk the ways of men, how often she spoke those words; and her mission would be the salvation of souls through love, the sanctified love that she had purified in her life of suffering.

One day, not long after Thérèse had had her profound mystical experience, Mother Agnes was sitting with the other nuns and novices at recreation when Thérèse started to talk to them about her own childhood, of the happy home they had all shared with their parents, and of the longing and aspiration she had had to enter Carmel while she was still only a child. Overriding the simplicity of her words was an undercurrent of sincerity that made her easy phrases sound like the music of heaven echoing through her lips to the children of earth. How transient the spoken word is. How often we wish we could recall a conversation we have had with a friend that has now blurred itself on the far side of memory.

Mother Agnes pondered for several days over the talks she had heard Thérèse give on her life and then came to a decision, the implications of which were quite unknown to her at the time. She ordered her sister, under obedience, to write the story of her childhood and her early days in Carmel, and it was in this way that the first eight chapters of the *The Story of a Soul* came into being.

Later at the request of her sister, Marie, she wrote the famous eleventh chapter in which she outlined her own teachings on the way of spiritual childhood, and in 1897, the year when she had once more been elected Prioress she handed to Mother Gonzague the remainder of the story, thus completing the manuscript as we know it today.

I write 'as we know it today' deliberately, for the first, and in fact all, the early editions were a censored and abridged version of the book that in many ways detracted from its spiritual significance. The first complete version in an English translation was by the late Father Ronald Knox, and published in 1958.

An interesting point about the manuscript itself is that just as Thérèse Martin had written her poems and hymns on any scrap of old paper she could find, such as the backs of used envelopes in order that she should not waste the property of the community, so in writing this book, fulfilling a disciplined order that made it part of her work in the convent, she made use of the cheapest notebooks that could be bought and crammed as much on to every page as possible. It is that all oneness of her outlook and character that we find permeating everything she said and did from her first hour as a novice to the last of her life on earth.

Before examining the contents of the book itself it would be a wise course I feel to dispel some of the illusions that have arisen around it. When it first appeared in English under the title of *A Little White Flower* it lost a certain amount of its meaning at the hands of the translator. He saw Thérèse as a sugary confection, in some ways very like the faked portraits of her I have already referred to. I know that when I first read the book myself, and I have talked to many devout souls who have had a similar experience, in spite of the fact that I recognised that here was the promise of a classic of the spiritual life I found its language too flowery and its impact on me rather sickmaking. I did not know then of course that whole passages of the book had been cut out and that the translator himself had only had as a source book the carefully edited and censored French version of the text.

The major fault of this book, however, was that it did much to rob Saint Thérèse of the Child Jesus and Holy Face of her full stature and significance. It belittled her spiritual struggles, it almost erased altogether the frightening stories of the temptations that had beset her as she trod the pilgrim's road towards beatitude, and she emerged from this maltreatment of her own story like a cross between a pretty little child, full of whimsy and innocence, and a tinselled angel perched on top of a Christmas tree.

The facts relating to the publication of Thérèse Martin's autobiography, *The Autobiography of a Saint*, present us with one of the most interesting problems in the annals of literature, for even today, in spite of the carefully prepared version in French that has been translated into English, as already stated, by the late Father Ronald Knox, we are not at all sure that we have the story as she wrote it during her last three years at Carmel.

It is important to realise that the manuscript from which this definitive version has been prepared and edited was the result of a very careful and critical examination of the three manuscripts that formed the basis of the original book when it was published under the English title of *A Little White Flower*. The three manuscripts each take the form of a letter, each addressed to a different person, and each written with a specific purpose and from a particular point of view so that there is no underlying principle of unity or continuity linking them together. The first manuscript was the letter she wrote under obedience, and addressed to her sister, Mother Agnes of Jesus, who was at that time Prioress. Because of the way in which Thérèse approached this task, seeing it as a personal account that she was writing mainly for her own sister, although from something she said later we can assume that at the back of her mind she had a vague idea of its later publication, it is a simple personal narrative of the life they had shared together both at Alençon and Lisieux with little literary merit. It is an intimate, gossipy story of saintly parents, noble sisters, a happy childhood and of her own constant striving after perfection. It is doubtful whether if it had been published in its original form it would have had much appeal to the general reader. One point to stress is that the Mother Prioress herself thought so little about it that once Thérèse had completed it and handed it to her she left it unread for four months herself.

The manuscript that formed the second part of the trilogy was a second letter, written to, and at the special request of her sister, Sister Marie of the Sacred Heart and was concerned mainly with the development of the interior life and the various stages in prayer. Sister Marie, the most intellectual member of the family, had often listened to Thérèse instructing the novices, and had also been fascinated with some of the ideas she had expressed on her life as a nun during community recreation. She felt she would like to possess for herself a more permanent record of these things.

This letter, as you will realise, was completely different in style and content to the first one, having very little to do with the saint's external life, centring as it did far more on her ideas about her inner development as a religious. It had been erased and rewritten, scored out and corrected in many places, and the original manuscript proves that Thérèse herself had given a great deal of thought and exercised a great deal of care in its writing. No doubt she recognised that if people in the future were going to take any interest in her at all, it would be as a religious aspiring to a life of perfect sanctity that they would approach her, hence a treatise on the inner life must be as near to perfection as she could make it.

The third manuscript came into being in quite a different manner to the other two. Sister Agnes had been succeeded by Mother Gonzague who had once more been elected Prioress, and having read the letter her sister had addressed to herself was so impressed with it that she approached the Prioress and suggested that she, the new Prioress, might order Thérèse to write a fuller account of her life in the convent as this aspect of her life had only been scantily touched upon in the first of the three letters.

Mother Gonzague assented and so a third letter, this time addressed to herself, was written, and once again because of the circumstances underlying its composition it was much more formal than either of the previous two letters had been. Three documents, not related to one another in any way and having no common underlying theme were thus in existence when Thérèse died in 1897. It was from these three letters that the formal letter *In Memoriam* was compiled and circulated to the other Carmelite Houses in France, and later at their request to other Carmelite Houses in many parts of the world. One point must be stressed here, and that is that Thérèse herself had given her sister Pauline permission to cut and edit the manuscripts in any way she pleased if ever it was decided to publish them for general circulation.

Within two years of her sister's death Pauline had persuaded Mother Gonzague to allow her to prepare a life of her sister based on the authentic documents for general circulation. At first the Prioress seems to have been a little doubtful as to the wisdom of this step, but later she agreed on condition that the book should be prepared in such a way as to make it appear that all the three letters had been addressed to her. To do this presented Pauline with a very formidable task. The matter in the three documents was of an entirely different nature. They had been written with a different approach to each one in a completely different style. The first letter, addressed specifically to herself, had little in common with the much more formal note in the third letter addressed to Mother Gonzague. The second letter had nothing in common with the other two as we have seen, and if this was to be used at all it must be treated in such a way as to appear part of a consecutive and coherent whole.

It is difficult to understand why the Prioress laid this peculiar condition on the question of their publication. Some of her critics, and they are among those who have tried to belittle all that she did and stood for in the life of the saint, have suggested that her sole motive was personal vanity.

I cannot share this view for I am convinced that in spite of her obvious worldliness in some things Mother Gonzague had a deep and profound humility in her ultimate attitude to Thérèse Martin. It may have been that she sensed a danger in Sister Agnes preparing the final script, and felt that by insisting on the fact that it should be dedicated and addressed to herself she could in this way override the personal approach that she felt sure would colour the saint's sister's approach to the task. After all, Mother Gonzague had been one of the first to sense the underlying sanctity in Thérèse's own life, and I think it is fair to assume that she adopted the attitude she did towards the book itself in order that she could do her best to ensure that that sanctity was presented as clearly and objectively as possible to its readers.

Pauline's approach to the editing itself was of a peculiar and interesting nature. First of all, she cut out many passages that she felt might present her sister in an unfavourable light to a wider audience than that of Carmelite communities. Having decided what the final content should be, she then rewrote the book completely herself so that the first published version was Pauline's account of the life of the saint, based it is true to a limited extent on what the saint herself had written. The first two thousand sold out very quickly and in the twenty years that followed the sales of this rather prettily written and sugar coated volume had run into millions of copies. In spite of all the editing, all the omissions, all the revisions, Thérèse herself does emerge as a living being in its pages. The tragedy of the book in my opinion is that it belittles her and prevents the grandeur of her stature from emerging in its full glory.

At the time the Process for her Canonisation was opened both the manuscripts, the saint's own version and Pauline's carefully edited one, were sent for examination to Rome where the Holy Office decreed that Pauline's version was the one that must continue to be reprinted and circulated to the general public. When a further edition was published in French, to which had been added some of the saint's poems and letters and an account of some of the miracles that had occurred after her death the more discerning readers commenced to wonder if the life had been written by the same person who had written the letters that were included in this volume. Eventually pressure was brought to bear on the Holy See to consider the question as to whether the time had not arrived to allow the original manuscript to be published in its entirety.

In August 1947 the Bishop of Bayeux and Lisieux gave the necessary permission for the full text to be published, and the Definitor General of the Carmelite Order wrote to Mother Agnes stating:

> The Church has spoken. The sainthood and the doctrinal mission of St Thérèse of the Child Jesus are universally recognised. To avoid and to refute partial or mistaken interpretation of her doctrine, and in order that her doctrine and her soul should be still more deeply understood the documents which you have so generously given us are insufficient. Only the original text can allow us to discover the movement in her thought and its living rhythm, and disclose all the light contained in her definitions which are usually so firm and so precise.

This order came as a shock to Mother Agnes and she herself seriously considered the whole question of the publication of the original text. Why did she hesitate? Was it because she knew that she herself had been responsible for erasures and alterations and omissions? There can never be a definite answer to this point, but we know that out of deference to her wishes it was decided that the full version of the book should not be published during her lifetime, although at the same time it was agreed that the original documents should all be carefully examined with a view to their ultimate publication.

The task that lay ahead of those who had undertaken this work was phenomenal. First of all there were the saint's own alterations. Which of the scoring and erasions had been hers and which were the work of a later hand? Parts of it had been written and rewritten several times and it seemed almost impossible to reach any final decision about a definitive text. However, by examining every page of the manuscripts line by line, by subjecting them to all the knowledge that science could place at the nun's disposal who had undertaken to do this work, by subjecting doubtful passages to a careful and critical scrutiny under ultra-red and ultra-violet rays much could be done and was done to arrive at what was by common agreement the nearest approach to the original text that could be arrived at after the passage of time. Mother Agnes had bequeathed to the only sister who remained alive in the convent, Sister Geneviève of the Holy Face (Céline), the task of seeing that a facsimile of the manuscripts was published after her death. Sister Agnes died in July 1951, and a year later permission was sought from the Holy See to publish the facsimile that had been so fully and so conscientiously scrutinised.

On the 19th September, 1952, the decree imposing the ban against their publication was lifted. Father François de Sainte Marie was responsible for supervising the publication of the French version of *The Autobiography of a Saint*, and it is this version that was used by Father Ronald Knox in preparing the English version of the same book. We must realise, however, that even today we cannot be sure that this is the exact version as the saint herself wrote it.

I have felt it necessary to give this detailed and carefully documented account of what happened to the saint's own account of her earthly life before continuing her story as it is only when you read the final version of it in Father Knox's somewhat unimaginative translation, that you see how what was looked upon in the past as the Little Way of Spiritual Childhood is within itself the great highroad to personal sanctity, and that a nun who had been referred to as a Little White Rose is seen as one of the most magnificent and rare orchids in the gardens of paradise. The grain of wheat had to fall to the ground it is true, but it has taken over half a century for it to come to its full fruition.

The letter addressed to her sister, Sister Marie of the Sacred Heart, is a vitally important document that calls for a very careful study if we are to understand Thérèse's own spiritual development. It is, in essence, her own account of the way in which she made the ascent of Mount Carmel, and as such needs to be fully comprehended if we are to place the correct valuation upon her sanctity. If we look upon Thérèse Martin as a Normandy peasant girl, shut off from the ways and affairs of the world in the pleasant security of her convent home we shall be highly mistaken. She was a wide-awake, alert person who was well informed as to what was happening to the Church and the world during the closing years of the nineteenth century. The anti-clericism that had swept over France troubled her deeply, while the internal dissensions within the Church itself that had arisen as a result of the Vatican Council's declaration of the doctrine of Papal Infallibility had caused her great distress. She offered up prayer daily for those priests who for one reason or another had broken away from Rome, and in her correspondence with priests and missionaries she showed a watchful and eager mind and expressed an outlook that had much in common with the trend in the Catholic Church of today that is seeking some way to assist in the healing of Christendom.

With the advances that were being made in the realm of science a great deal of speculation had arisen as to the relationship between science and religion. On the one hand you had those who were the fore-runners of the rising wave of materialism that has to a large extent engulfed the present generation. On the other you had the die-hards, the bible thumpers who still upheld the concept of a six-day creation and who looked upon God in purely anthropomorphic terms.

The idea of God was not something you could prove in the same way you could a mathematical equation. It was an inner experience, a knowledge that sprang from deep down in the human soul, and it was from that knowledge that the whole of her interior life was directed. She knew, as many of the greatest mystics had known before her, that just as poetry is capable of nuances that cannot find expression in prose, so the spiritual life is one that moves in a totally different direction to the material order. Thérèse leaves us in no doubt at all about this for she says that 'human speech is incapable of reproducing those experiences which the human heart only perceives confusedly'. Here we have a very clear echo of the words of St Augustine when he warned his followers that 'the heart has reasons the mind knows not'.

The point of departure for the mystic is this personal awareness of God. This is an awareness that moves outside the region of relatives giving to those who know it and share it an absolutism that merits no contradiction. Her advice of how to achieve this is quite clear and decisive.

> You want a guide to dictate your actions to you? Then you must read in the book of life, which contains the whole science of loving. The science of loving, yes, that phrase wakes a gracious echo in my soul; that is the only kind of science I want – I'd barter away everything I possess to win it.

As she moves deeper into this brilliant exposition of the soul's journey from its source to its goal Thérèse leaves us in no doubt as to her own achievements. 'Our Lord has seen fit to show me the only way which leads to it, and that is the unconcern with which a child goes to sleep in its father's arms'. The writer is not only conscious of her own inadequacy to convey the fullness and richness of her own experience but warns the reader, 'How am I to express heavenly mysteries in the language of earth?'

Her own thoughts carried her away to the point where she touches a state of ecstasy and the letter moves from the personal analytical note on which it opens to a rapturous psalm of praise for Jesus her beloved Bridegroom. 'Jesus, my well-beloved' she writes as she opens up this second phase of the letter,

> how considerate you are in the treatment of my worthless soul; storms all around me and suddenly the sunshine of Your grace peeps out.

There are moments, wonderful moments when she takes us by the hand and seems to sweep us with her into the heights where her freed soul is soaring. A dream of seeing three Carmelites, of one lifting her veil and revealing herself to be the Venerable Mother Anne of Jesus who had founded the Carmel at Lisieux.

> How soon, she asks, will my earthly mission be accomplished, when will God come to take me to Himself?

Soon, very soon was the simple reply, and the assurance these words brought her caused her to soar like an eagle to the veritable ramparts of heaven itself. Were her little sacrifices sufficient? Had she found in her daily acts of mortification the royal road to the heavenly marriage?

As we ponder on these words our thoughts turn to other great souls in the past who have had a similar experience. Teresa of Avila, Catherine of Siena, Dame Juliana of Norwich, each of these had borne witness to this inward moving of the soul where it seemed to be temporarily released from the body and living poised on the brink of eternity. Timelessness, a sense of the past, present and future all contained in a state of being outside the confining orbit of time and space.

> The Magdelen,

she tells us,

> by stooping now and again into the empty tomb was at last rewarded for her

search; and I by sinking down in the depths of my own nothingness, rose high enough to find what I wanted.

The eagle soars still higher:

To be nothing else than love, deep down in the heart of Mother Church; that's to be everything at once, my dream wasn't a dream after all.

The limitless horizon beckons her onward and upward, the spiritual marriage is finding its completeness in a negation that is more positive than the loudest affirmation of 'yes' the soul dare make.

And love has chosen me, weak and imperfect creature as I am for its burnt offering. Love cannot be content without condescending – condescending to mere nothingness, and making that nothingness the fuel of its flame.

Thérèse Martin leaves us in no doubt as to what she feels within herself has happened to her: 'here I am' she says, 'a child, the child of Holy Mother Church, a King's Bride.' Life, she goes on to remind us, demands that we shall do the least unimportant things in the right way, will call for endless small sacrifices. Love and suffering, these are the twin themes that run right through this remarkable document and these same two themes dominated the whole of her earthly life. She recalls for a moment a phrase from St John of the Cross who had said that the slightest movement of disinterested love had more value than all the other acts of the human soul put together.

She mounts higher still, nothing can hold her any longer in bondage to this world. The moment of consummation has arrived, the declaration of complete surrender must be made. There is an underlying note of terror in her affirmation as she cries out in ecstatic phrases:

I must be allowed the folly of entreating these eagles of yours, my elder brother, to win me the grace I need, that of flying towards the Sun of Love on the eagle wings you and you only can lend me. As long as it is your will, my Beloved, I am ready to remain without any power to fly, as long as I may keep my eyes fixed on you, fascinated by your gracious regard for the prey of your love. And one day I hope you will come down from your eyrie and carry off this poor creature of yours, carry it up to the very centre of love's furnace; to which it has offered itself as a victim.

To anyone who is familiar with the language of mystic experience these words convey their own truth. They are an attempt to speak the unspeakable, to catch in cold words the fire of truth itself. The soul of the victim who is also the victor is moving in ever-widening circles until it touches the fringe of what has been called cosmic consciousness, a state undefinable in prose but at times hinted at in the works of great poets like Blake and Browning.

Having become as nothing, the victim feels she had become all things, a fighter, a priest, a doctor, an apostle, a martyr. All she desires in her moment of complete victory is to be scourged, to be crucified, to be flayed alive, to be immersed in boiling oil, to offer her neck to the executioner, to be burned at the stake. What human lover has not felt these things when he has finally and completely possessed the body of his loved one? How much more then does the great mystic feel when having forsaken all the ordinary joys of physical love she finds her completeness in the unfading and undying love of her crucified Saviour?

It must be remembered, in fact I cannot emphasise it strongly enough, that Thérèse Martin did not seek these things as an end in themselves, hers was no road to selfish perfection. What she was striving for was to so completely abase her own will before the Will of God that she might become a worthy vehicle through which His love might pulsate to mankind. Time seemed too short, her years seemed too limited for her to accomplish all she knew within her heart she was striving to achieve.

> I should want to be a missionary (of divine love) ever since the creation and go on being a missionary until the world came to an end.

She knew at that moment, at the age of twenty-three, that the whole world had been offered to her by God as her parish.

We must try to realise that she knew, once she had been pierced by the dart of love, once she had reached her own fulfilment in her spiritual marriage, once she had been privileged to soar to those heights that lie outside the orbit of ordinary mundane experience, she knew that she must return to a life of bitter and relentless suffering. Beyond the Gethsemane into which she was moving stood Golgotha, and on that hill stood the cross that she herself must be nailed to if she was to find her place among those rare souls whose eternal mission is to share in the creative redemption of love. The miracle of her own complete self-abnegation was, as we shall see, to find its fruition in the miracles that her life and death were to bring about in the lives of others.

Love knows no barriers, surmounts all barriers, and I am convinced that in that moment, when she accepted without question the agony that lay ahead of her, she knew she was becoming a victim for a universal love that should have as its final mission the reunion of the church and the healing of nations. God would use her innocence, her simplicity, her childlike trust in such a way that He would raise her to the Altar of the Church, that as a member of the Church Triumphant, she might also be a guiding light to the Church Militant here on earth.

Mother Gonzague stood looking along the avenue of chestnut trees that led to the Lourdes Grotto at the end of the convent garden. Two hours earlier the community had been awakened for the first office of the day as the castanets clicked out their call to rise from their beds and proceed to chapel. It was a spring morning in 1896 and everything, the trees, the earth and the sky seemed to be touched with the ageless magic of rebirth. The waxen buds on the trees were showing the gentle green of their first leaves. The sky had that subtle iridescent quality that all who know Normandy at this time of the year are familiar with. The bird songs from housetops and hedgerows were cascading through the stilled silence of the morning air.

In spite of this unearthly beauty, this sense of God's signature upon His creation, Mother Gonzague was low and despondent. Her conscience was strangely disturbed by the look she had seen on Thérèse Martin's face the previous evening. The young face, that almost childish look that had been so enchanting to look upon, seemed to have completely disappeared. In the low lamplight of her cell where she sat writing on the scraps of paper she had saved from used envelopes she looked very old and very tired. Her eyes were deepsunken and her cheeks had a strained and hollow look.

'Are you ill child?', there was a slight petulance in her tone as Mother Gonzague addressed the question to the nun sitting there in half-darkness.

'No Mother,' the answer was as simple and direct as every phrase was that passed Sister Thérèse's lips.

'I heard you coughing and you seemed to walk very slowly up the stairs this evening'; there was still a doubtful note of interrogation in the voice. She hated illness, perhaps it was a reaction of her own fear of death that hardened Mother Gonzague's heart a little when any member of the community complained of sickness of any kind.

'I say a little prayer on every stair offering myself completely to the will of God.' The remark startled her. Coming from any other nun it might have sounded slightly presumptuous, but the words on the lips of Thérèse had a quiet sincerity that dismissed any thought of presumption or arrogance. It was this inexplicable quality, this sense of complete submission that made all that the nun did stand out in some bewildering way. Here was a life so completely dedicated to its vocation that its every minute was a challenge to all who came into contact with her.

As these memories flashed through Mother Gonzague's mind she noticed that Sister Thérèse was walking slowly along the avenue to the grotto itself. Each step she took suggested that she was in pain. Suddenly her shoulders shook a little and the hacking cough that had plagued her for some weeks cut through the still air of the silent morning. The older nun suddenly realised that she hated something inside herself, that something that always seemed to act as a barrier between herself and the other members of the community. In her heart she longed to feel that she really was a mother to all those who had placed themselves under her care, and yet in her mind she knew that many of the nuns despised her.

What a stupid thing human ambition was. How easily one found oneself ensnared by the devil through one's own arrogance. Those wasted years, and in her heart she felt they had been wasted, seemed to be mocking her as she stood in the breaking sunlight of another day. Where had her hopes, her dreams, the visions of her youthful ardour gone to? Then, she had seen herself as a worthy abbess of a great and mighty foundation. Now, all she was was the prioress of an obscure convent on the northern plains of Normandy. The will of God, surely that was the guiding rule for every Carmelite. Sister Thérèse submitted to it completely, absolutely and without question. She herself found it the most difficult part of the daily round to accept.

'The Martin club,' she thought of the phrase that she herself had used to some of the older sisters when Céline had entered the convent as a novice. There were times when she saw the division in their ranks, herself on the one hand and the three Martin sisters, Marie, Pauline and Céline on the other. Once again Thérèse's conduct baffled her. She seemed to stand apart from, even to remain deliberately aloof from the rest of her family. No one in the community seemed to understand Thérèse completely. Even her confessors had confided to the Prioress that at times Thérèse seemed to have too many scruples, to place too fine an edge on the province of evil.

A sense of complete frustration filled the Prioress's heart as she pondered on her own frailty and found herself seriously considering her own shortcomings. Power, that was her greatest temptation, and humility was the cross that she herself must learn to accept without reserve of any kind. Thérèse had taken from her shoulders all the burden of caring for and guiding and looking after the novices, and yet she herself had never had the courage to relinquish the nominal position as Novice Mistress. As she moved back through the open door into the convent itself, she noticed that Sister Thérèse was walking slowly back towards the house. Her face was racked with pain. Her shoulders were shaking as each spell of coughing shook her fragile frame. What did the novices think of her, this ailing woman, grown old before her time, who had directed them with such care, such patience and such unceasing devotion?

Sister Ann sat in her cell gazing at the ceiling. She had a blank look on her face. Life had never been easy for her and she found herself wondering what it was that had led her finally to the portals of Carmel. She did not know much about her early life. She had never known her parents for she was what the French call a charity child, that might mean she was either an orphan or a bastard. Her name, simply Mary of Ospanias, after the village where she had been born and where she had worked as a child on a farm. No one had ever thought it worth while to be kind to her. She was the household drudge, the unpaid labourer, the maid of all work who was beaten regularly by her employers if she did not satisfy the unceasing demands they made upon her. The floors to be scrubbed, the cows to be milked, the meals to be cooked and all for a mere pittance and her keep. When the time came, when she was old enough to openly rebel against the harsh treatment meted out to her, she had run away to a nearby town and taken a job as maid to a middle class family who were as bad, if not worse than her foster parents had been.

How Mary longed for a little human affection. There were moments when, tired and listless after a full day's hard work, she would lie down and cry herself to sleep. No one noticed her. The family very seldom spoke to her. It was 'get this', 'fetch that' from early morning until well after eleven at night. She knew that she was not very bright but wondered why it was that no one ever showed her any of that human sympathy that would have meant so much to her aching and lonely heart.

Mary recalled the day that she had decided to leave her cruel employer and seek admission to Carmel. If working for men and women was so terrifying then surely working for God must be much better. Sister Thérèse had always been gentle with her. All that talk though, what did it mean? She was always telling the novices that they must try to be like little children and learn to have a complete trust in God. There was something in Sister Thérèse that almost frightened Sister Ann, as Mary was named in the convent. She was so good, so kind, so patient. No matter what was said to her she never lost her temper.

Sister Ann remembered the day when she had deliberately insulted the novice mistress just to see what she would do. Her old employers would have raved at her and probably given her a beating. All Thérèse had done was smile at her very gently, put her arm round her shoulders, and placed her finger to her lips as the bell proclaimed the great silence, and had led her to the convent chapel. The lay sister lay on her straw palliasse and settled down to sleep. Different, that's what Sister Thérèse was, just different, but then it takes all kinds to make a world, even the little world of a Carmelite convent.

Sister Marie-Gabriel was working as usual in the linen room. How different life was in Carmel to what she had expected it to be when first she entered the Order. Peace ought to have been waiting for her there. How much she longed for peace. Deep down in her heart how much she needed a simple affection that would take away the shadow of fear that clouded all her days. Prayer, that seemed to help so little. Discipline, well, even that had lost its meaning and significance for her. She thought of how at times she had flayed herself with nettles to try to subdue the unruly thoughts that never seemed to cease tormenting her. Why had it always to be like this? Where was the centre of serenity, that haven of respite that had seemed to beckon her when first she heard the call of Carmel?

Her past life always seemed to be betraying her into a sense of despair. She thought of the draper's shop her father had kept at Nantes. Her life there as one of a large family of ten children had not been a happy one. Her father had never been unkind to her, In fact, all the town looked upon them as a perfect Catholic family. And yet somehow she had always been afraid of him. His life was lived within the narrow confines of the rules of the church, it lacked love and through that he seemed quite unable to give any real understanding to those around him.

How different life had been in the Martin household. She had often heard the sisters talk of their early life in Alençon and Lisieux during recreation. How they had loved their mother and how deep and profound had been her understanding of the life they were all seeking. She recalled how Sister Agnes had once mentioned that her mother had wanted to be a nun when she was younger, and how she had dedicated herself to family life in exactly the same way as she would have dedicated herself to a religious vocation. What was it that Sister Thérèse had called her, Marie Gabriel? 'A lily in a pot', an earth-bound soul that would blossom in beauty in spite of its cramping outlook and environment. How she had resented that remark.

Thérèse Martin, now there was an oddity to find in a Carmelite Convent. Why was she always seeking her out and what made her offer to help her in the linen cupboard? Nothing ever seemed to disturb her inner peace. No matter how unkind, or unjust as it seemed at times to the other nuns Mother Gonzague might appear to be, to her she never murmured a single word of protest but smiled as she did exactly what was demanded of her. There was something in Marie-Gabriel's nature that longed to open up, to accept the gentle flow of love that Sister Thérèse offered to all she came into contact with. And yet the older nun felt closed in, shut off, from the simple affection that was a fundamental part of Sister Thérèse's way of life.

How odd she had been at moments. That day when they were putting away the rough sheets, when Thérèse had said that laying one on the other could be a rosary, an offering to God of simple service. Sister Marie-Gabriel's God was not like that. He was a fierce and disturbing being, a projection of her own father who had always been ready to punish her for the least of her faults.

That was why it had been so hard for her to understand what Sister Thérèse meant when she said that we could always approach God like little children who were always sure of their father's love. If only the spiritual life could be as easy as that, but fathers could be cruel and unjust and perhaps God was very much the same. Her doubts grew more frightening each day, and somehow Sister Thérèse seemed to know of the valley of shadows through which she was passing. At recreation she would single her out and sit next to her, and try to amuse her with stories about her adventurous journey to Rome when she had gone to see the Pope. Those imitations she gave of some of her fellow travellers. Never cruel, never unkind, but so funny that the novices gathered all around and shook with laughter. Even the stern face of Mother Gonzague broke into a thin smile once in a while. 'Try to become like a little child again,' Thérèse would say to her. 'Realise that God loves you and wants you to trust Him completely. Never be afraid of Him because it doesn't matter what you have done. You can always be sure that if you are really sorry He will forgive you.'

Would God really forgive her, Sister Marie-Gabriel of the Conception, for the fear and hatred she felt of Him at times in her heart? Could He really understand the terror that overshadowed each day of her life as she found herself becoming imprisoned more and more in self-hatred, a victim of self-loathing and abject despair? The little way of spiritual childhood, that was what Sister Thérèse called it, might be all right for novices who were still close enough to their own childhood to have remembered some of its innocence, but for an older woman like herself it was far from easy. Fear had overshadowed all her days, fear of life and now, as each night came, fear of death. A solitary tear was falling down her cheek. She gazed steadily at the crucifix on the wall opposite. Was that the answer, suffering and death and apparent defeat? Or was Thérèse Martin right in her simple acceptance of love as an ultimate that lifted us beyond sin, that transformed suffering, that gave us an inner tranquillity that nothing or no one could disturb. An old prayer from the ancient liturgy of the church rose to her lips, 'Lord I believe, help thou my unbelief'.

Something inside her seemed to be breaking, the core of hardness that she clung to and hated at the same time seemed to be cracking. Was Sister Thérèse right after all, and was it only when we had that childlike acceptance of the love of God that we escaped from the fear of His justice, a fear through which we often imprisoned ourselves in a picture of God as being as imperfect in His justice as is the justice of men?

Coryside Chantal, Marie de la Meilleays, was the daughter of a wealthy family in the Province Indre-et-Loire, and had been given an education that befitted the child of a noble household of France. She was a little wild, a trifle headstrong, but took to long walks in the countryside where in the solitude that surrounded her she would ponder for hours on end the meaning and purpose of life. The easy, slightly arrogant, arid intellectual background in which she had been brought up failed to satisfy some inner longing, some deep need for adventure that was always challenging her. The life of the great Teresa of Avila fascinated her. She too would like to be a missionary for God, living under His direct orders, dying for Him if He so demanded. How she loved the writings of St John of the Cross and how deeply she was moved when she read the life of St Catherine of Genoa. These were the rarified souls. These were the ones who had been courageous enough to offer everything they were and all that they possessed to the service of God.

For several years these thoughts were her constant companions, and the more she meditated upon their meaning for her the more discontented she became with what appeared to her to be the useless life she was living in the world. To the surprise of many of her friends, and in spite of the slight annoyance of her family she had decided to seek to become a Carmelite nun and now she was in the convent at Lisieux known as Sister Jacob.

She was sitting in the convent garden pondering over the many things that had happened to her since that first day when Sister Thérèse had led her to her cell when she entered the Novitiate of the Order. All the arrogance in her had risen up and rebelled against the subservience that she had to learn if she was to adapt herself to the daily life of the community. It was very hard when you had been giving orders all your life to suddenly find that you were the one who was expected to take them. It would not have been an easy business for the lady of the manor to have become a parlourmaid, and it was certainly not an easy matter for Sister Jacob to accept Thérèse Martin as her 'angel', the one appointed by the Mother Prioress to guide her footsteps during her first year in the convent. On that first day, when Thérèse had opened up the shutters and pointed out to her the railway line that ran alongside the convent garden as though to remind her that they were not completely cut off from the world, she could not help noticing how shabby her habit was, how worn her sandals, and how chapped and coarse the hands that held the shutters open to fasten the catches.

Those first months had been far from easy. Instead of finding herself facing a stern taskmaster she had discovered that Thérèse always went out of her way to make things easy for the novices in her care. She talked to them very little about the Spiritual Life. It us true that she read to them from *The Imitation of Christ* and that occasionally she would open a book by the Saint of Avila and commence to read a passage from that, but more often than not she would put the books down and talk to them in simple friendly terms about the Gospel story. Was this the reason that she, Sister Jacob, had given up her life of intellectual companionship and leisured ease? Was Carmel only a kindergarten for small children who were taught by someone who seemed to know less than some of her pupils? That day for instance when she had asked Sister Thérèse to teach her to pray. As they sat together the novice waited to hear a learned and profound exposition of the way of interior prayer such as she had read in some of the mystical books in the library at home. How surprised she had been when all the novice mistress had said to her was, ' I usually say nothing – just kneel in silence loving Him'.

Then there had been that first frightening moment when Sister Jacob had realised for the first time that Sister Thérèse was in some strange way in direct communication with God. She had been talking about Jesus in those homely phrases that seemed in some way slightly alien to hear from the lips of a nun. It was not that they were lacking in reverence but merely that they seemed, when first you listened to them, to be so ordinary, so commonplace and it was only later that their depth and intensity opened itself up to you. 'Jesus,' she said to them all one day as they sat in the novices' room together, 'has told me that the way to glory is to be as nothing. We must try to become as tiny as a grain of sand so that only God can see us.'

How terrible she felt now as she thought of that dreadful day. When Sister Thérèse had uttered these words, she, Sister Jacob, had simply shrugged her shoulders to show her annoyance at such trivialities and had then commenced to walk away. Thérèse had followed her, and gently placing her arm on her shoulder had asked her quite simply why she was so unhappy. The phrase irritated her beyond measure and suddenly the temper she had been subduing for weeks burst in its full fury.

'What do you know about my soul?' she had shouted as the older nun stood silently beside her. 'I came here to do great things for God. I want to die for Him, not to sit and listen to childish prattle like yours'.

All Sister Thérèse had said to her, so quietly that it seemed like whispered phrases on the morning air, 'So do I. But we can only die for love of God if we live by love. So make a start, try to be good for a whole day.'

Suddenly, in a blinding light Sister Jacob had been given for one moment a glimpse of the Divine Vision of God in His Glory, and she saw that it was because of this that Sister Thérèse was trying to teach each of them to walk in the simple way of love. Martyrdom, that was easy compared with the daily humiliation that Thérèse Martin accepted without question. Fighting for the glory of the church, that seemed trivial when you weighed it against the hourly fight that Thérèse was striving to teach them to wage against temptation. To die for the faith, what was even that compared to the constant struggle to live by faith that was the message of Thérèse's own life?

The words formed slowly on her lips. Her throat felt parched. Sister Jacob had to struggle to utter them. 'He hath put down the mighty from their seat and hath exalted the humble and meek.'

Madeliane Aumuerier, how strange the name sounded now, and how lonely were her surroundings; a bare room, a plank bed, a wooden chair and table and a crucifix on the wall. What a vivid contrast to her father's house, her father one of the most prominent bankers in Toulouse and one of the most respected members of the community. How often, when she had sat round the table at home, years ago, had she found herself wondering where the endless spate of words were leading them all to. The company was always a little too bright, the words always seemed a trifle too brittle, the arguments all sounded a tiny bit too intellectual. They dismissed God with a few words, His Church with a few phrases. Agnosticism was the label that all rationalists used in their arguments, arguments that appeared to go on endlessly and lead them nowhere. It was hard to realise that she too had once been in the ranks of the unbelievers. How she had sneered at religion. How she had laughed at the foolish women, the holy sisters as she sarcastically called them, who spent their lives out of the world, doing nothing but praying behind the high walls of the convent's enclosure.

A smile crossed her lips as she pondered on the merry parties, the gay balls, the abandoned life of pleasure seeking over which she had presided. What a flirt she had been. How close she had sailed to the easy way of life that was the hallmark of the rationalism that was sweeping through France when she had been a girl in her late teens. What was it that had awakened her from this drugged life of idle pleasures? It was difficult, even now, for her to find the true answer. Satiation with too many of the good things of the world? A growing tiredness of the ceaseless flow of clever epigrams that spelt an inner emptiness and were as hollow as the deeply charged note of a bell tolling over another grave-bed? All of these things perhaps, but something else as well. A deep and profound dissatisfaction with everything that was going on all around her.

There was that moment of silent horror when she had announced to her father that she wanted to become a Carmelite nun, and she had had to wait until she was of age before entering Carmel as a novice because she knew that if she had attempted to do so earlier her father would have refused his consent.

Well, those days lay behind her, and here she was now, Sister Louis of the Cross. The Cross, her title seemed in some ways to be the final irony, for the cross was the one thing she could not fully comprehend, the baffling mystery that challenged the whole of her rational and intellectual upbringing. Why did the memory of Sister Thérèse's face always haunt her? From the first moment they had met she had felt a slight repugnance, an apathy towards her. This girl who couldn't even sweep a floor properly. This infant whom some of the nuns already looked upon as a budding saint and yet who did nothing outstanding of any kind. All she seemed to do was talk about love, her need of God, yes, and as a final blasphemy, His need of her. The Cross, that was a thing of pain, of agony, of dying into life. She, Sister Louis, would show all of them what the life of faith meant. Blazing a trail to glory, triumphantly riding on a rising tide of faith until she was engulfed in ecstasy. How easy it had all seemed then, but how difficult it was now.

Did Sister Thérèse possess some spiritual sense that had eluded another of the nuns, Sister Joan? If not, what was it that had led her to come to her cell that afternoon, not so very long ago, and talk to her gently and quietly about faith residing in the heart. The soft voice, the easy phrases had driven her into a frenzy. 'We must always remember, Sister Joan, that God will forgive everything just as Christ forgave the penitent thief'. Her own words seemed to be mocking her as they echoed through the dark silence of her cell. 'I despise all unbelievers. God will never forgive them. They belong to the outer darkness throughout eternity.' What was it that Thérèse had said?

'I have sat at the table of the unbelievers. I often doubt Eternity itself. I hear a voice mocking me saying: hope on, hope on, go on longing for death. But it will give you not what you hope for, but a night darker still – the night of utter nothingness. And yet I have done more acts of faith this year than in the whole of my life.'

Was it at that moment that she had seen a martyr's crown round Sister Thérèse's brow, she, who knew more than any other nun in the convent what it was to live perpetually in a martyrdom of doubt? All she knew, as she sat taunted by the mocking shadows that seemed to rise up in every corner of her cell was that Sister Thérèse of Jesus was giving herself and her love and her faith unceasingly to everyone who lived with her in the quiet solemnity of the convent walls. Would she, Sister Joan, ever conquer her own doubts? Would she ever escape from the burden of unspoken dread that always seemed to weigh so heavily on her shoulders? If she did, she knew it would be because of the example that Sister Thérèse set before each of them every day. A strange peace was filling the ghost-ridden room with a hallowed silence. A voice, a child's voice, seemed to be saying softly and insistently, 'Be still and know that I am God'.

Sister Joan turned down the wick of the lamp on the bracket above the table. Folding her habit closely around her as though to protect herself from any further attacks of the temptations that were always assailing her she knelt down and whispered very quietly – 'O God, loving Father give me the humility to understand that until I too become as a little child I cannot enter Thy Kingdom.'

Sister Agnes of Jesus was tired. It had been a long and difficult day and Mother Gonzague had been in one of those moods that she found so irritating and difficult to cope with. There was always an inner feeling of antagonism between them. It was a hard task to try to feel kindly to the one person who could have made Thérèse's life a little easier but who seemed to take an almost malicious delight in making it more difficult. That cough that shook her body until it seemed it must break under the strain. The pallid look on her cheeks, the thin bloodless lips, and the body once so straight and tall that now seemed to crumple up like the ageing frame of an old woman. It was a hard thing to have to learn to stand aside, to detach oneself from family ties and sisterly affection and see her Thérèse, the baby she had nursed, the child who had run to her for protection, the happy girl who had danced among the sunbeams along the Normandy lanes, and who now looked so ill, so pale, so wan, without uttering harsh words of protest to her Superior.

It was true that Thérèse herself never complained, never grumbled, never even asked for those slight concessions against the hardness of the rule that her failing health gave her a right to. She could see her now standing in the darkest and clammiest corner of the laundry scrubbing away at the clothes with her chilblained hands that must have found the hot water a constant irritant. Even she, Pauline her sister, had not even troubled to thank her for the manuscript of her early life that she had commanded her to write under obedience when she, Sister Agnes of Jesus, had been Mother Prioress. Thérèse had never questioned her about it, never even asked her if she had read the closely written pages. To her it had simply been a task to be accomplished, to be offered up to God in an oblation of love and then apparently forgotten. Was the road to sanctity always to be full of sharp stones that pierced the feet, and was the crown one was making for oneself always to be of thorns and never of roses?

The evening light was folding the garden in a haze of turquoise mist. The winter sun was setting in blood red splendour. The path to glory was the way of suffering. Zélie Martin, her mother, had trodden that way before them all, and now her youngest child Thérèse Martin seemed to be destined to follow in her footsteps. Only that morning when she had spoken to Thérèse as they moved into recreation saying to her, 'Are you in much pain sister?', Thérèse had looked at her and said very simply, 'I do not want to suffer less, Jesus suffered so much for all of us so why should we worry about a little pain for Him?'

Prayer, constant prayer, that was the ultimate answer to all things. The mind might be in a state of turmoil, the heart might be full of a hopeless restlessness, even the words might seem dull and empty, but prayer, that was the Alpha and Omega of a Carmelite's vocation. Sister Agnes drew her cloak around her and walked quickly to the chapel. The light in the sanctuary picked out with a startling clarity the suffering face on the cross above the altar. Prayer, what was prayer? – a silent surrender to God, an unquestioning obedience to His call, an unstinted acceptance of His will. Thérèse Martin knew these things, they echoed in her every word and revealed themselves in her every action. Even in the darkened places of this world she seemed to walk in the light of His Glory. All Sister Agnes could do was kneel in complete silence, knowing in her own unworthiness that some tremendous task lay ahead of her.

Part Three

The Pathway to Glory

'Since I am coming to that Holy room,
Where with Thy choir of saints for evermore,
I shall be made Thy music. As I come
I tune the instrument here at the door,
And what I must do then think now before.

So in his purple wrapped receive me Lord,
By these His thorns give me His other crown,
And as to other souls I preached Thy word,
Be this my text, my sermon to mine own,
Therefore that he may raise the Lord throws down.'

John Donne

CHAPTER IX

Into Thy Hands

The illness and death of Sister Thérèse of the Child Jesus and Holy Face has always been the subject of a great deal of controversy. The devout Catholics, who can at times be as narrow-minded as a Seventh Day Adventist, regard it as a willing form of martyrdom. There are others, however, many of them practising Catholics, who do not find it at all easy to accept this purely sentimental view of the situation. Has anyone the right to willingly seek death rather than try to cling on to life as long as possible? Is a voluntary movement towards death a form of suicide? Why were not steps taken, much earlier than they were, to seek medical advice and treatment for her consumption in its early stages? Was the Prioress, Mother Gonzague, guilty of wilful negligence to one of the nuns placed under her care and direction?

The main difficulty that faces the critics is that they are looking at the whole matter from outside the walls of the convent enclosure. They seek to measure the meaning and purpose of Sister Thérèse's life against their own worldly standards and in doing so miss much of that life's meaning and purpose. The Carmelite Rule is undoubtedly one of the strictest among the religious orders, and at the end of the nineteenth century it was a little more severe than it is today. The aim of the true Carmelite is to sacrifice herself completely to the love of God, to become in fact as Thérèse Martin did, the victim of Divine Love. The rigidity of the discipline and the harshness of life lived in the enclosure demands a totally different standard of values to those we use when we are judging day to day events in our ordinary worka-day lives.

As we shall see, Thérèse herself made no complaints about ill health, in fact no one appeared to be aware of how ill she really was until she had her first haemorrhage. A perfect life and a goodly death was the aim of every inhabitant of the enclosure, and when Mother Gonzague realised that Thérèse herself wished to accept the burden of suffering that her illness brought with it she saw in this a complete acceptance of the Carmelite rule. Had the nun asked for medical treatment before the doctor was summoned to visit her and diagnose her complaint she would have been given it without question.

We have already seen that for her mortification did not consist of spectacular demonstrations of physical violence against one's own body, but in the willing acceptance of the little acts of suffering that formed part of her daily life of complete dedication to the will of God. When she was mis-judged she never attempted to justify herself. When she was misunderstood she never sought to escape from the consequences of her own actions. When she was falsely accused of some act that was frowned upon by her Superior she never tried to escape from the punishment meted out to her. The strength and power of her Little Way lay in the offering of each minute of every hour as a perfect gift to God. She lived on a level of absolutes where other people exist in the framework of relatives. So perfect was her example to others that as she lay dying the priest who heard her last confession openly declared that he doubted whether she had ever committed a mortal sin. Her spiritual power lay in her ability to come down to our level of understanding in order that she could lift us to her level of Grace.

We find it difficult at times to accept the fact of the existence of God, so did Thérèse Martin. We find that our own spiritual endeavours are often clouded with the dark shadows of doubt, so were Thérèse Martin's. We are at times the victims of an overwhelming sense of despair, so was Thérèse Martin. It is because of these things that her life touches ours so closely and seeks to transform us into becoming more like the creatures that God meant us to be. Her sanctity was so simple, so practical, and so devastating, that we are inclined to reject it when first we try to understand it. The prophetic element that underlay every moment of her earthly existence is alien to our so-called practical natures that revolve much more round the pragmatic than the spiritual. Thérèse Martin accepted the central fact of Christianity, the resurrection of her Divine Lord without question. We are much more akin to the disciple Thomas who wished to touch the nail-wounds on the hands and feel the spear slit in the side before we are prepared to accept the resurrected Christ as our Saviour. As we follow Sister Thérèse's painful journey to her personal crucifixion, we must try to realise that a saint is God's signature in history to show us that He is not dissatisfied with His world.

It is also important to remember when we are considering the role that Mother Gonzague played in the closing two years of Thérèse's life in Carmel that the Prioress was firmly convinced that, unworthy as she might be to fulfil such a role, she had been placed in charge of a nun who was destined to become a saint, and who herself had always sought the way of suffering as a method of mediation for all mankind. After all, it was her own sister Pauline, Mother Agnes, who was Prioress when first Thérèse realised that she was suffering from the first phases of the disease that eventually killed her. She did not confide to her sister the fact that she was ill, and, although several of the nuns noticed the change that was taking place in her physical appearance, her sister, who must surely have noticed it as well, did not seek to obtain medical advice as to Thérèse's condition.

We may never be able to discover the full facts about the final phase in her life as the underlying antagonism between the two Prioresses, Mother Agnes and Mother Gonzague, who were each in turn very closely associated with her, may have kept their counsel on certain points right up to their deathbeds. If Mother Gonzague had taken a gentler line and relaxed the discipline of the order in her dealing with Thérèse during her illness Mother Agnes would undoubtedly have charged her with having interfered with the road to martyrdom that Thérèse herself wished to travel. As it was, because Mother Gonzague followed in the strictest possible way the rules laid down by the Foundress herself for the Carmelite Order, after Thérèse's death Mother Agnes criticised her for the 'unnecessary suffering' that her sister had gone through in the closing weeks of her life; completely ignoring the fact that Thérèse herself, far from trying to seek a negation of suffering in any way, had asked that her suffering might be intensified so that she might align herself completely with the sufferings of Christ Himself in his death agony.

It is only when we see the final phases of the saint's life against this background that we can hope to gain some understanding of it, and it is because of this fact that when I am dealing with the final stages of her soul's journey I shall use her own words in writing about it as far as possible.

Let me remind you that it was on 9th June, 1895, that Sister Thérèse had offered herself as a willing victim to the merciful love of God. She realised that the cause to which she had dedicated her life in Carmel, the helping of priests and missionaries and the seeking to bring to all men a knowledge of the power and the love of God, demanded from her a wholehearted acceptance of whatever God wished to bring into her own life. If she was to seek to perfect herself in love she must also recognise that love always involves suffering. The image she built up for herself of her Divine Spouse was that of the Suffering Servant, offering Himself daily on the Cross for the salvation of all humanity. The complete allying of herself with that suffering was her objective and her illness and death was one of the means by which she knew that this objective could be realised.

During the opening months of 1896 it became obvious to many of the novices with whom she was so closely associated since she acted as novice mistress, and also with some of the nuns whom she met at work, in chapel and at recreation that Sister Thérèse was far from well. They noticed how at times, when she had performed any duty that called for physical effort how she would lean for a few moments against a wall or catch hold of the back of a chair to steady herself while she struggled to get her breath. To watch her climbing the stairs at night when she was retiring to her cell was a frightening experience. She would mount the stairs one step at a time, pausing for a moment on each to get her breath, and when she reached the top would stagger along to her cell, her whole body shaking with a cough that shook her frail frame. In spite of this she made no complaint of any kind to her superiors and was allowed to go through the rigorous fasting during Lent of that year which must have accentuated the progress of her illness.

On 3rd April, the Thursday before Good Friday, she had retired to her cell for the night when she had her first haemorrhage. To Sister Thérèse this was 'as it were a far away murmur announcing the coming of her Divine Spouse'. Let me quote her own description of this incident that was the first obvious evidence of the serious illness that had already started to waste her body away.

> At the beginning of Lent I felt stronger than ever before and this feeling of strength, notwithstanding the fast which I observed in all its strictness, continued until Eastertide. But at the very first hour of Good Friday Jesus gave me the hope that I would soon join Him in His beautiful heaven.
>
> Oh, how sweet this memory is to me. Not having obtained permission on the Thursday evening to remain at the sepulchre all night I went to our cell at midnight. No sooner did my head touch the pillow than I felt a burning stream rise to my lips. I believed that I was going to die and my heart was filled with joy. However, I had just extinguished our little lamp so I mortified my curiosity until morning. At first, when the signal for rising came I reflected immediately that there were glad tidings awaiting me, and going to the window my suspicions were verified by finding our handkerchief stained with blood. Oh, my Mother, with what hope my soul was filled. I was intimately persuaded that my Beloved, on this, the anniversary of His death, let me hear the first call and distant call and distant murmur which announced His blessed coming.
>
> With great fervour I assisted at Prime, and afterwards at Chapter. I then hastened to kneel beside you, Mother, and confide in you my joy. I did not feel the slightest fatigue or suffering and so I easily obtained permission to finish Lent as I had begun. Thus, on Good Friday, I shared all the austerities of Carmel without any mitigation. Ah, never before had these observances seemed so sweet to me. I was in transports of joy at the thought of going to heaven.
>
> At the close of that happy day I again went to our cell with a glad heart and was peacefully going to sleep when my good Jesus gave me, as on the previous night, the same sign that my entrance to eternity was drawing near. I enjoyed such enclouded living faith, that the very thought of heaven was my greatest happiness.

Just prior to writing these words Thérèse had been talking to her sister, Mother Agnes, about the autobiographical sketches she had written of her early life and her days in Carmel. It was one of those moments when she revealed quite clearly that there were moments when she was definitely gifted with prophecy for speaking of her manuscript she said, 'It is indeed the manifestation of my soul. These pages will do a great deal of good. Through them God's gentleness and sweetness will become better known. Ah, I know it, everybody will love me.'

Sister Thérèse had confided in her sister the story of her haemorrhage and Sister Agnes told her that it was imperative that she should seek out the Prioress and inform her also of what had happened. The Prioress listened to Sister Thérèse's account of the happenings of the preceding two nights, but on looking at her found her looking strong and well and on questioning her was assured that Thérèse felt quite capable of carrying on the rigid disciplines of the Order. We may feel a little surprised when we discover that during the intervals in the long offices for Good Friday the Mother Prioress directed her to clean the convent windows inside and out, and not at all surprised to learn that one of the novices discovered her in a state of complete exhaustion and offered to complete the task for her. The novice was unsuccessful in her solicitude for the ailing nun, and for the next few weeks Thérèse did all she could to conceal, even from her three sisters, the fact that she was definitely growing weaker and more tired with every passing day.

However, her reassuring manner and her constant statement that she was feeling much better could not stop the increasing ravages that her complaint was making upon her weakening condition. Her face grew pale and wan, her body thinner and seemed to be shrivelling up with old age. Her cough grew harsher and more persistent and before long the Mother Prioress recognised that the time had come for her to take some positive action in the matter of Sister Thérèse's failing health.

The two doctors who looked after the health of the community at Lisieux were both called in and after they had examined Sister Thérèse saw no immediate cause for alarm. In view of the haemorrhage she had had, however, and in an attempt to stay a recurrence of these, they gave her the very painful cauterizing treatment with hot needles that was the only remedy known for a lung complaint of this nature at the time. As they burnt, cupped and blistered her, Thérèse never winced in any way, although the pain these treatments accorded her were worse than the illness itself. She smiled serenely at the doctors as they carried out their treatment and thanked them gratefully each time after they had completed subjecting her to what must have been a daily torture.

The rules of the order were relaxed, the invalid was put on a strengthening diet and she seemed to grow stronger as the summer proceeded. Her hopes of a speedy death were gone, and yet, in spite of her longing to join her Beloved in heaven, she jokingly said to the novices one day, 'Sickness is truly too slow a conductor, I rely on love alone'.

It was at this time, when for a short while she thought she might be destined to some kind of miraculous recovery from her illness, that she once more considered the idea of joining a Carmelite Community in Hanoi to assist them in their missionary work there. The Mother Prioress, however, made it quite clear to her that there was no hope of this wish finding fulfilment unless her malady was completely cured and she was given a clean bill of health by the doctors who were attending her. Not content with mere physical help she decided to seek spiritual assistance as well, and at the beginning of November 1896 she commenced to offer up a novena of prayers to the Venerable Theophane Venard invoking his aid to help her to move on to the missionary venture.

The hand of God, however, soon showed her quite clearly that her destiny was not to journey to Hanoi, but was to die here, in her convent at Lisieux. At the end of November she suffered a serious relapse, followed by an intense and continuous fever. This was followed by an upset of her digestive system and before long she was in a very poor condition indeed. It is dicffiult to understand why the Mother Prioress had allowed her, after her apparent partial recovery, to resume in all its strictness the daily regime of life in Carmel. Each evening found her so completely exhausted that she would literally stumble up to her cell and sink in a fevered condition on the hard palliasse, wrapping the two rough blankets round her, her only bed-covering in the severe cold of a Normandy winter, and lie there lost in prayer awaiting the rising clapper of the castanets that would summon her to another day's duties.

What was it that motivated this strange course of action on the part of her Superior? It is very difficult to find any logical explanation of what, on the surface seems to be a cruel and unnecessary strictness in the application of the rule of the Order to one of the community who was obviously not strong enough to stand up to the rigours of the daily discipline. We know that Mother Gonzague was hard herself, that she had little patience with sickness of any kind. We can also discover by carefully examining her behaviour at this time that since she considered the Carmelite's whole vocation was the acceptance of a living death, then the fact of illness and physical death seemed to be relatively unimportant to her. We must also take into account that Thérèse herself had no desire for the way of life she had chosen to be relaxed in any way, and as we have seen already believed in her own heart that her death was imminent. Looked at from the spiritual level it is possible to suggest that Mother Gonzague was allowing herself to be, to a certain extent, the instrument of the Divine Will and that that Will desired that Thérèse herself should become a willing victim to a disease that was to lead to an agonising and terrifying death.

At last, after carefully examining the invalid again the doctor said that her case was hopeless and that he would not be able to cure her, adding, 'but I am convinced that this beautiful soul that rests and trusts so completely in the love of God is not meant for this world'.

Each week the dreadful disease was taking its toll of her. The treatments that caused her so much pain were intensified. Thérèse lay for hours in agony after each of these but never uttered a single word of complaint, but seemed to literally hug the suffering she was going through to her heart. A few of the nuns were staggered at her bravery, but to others she was merely a young woman, dying of consumption and being given the best possible treatment for the disease that medical opinion had knowledge of at the time. Thérèse knew that her oncoming death was a constant source of conversation, and one day as she lay quietly in her cell she heard a sister who was working in the nearby kitchen say, 'Sister Thérèse of the Infant Jesus will soon die, and in truth I ask myself what can our Mother say of her after her death in the notification and memoir she sends out to all the Carmelite Houses in France? She will be embarrassed, for this little sister, amiable as she is, has surely done nothing worth recounting.'

The infirmarian, who happened to be with Thérèse at the time and also overheard this remark looked across to the invalid and said in a somewhat soured voice, 'If you had set any value on the opinion of creatures you could indeed be sadly disappointed today'.

A gentle smile played upon Thérèse's lips. There was a radiance, a hallowed light that seemed to be playing round her head as she replied, 'The opinion of creatures? Ah, happily the good God has always given me the grace of being absolutely independent of them'.

The infirmarian looked at her once more and said to her in a gentle tone, 'It is said by some that you have never suffered very much'.

Thérèse Martin smiled and pointed to a glass phial containing some red liquid as she answered, 'Do you see that little glass? Looking at it one could believe that it contains a delicious liquid; in reality I take nothing more bitter. Well, that is an image of my own life. To the eyes of others it had always appeared in radiant hues. To them it seemed that I drank a delicious cordial, whereas in reality it was a cup of bitterness. I say bitterness, and yet in reality my life has not been bitter for I have known how to turn every bitterness to sweetness and joy and love.'

Even the infirmarian was a little dumbfounded at this remark. She looked very gently at the girl, for she looked little more as she lay in bed, and said very quietly, 'You are suffering very greatly at this moment are you not?'

Once more the reply came in a few crystal clear words, 'Yes. But then I have so much desired it.'

As a child she had sensed it from afar, as a girl approaching her teens she had known it was the desire of her heart, as a professed nun she had realised that this, more than all else, was her vocation; to so perfectly ally herself to the will of God in terms of a complete abnegation of the self to the unfolding of a perfected love that she might in a state of complete surrender become as one with Christ in His Passion. There had been a deep sadness in Sister Thérèse's heart when they had moved her from the cell that had been her hermit's retreat to the infirmary that she knew was the gateway to Gethsemane. Her mysticism, and those who deny that she was a mystic at heart prove how little they have studied the undercurrents to her spiritual unfolding that had filled her with interior grace. She knew within herself the love of God as an intimate and personal revelation of His will for her life in Carmel, and the life that she knew now lay beyond the walls of the enclosure in the quiet silence of the grave. The gathering darkness of that night in the garden beyond which stood a hill called Calvary was claiming her for its own, and as she moved deeper and deeper into the shadows strange and bewildering fears filled her soul.

Physical pain was easy enough for her to bear. The atmosphere of emotional misunderstanding that had often surrounded her had been accepted by her as an inevitable part of the pilgrim way ever since she had made her profession and taken her vows. The mental anguish of aridity that she acknowledged as being fundamental to a life of prayer no longer held any terrors for her. And yet now, as she lay on her sickbed, new fears tormented her. Thérèse Martin found herself being tempted every hour of the day and night against faith, the one factor that had been her bulwark throughout the years. Man seemed to have forsaken her and God appeared to have abandoned her. She was alone in a place of evil shapes that all the while taunted her and made a mockery of all that she had striven to accomplish.

Spring came along and still she lay racked with physical suffering and worn out with mental conflict. The kindly messenger of death that had seemed so close to her a year ago now seemed to be further away than ever. All she could cling to was the knowledge that only in perfect abandonment to the desert wastes of spiritual aridity could she hope to rediscover the way to peace. The words, 'Though He slay me yet will I trust in Him' were constantly on her lips.

Towards the end of May 1897 Thérèse appeared to regain some of her old liveliness and tranquillity. One day Sister Agnes of Jesus was talking to her sister about the fact of death. Thérèse listened to her words and when she was asked what her own attitude was to dying answered very simply, 'They say that I shall be afraid of death. That may well happen; if only they could know how little confidence I have in myself. But I wish to enjoy the dispositions that the good God now gives to me. It will be time enough to suffer the contrary when it comes.'

The amazing thing about this long period of purgation is that no matter how much her body might be tortured with pain her thoughts were always turning to the well-being of others. Each day she sent a message of hope and joy to the novices whom she had always cared for so deeply. The missionary priests to whom she had dedicated so much of her own interior life were constantly in her thoughts, and in spite of the fact that she found it difficult to hold a pencil in her fingers that were crippled with a form of developing paralysis she still managed to write to the young priests in a seminary where they were training for the mission field. Her letters were full of common sense and spiritual consolation. One of them wrote to her to tell her that he was very unhappy at the thought of her possible death while she was so young as he had hoped that she would have been able to pray for him and his work for many years more. Let me quote a couple of paragraphs from the letter she sent to this young priest.

> Perhaps when you receive these few lines I shall be no longer on earth, but in the midst of eternal delights. I do not know the future; yet I can say with certainty that my Spouse is at the door. A miracle would be required to keep me in exile, and I think Jesus would not work a useless miracle. Oh, my brother how happy I am to die. Yes, I am happy, not at being delivered from suffering here below, for, on the contrary suffering united to love is that only thing that appears to me desirable in this valley of tears. But I am glad to die because I feel that such is God's will, and because in heaven, far more than here, I shall be able to help the souls dear to me, especially yours.
>
> When my brother sets out for Africa I shall follow him not only in thought and in prayer. *I shall be always with him, and his faith will know all how to discern the presence of a little sister that Jesus has given him to be his helper not only for two short years but to the end of his life.*
>
> These promises may seem fanciful to you, but you must begin to realise that the good God has always treated me like a spoilt child.

It is difficult to accept the full impact of these words. Once again Sister Thérèse has moved from the temporal to the eternal, once again she looks to the future with a prophetic vision that was later to find its justification in the findings of the Church when it examined her cause. Pain did not matter, anguish was unimportant, all she really sought for was that complete self-abnegation that would enable her to offer herself as a willing sacrifice for the well-being of all those who might need, or might seek her aid. It is the simplicity of her assurance that gives such a stupendous momentum to her message. Death for her was in fact the gateway to a fuller life of service than she had been able to offer while imprisoned in the confines of the flesh.

When Sister Agnes called in to see her one evening, although her body was a pitiable parody of what it had once been her face was alight with an inward happiness that many who witnessed found almost impossible to comprehend.

'Why are you so joyful today?' her sister asked her.

'Because I have had this morning two little trials, and very painful they were. Nothing gives me little joys so much as little trials. I know I am going to die soon but when will it be? Oh, it comes not. I am like a child to whom a cake is continually being offered, it is shown him from afar, and then, when he draws near to take it, the hand that offers it is withdrawn. But I am wholly abandoned to the will of the good God.'

In death as in life her one thought was always for the well-being of others. 'You must not let people give wreaths to place around my coffin. Ask them to use the money to rescue little negroes from slavery. Tell them they will please me by so doing.'

It is tragically easy to misinterpret and not understand her words. The simplicity of her language can deceive us into belittling all that she was striving to accomplish from her bed of sickness in these, the last few months of her earthly life. Some of us might prefer more sonorous phrases, or hope that she would offer spiritual advice couched in much more intellectual language. What fools we are and how much we stand to lose if we embed ourselves in our folly. Here was a saint for the simple as well as the profound. Here was a teaching of the way to God that could be understood just as easily by the semi-illiterate native in the mission compound as by the most learned and intellectual theologian in the church. I believe that Sister Thérèse stood so near to Christ in her final agony that she had become in His hands as a little child.

As summer approached the dying nun appeared to grow a little stronger. The doctor said that she might be wheeled on sunny afternoons along the avenue of chestnut trees in the convent garden. These were happy moments for her on summer afternoons. A hen, nestling down and tucking her chickens under her wing, brought tears of joy to her eyes as she saw it as a symbol of the way that God had cared for her throughout her life. One afternoon when she was being wheeled along Thérèse insisted on getting out of her chair and walking a few steps unaided by her companion. One of the nuns who saw what she was doing admonished her and told her she had no right to tax her strength in this way. Sister Thérèse winced with pain at each step she took, but with a gentle look of compassion on her face looked up at the nun and told her she was walking to help a missionary who was having a difficult time in Africa.

Several novices witnessed this incident, and one of them passed a remark to the others about Sister Thérèse's amazing courage.

'I have often been told,' Thérèse said very quietly, 'that I am courageous, and it is far from being true. I was afraid people might be led astray by such remarks so I set myself to acquire courage by the aid of grace. I have no fear of the final combat, nor of the sufferings that sickness brings no matter how great they may be. The good God has helped me and led me by the hand from my infancy. I count on Him: I feel that He will continue to help me to the very end. My sufferings may indeed be extreme, but I am sure that He will never abandon me.'

The weeks dragged on and still there was little or no respite from the increasing pains that had now become her constant companion. She still did a little embroidery and tried to paint religious pictures to give to the novices. By the beginning of June she commenced to suffer acutely·from a constant series of stabbing pains in her side. The thought of death was now an ever present reality, and on 4th June, 1897, when her three sisters were sitting round her bed she took the opportunity to bid them farewell.

Her eyes were radiant with happiness as she spoke to them. 'Oh my little sisters, how happy I am. I see that I am soon to die; I feel sure of it now. Be not astonished if I do not appear to you after my death, or if you see nothing extraordinary that would make my happiness known to you.

Remember that it is my little way to desire nothing of that kind. I would, however, wish to have an easy death in order to console you. But do not be disturbed if I suffer greatly, and if, as I have said, you cannot see in me any signs of happiness at the moment of my death. Our Saviour was truly a victim of love and see how great was His agony.'

For a few moments the lying figure on the bed of pain seemed to become transfigured. Her eyes shone with an unearthly light as she eagerly looked towards the martyrdom that had been revealed to her that God was to demand.

The ideal that sustained her as she moved nearer to the valley of the shadow of death was the assurance that she had all her life as its one object the surrender of herself to the service of others. 'I shall never regret having worked for one purpose, the saving of souls. How glad I was to learn that our Mother Teresa herself was of the same mind.'

During July and August Thérèse grew steadily weaker and hardly a day passed in which she was not subjected to hours of agony. The medicines that the doctors had ordered for her did little to relieve her sufferings. At moments she would look clearly and confidently to the death that she knew could not be very far away; at others she felt lost in a place so full of horror that a terror seemed to hold her fast in a vice-like grip. And yet she feared death less and less the nearer she moved towards the gateway that to her would spell deliverance from the body of this flesh. When would He come? At what hour would the Divine Spouse take her in His everlasting arms and enfold her in His all-embracing love? Like a Thief in the night, yes, that was how it would be.

'Are you not afraid of the Thief,' her sister said to her one day, 'now you know He is at the door?'

'No. He is not at the door. He has come in. But what is it you ask me, little mother? How could I fear One whom I love so much? The words "Though He should slay me yet will I trust in Him" have delighted me since my childhood. But I have taken long to attain this degree of abandonment. Now I have reached it. The good God has taken me and placed me there.'

Time was passing, life was passing, death was hovering nearer to her each day; not the kindly death of slipping slowly away into quietness, but a cruel and callous enemy racking her frail body with pain and tormenting her mind with doubt. There were moments, frightening moments when she cried aloud in her agony that with a swift stroke of the sickle the silent reaper might make an end to her suffering, and then, almost before the silent wish had had time to take upon itself a conscious form she would confess to her own weakness in trying, even for a moment to push away the cup that held the bitter draught that she was destined to drink to its final dregs.

Those sitting in grave silence round her bedside were staggered at her patience and fortitude. Her life had been lived in a complete dedication to the well-being of humanity and her death must be the final offering she could make for their salvation. Even the doctor who attended her had to admit that he had never seen suffering accepted so willingly in such a spirit of supernatural joy. August came and went, and still she lay, fully conscious all the time, enduring without a murmur the increasing sense of suffocation and the terrifying ordeal of her bone breaking through the fragile flesh and forming gangrenous sores.

Early in September the doctor prescribed for her some strengthening remedies, not hoping that they would cure her, for now he admitted that this was impossible, but feeling that they might do a little to alleviate the constant pain that held her in its grip.

Sister Thérèse had no illusion about the various potions that were being administered to her. 'I am convinced,' she said, 'of the uselessness of remedies as regards curing me; but I have arranged with the good God that He will turn them to profit for the poor missionaries who have neither the time nor the means to look after themselves.'

Her throat seemed to be in a state of constant dryness and she was consumed with an intense thirst that nothing seemed able to alleviate. One day, when they had applied remedies to her chest that almost seemed to be like living coals of fire placed upon her bare flesh she called out, 'My Jesus, Thou seest that I am burning with fever, and they bring me yet more heat, more fire. Ah, if I had instead but half a glass of water how relieved I should be. Oh my God, Thy little child is consumed with thirst. But she is happy nevertheless to have this opportunity of doing without what is necessary so that she may better resemble Thee and save souls.'

There is a startling assurance in these words that staggers us once we strive to comprehend their full intent. No matter what those looking on at her hourly torture might believe or think, she knew that she was moving into a state of complete and fully realised sanctity. We might almost say in complete reverence that she had canonised herself before her death, and all that was done later was to give official sanction to what the dying nun already knew in her own heart. The closer she moved towards the shadows that were gradually closing in upon her the more she realised that the fullness of time for her complete consecration to her final purpose had at last arrived.

One day, one of the nuns who knew how as a child she had loved the golden cornfields of Normandy, splattered with the red stains of poppies, had brought to her bedside a full-grained ear of wheat. Thérèse looked at it intently for a few moments and then looking into the eyes of Mother Gonzague who was standing by her bedside told the Prioress how it reminded her of the good graces the Lord had laden her with for the benefit of others.

On 11th September as she lay holding firmly to the crucifix that hardly ever left her hands she admitted that she had from time to time experienced a fear of death, but that the moment this fear tried to take possession of her she abandoned herself completely to the love and will of God. Even this fear she felt might be offered up for the benefit of others, who when they entered upon this final phase of life's journey might know only joy and peace because she had accepted her own doubts and sufferings on their behalf.

Three days later a rose was brought to her. Very gently and with a wonderful tenderness she picked off the petals one by one and let them fall around her bed. As she plucked each petal she held it against the wounds of the figure on the cross. Turning to the sisters grouped around her she said to them with a benevolent simplicity that brought tears to their eyes, 'Gather up the petals, later on they will enable you to bring joy to others', a prophetic utterance that as we shall see was to be fulfilled in a thousand and one ways.

Each evening as the shadows of twilight fell across the window of the infirmary where she was lying, she would look eagerly to the darkening night wondering if for her it would bring the final darkness on earth, and each dawn as the September sun streamed in at the window she would welcome a new day as another opportunity to help other souls in torment.

One morning, after a night of drawn-out pain that convulsed her body from hour to hour, she turned to her sister, Pauline, and said very quietly, 'I am like a little child; I have no thought except simple consent to everything God wills, suffering what He sends me from moment to moment, without being preoccupied about the future. I only rejoice in death inasmuch as it is the expression of God's will for me. I do not desire death more than life. Following natural choice I prefer death; but if I had the choice I would choose nothing: what the good God does I love.'

The doctor who attended her, the priest who listened to her spiritual confidences, the nuns who looked after her were all at a loss to understand how she could accept pain with such cheerful confidence and unremitting patience. Here was a heroism so staggering that it could only be understood if it were seen from a supernatural level. Her cries of agony were transformed into tears of joy. Her prayers for a release from the anguish of the flesh that held her in bondage were at the same time a psalm of thanksgiving that God was allowing her to share in some small way the suffering of her Saviour.

As the cold hand of death drew nearer she became completely identified with what she now knew to be her eternal destiny, to continue until the end to labour for the good of others and for the spiritual wellbeing of the whole world. This was her period of transfiguration, in which she saw with a clarity that appals and astounds us at the same time that just as she had sacrificed every moment of her earthly life in preparation for her divine mission after her death, so she would also sacrifice her eternal felicity to aid all those who sincerely called to her for assistance in any way.

There was nothing egocentric in her attitude or aspirations. She was so absorbed in grace, so abandoned to love, so God-centred in her final agony that a hallowed radiance seemed to surround her during the last few days of her life. With eyes aflame with an unearthly joy she called out in ecstasy, 'Oh my God, how good Thou art to Thy little victim of merciful love. Even now, when Thou dost join exterior suffering to the interior trials of my soul I cannot say, Thy anguish of death has encompassed me, but call out in gratitude, I have gone down into the valley of the shadow of death, yet I fear no evil, for Thou my Saviour art with me.'

The days seemed to stretch out in monotonous bouts of never-ending pain, while the nights were like heavy layers of enfolding darkness that in their fearsome silence appeared to increase the mounting feelings of agony and terror. Sister Thérèse was hovering all the time in that half-world between life and death, a hollow place of fear and loneliness where all human affection seemed to have deserted her, and where even the knowledge of the grace of God no longer offered her any consolation. It was indeed the final phase of the flight of the alone to the alone. Emptiness, nothingness, annihilation, these were the ghostly shapes that were constantly pressing in upon her from the surrounding darkness. The strange thing is that something in her diminishing consciousness of the ordinary world held her secure in her conviction that this was the inevitable phase of her final surrender, her last agony.

Those who watched by the bedside noticed her appearing to try to draw out the nails from the hands and feet of the figure on the cross that lay on the counterpane, or watched with an awed fascination her hands as they seemed to be trying to lift the crown of thorns from the head of the Crucified. Here was a final witnessing to her perfect atoneness with her Divine Lover. She longed to pierce her own burning flesh with the nails and to press the thorns on her own fevered brow. There was no suffering He had undergone in which she did not desire to share. Just as in that one terrifying moment that has echoed throughout history when the strangled words had been uttered by her Saviour, 'My God, my God, why hast Thou forsaken me,' so now, she too knew the dread of isolation from both God and man. She had dragged her weakened and tired body up that stone ridden hillside, she had willingly nailed herself to the cross of almost unbearable pain, she had offered herself as a willing victim to redemptive love, all that was now left was the waiting, the apparently endless waiting for the ultimate release that the world might look upon as defeat but that she herself knew would mark the commencement of her timeless mission among all mankind. Even when, a few days before Sister Thérèse died, a Mass was offered up for her and she was reminded by her sister that it was for her good, her only comment was 'My good . . . that, without doubt, is to suffer'.

On the evening of 28th September as she lay fully conscious of all that was happening around her, a robin hopped on to the window ledge of the infirmary window at the foot of her bed. Her eyes, so tortured with pain, lit up with a happy smile. This seemed to her to be a symbol of the benevolence of God, a sign of His undying love for her little soul. Almost in a whisper, in fact the words were barely audible to those around the bedside so her sister, Céline, Sister Geneviève of Jesus, repeated them quietly, she murmured, 'The voice of the turtle is heard in the land. Arise my love, my dove and come for winter is now passed.'

On the morning of the next day, 29th September, the death rattle started.

At one moment she would appear to be slipping away into the calm embrace of the final visitor, at the next she would be fully conscious and talking quietly to the Mother Prioress who sat at the bedside. 'My Mother, is this my death agony, how am I to prepare for death?' The Office of St Michael was read to her in French and the nuns commenced to intone the prayers for the dying.

'Is it today, Mother?'

'Yes, my child.'

The clock ticked along, each tick seeming like a merciless mockery of time seeking to hold one in bondage who longed for eternity. Periods of intense pain would be followed by short spells of complete calm.

Once she muttered, 'I am utterly exhausted. I can do no more. All pray for me. If you only but knew.'

The clock ticked on, the hours passed by and at midnight she was still hovering between life and death. Another dawn broke over Lisieux and the nun still lay waiting, hoping, praying and longing for death. Turning her head a little to one side she smiled with serenity as she fixed her gaze on the statue of the Blessed Virgin that stood on a table by the bedside and said very quietly, 'Oh, I have prayed to her so fervently, but it is pure agony without any measure of consolation. If this is the agony what then is death?'

It was obvious to the onlookers that a subtle change was taking place on the face of their dying sister. During her long and protracted illness it had grown old, lined and wrinkled; pain had marred the serenity that had always been a marked feature of her gentle face, but now the lines were disappearing, the wrinkles smoothed out, her face was regaining its calm look of complete resignation, the outward sign of the inner state of grace towards which her soul was moving.

'Oh my Mother,' she called out to the Prioress, 'the cup is full to the brim. Yes my God, do whatever Thou wilt but have pity on me.' Her sisters could not withhold the tears that seemed to be stifling them, so turning to them she said very simply, 'My little sisters, pray for me,' and as the pain racked her whole fragile form once again, 'My God, why art Thou so good to me, oh yes, Thou art good, I know it.'

Nothing mattered now except that the wicket gate she had journeyed towards for so long should open wide that she might pass through its portals to the bliss she knew now was to be her reward from her heavenly Spouse.

Her thoughts turned to Our Lady of Mount Carmel, she found her mind conjuring up the image of a desolate mother standing at the foot of a lonely cross. 'Oh, my Mother, present me to the Blessed Virgin without delay. Please prepare me to die.'

The Mother Prioress, living at this moment in the complete spirit of the rule that controlled the life and death of an inmate of Carmel asked her very quietly was she sure that her life had always been lived in a spirit of complete humility.

'Yes,' answered Thérèse Martin, 'I have never sought anything but the truth. Yes, I have understood humility of heart. All that I have written of my desire for suffering is true. I do not repent of having surrendered myself entirely to love.'

At five o'clock in the afternoon of 30th September, 1897, Sister Agnes of Jesus was watching alone by the bedside when she noticed a distinct change in the appearance of Sister Thérèse. Hastily she rang the bell to summon the whole community to return to the bedside for she realised that her last hour had arrived. The figure on the bed smiled affectionately at each of the nuns in turn, then she slipped away into silence, her eyes fixed in contemplation on her crucifix. The rattle grew louder, it seemed almost like a frightening thunderclap in the quietness of the room. A couple more hours passed and still the pain was causing her frail body to twist and writhe as though to escape from its callous stabs.

Looking with tenderness at the Prioress once more she whispered, 'Has the agony come at last Mother?'

'Yes, my child, this is the final agony but the good God wishes perhaps to prolong it for a few hours.'

Suddenly the voice of the dying nun took upon itself a strength, a resonance, that startled the watchers kneeling around her. 'Well then, let it be so. I would not wish to suffer less. My God, I love Him. Oh, my God, I love Thee.'

Those were her last words, but a few moments before her last breath was to be drawn she raised herself up in the bed, opened her eyes, and fixed them with a gaze of ecstasy on the crucifix that was being held up before her. A nun who was present at the time stated later under oath that the ecstatic state lasted for almost a minute.

Sister Thérèse fell back on the bed and at 7.20 p.m. slipped away into the gentle peace of death. Within an hour of her death her features had regained the youthful serenity of the novice of seventeen. They clothed her in her religious habit, placed a wreath of white roses on her head, laid her on a palliasse and carried her mortal remains to the convent chapel where, according to the rule of Carmel, she lay behind the grille with her face uncovered that the people of the town might come and pay their last homage to one whom many had known and loved when she had been a girl living amongst them.

It was here, in the convent chapel, that the first of many miracles was to occur that was destined to make the name of Thérèse Martin famous in every part of the world. A lay sister, who at one time had had little patience with the nun, but who had been strangely moved and impressed by her exemplary death, knelt down beside the corpse and kissed its feet. For years the sister had suffered from cerebral anaemia but from the moment she knelt and asked the dead nun's forgiveness for the manner in which at times she had misjudged her she was completely cured.

And so it was that Sister Thérèse of the Child Jesus and Holy Face died at the age of twenty-four years and nine months. Some nuns claimed that immediately after her death the scent of roses pervaded the convent, others said that they had seen her in visions, there was one who said that she had heard her voice echoing along the corridor near her cell. We can discount this as being a slight form of hysteria, an emotional reaction to the strain of the last few weeks of her life among the community, or the product of vivid imaginations that were always seeking signs from on high. Sister Thérèse was buried in the portion of the cemetery at Lisieux which had been allocated to the convent. It was a simple service attended by many priests from the surrounding districts who had heard something of this nun's dedicated life and exemplary death.

Even her death, however, was not to be allowed to be marked by the unruffled dignity that such an occasion should have demanded, for Mother Gonzague and Sister Agnes had another little fracas about the inscription that was to mark the last resting place of the simple soul whose life had been a lesson in humility to both of them. The usual practice was to mark the grave with a simple inscription bearing the name of the nun, in this case, Sister Thérèse of the Child Jesus and the Holy Face, but Sister Agnes insisted that in addition to these the words 'I will spend my heaven doing good on earth' should be added to the usual terse statement of Born, 2nd January 1873, died 30th September 1897.

On the day of the funeral there was a strange silence in the convent itself. Most of the nuns felt sad at losing a companion who had shed so much love, radiance, compassion and understanding in all their lives. However, Sister Thérèse was dead, the usual notification would be sent to the Carmelite Houses all over France by the Mother Superior, and life for them would resume its normal disciplined way.

'Her life is over,' one nun said, 'and what a short and unimportant life it was.'

Little did she realise the irony that lay behind the words she had spoken in meekness and humility. Thérèse Martin's real life had only just begun . . . and in this fact lies the rest of our story.

CHAPTER X

Tell John

. . . tell John what your own ears and eyes have
witnessed; the blind see, and the lame walk, and the
deaf hear and the poor have the good news told unto
them.

THE NEW TESTAMENT

Mother Gonzague stood in the oppressive silence of her cell. Words, the
hollow flattery of men, how little these meant when one seemed to be standing face to face with the judgement of God. The tragedy that seemed to
underlie her own life was as dust and ashes when she thought of the lowly
splendour of the nun whose life had appeared to so many as uneventful and
whose death had had little significance except in the solemnity of her passing.
It was over, all was ended and now life in the Carmel at Lisieux would once
again resume its normal cycle.

Would it though? That was the question that kept tormenting the Mother
Prioress's active brain. Had something happened of which most of the
inmates had been completely unaware? Was the last spade of warm earth
that had been thrown on the very ordinary grave an end, or might it be
that it was also a beginning? Her own vanity, the egotism that had played
such a dominant role in her life, the inward sense of superiority that marred
the value of so many of her actions; what were these things to her now
and what value had they in the noble calling to which she had sought to
dedicate her life?

The tears flowed down her cheeks. It was almost as though once the
floodgates of her own inner repentence had opened up no power on earth
would be able to close them again. How stupid her petty tyrannies seemed
when she considered the conscientious way in which Thérèse Martin had
tried to live out every moment of her spiritual life. How silly the jealousy
seemed that at times consumed her with a feeling of malice and hatred when
she looked back upon the unceasing love that had permeated every moment
of Thérèse Martin's life. How foolish her arrogance and love of power were
when placed side by side with Thérèse Martin's daily humility.

A strange calm seemed to be pouring into her soul. No one would dare to
suggest that she was a highly imaginative woman who might easily become
the victim of hallucinations, and yet she had a presentiment that someone

189

else was in the room and a wonderful perfume played around her nostrils. Imagination, no, for had not all the nuns had a similar experience as they knelt in silent prayer by the corpse of the dead nun, and had not rose petals been found scattered round the bier that could not be explained away as having been scattered there by any human agency?

This strange woman, in some ways so unsuitable to have become a guardian of souls and yet in others the perfect example of what a great Prioress ought to be, made a vow in the lonely silence of the room in which she was standing. From henceforth she would try to live her own life in a manner that would be worthy of the lovely soul who had only lived among them in the convent for nine years and a few months.

The next morning, two days after the funeral, the Mother Prioress sent for Sister Agnes of Jesus to discuss with her how she should write the memorial to her sister, Thérèse, the obituary memorandum that was to be sent to all the Carmelite Houses in France. She had already made one or two attempts to write a brief account of her life during the time she had spent in Carmel. As the words flowed from her pen she realised how inadequate they were to say what she was trying to convey to those who would later read them. Thérèse Martin, a delightful child of middle-class origin, had sought admission to the convent at the age of fourteen and had been admitted after an amusing tussle with the authorities just after her fifteenth birthday. She had been charming with the novices when they were placed in her care. She had seemed to single out the nuns to whom she felt a natural antipathy in order that she could perfect herself in a way of loving that was basic to the kind of life they were all seeking to live in the community. She had painted pretty little religious pictures and decorated prayer book cards in a dainty way. Developing tuberculosis largely through neglecting to look after her health properly, she had died an exemplary death that was a wonderful example to all those who had been privileged to watch by her bedside during the final hours on earth. It all seemed so insignificant, so trivial, so unimportant, and in any case it did not convey what the Prioress was striving to say at all.

Sister Agnes, when the Prioress asked her opinion about the matter, had very clear and decisive views. Why not let her dead sister tell her story in her own words? Would the Mother Prioress like her to prepare an abridged version of Thérèse's own autobiography and then this could be printed to circulate among other members of the community in other towns and cities in France. The Mother Prioress demurred a little at this suggestion. It was, to say the least, somewhat unusual; in fact to her conservative outlook on life, it all appeared a trifle too radical a way of dealing with the business. In the end, however, she agreed to Sister Agnes's suggestion and authorised her to prepare the small book for the printers, agreeing that it should be called simply *The Story of A Soul*.

This, then, was how a book that has been the centre of more controversy than any book of its kind in the last hundred years came into being. Sister Agnes was to edit and select from Thérèse's own manuscript a shortened version of her story that would serve as an obituary notice for her among members of the Carmelite Community in France. It is very improbable that either of the two women who took part in the discussion that led to this momentous decision had any idea of what they were about to accomplish. A simply-told story of a middle-class girl's life in their convent was to prove a stick of dynamite to both the sacred and secular world. Controversy, sceptical comments, cynical asides, these were destined to be its camp followers for the next half-a-century and more. Fake, charlatan, fiend, these became common enough words among those who were to form the vanguard of the anti-Little Flower movement. Saint, martyr, angel of light, these were to be the description used by her enthusiastic devotees, converts, and fellow catholics.

Another problem that has never been solved, and is probably beyond solution now, is what guided her sister Pauline, when she came to compile the first version of the book that was to see the light of day. It is obvious that if the book had to be printed at the expense of the Carmel at Lisieux a certain amount of economy would be called for, therefore abridgement and selection would play an essential part. The fact remains that the parts which Pauline left out are the ones that lift Thérèse Martin to the heights on which stand the great figures of our Christian heritage, and by omitting these entirely she was turned into a simpering little sugar-candy creature who bears no resemblance at all to the nun as she was in life and death.

If you read the English translation of *The Little White Flower* in its original form that was prepared by her sister Pauline and compare it with *The Autobiography of a Saint*, the late Father Ronald Knox's translation of Sister Thérèse's own manuscript in its entirety, you will be astonished at the marked difference in emphasis the two books give to the same person's life. I am sure that much of the earlier criticism would have been discounted had those who sought to defend Saint Thérèse of Lisieux against many of the base charges made against her had had the original text to refer to as out of that alone they would have found sufficient ammunition to refute the most violent of her attackers and detractors.

We must however return to the main lines of our story. On 7th March, 1898, the Bishop of Bayeux gave his imprimatur to the book Pauline had prepared, thus giving to its publication the official blessing of the Church and assuring its readers that there was nothing in its pages that was in any way an effrontery or a denial of the fundamental theological and moral tenets of the Catholic Faith. In October of the same year the first printing of two thousand copies was delivered at the Carmel at Lisieux.

If, you might well ask, the book was only to be circulated as a memorial volume to the Carmelite Houses in France, why had Pauline considered it necessary to have so many printed? Some see in this the first move by her to one of the cleverest hoaxes ever foisted on an unsuspecting humanity, while others, of whom I am one, see in it the action of Divine Providence that was merely using Pauline as its humble and willing instrument. We do know that when the printer delivered the parcels of books to the convent one lay sister remarked, 'How on earth are we going to dispose of all of these?' Little did she know that she had one of the best sellers of all times on her hands that would be printed in nearly every language and would take its simple but profound message to every quarter of the globe.

The first copies were duly sent out to the various religious houses, were read by their inmates and then later passed on to friends of the convent living in the outside world. Soon a steady trickle of letters started to be delivered at the Carmel at Lisieux asking if it were possible to obtain copies of the book. Further printings had to be made, some found their way to Canada, others to the United States. People in Great Britain started to talk about it and before many years had passed there was hardly any part of the Christian world that had not heard of Thérèse, the saintly nun of Lisieux, and of the amazing book she had written giving an account of her life and teachings. The General of the Discalced Carmelites, writing from Rome, spoke of Thérèse as a precious jewel, and went on to add that her simple and pleasing virtue was both lofty and heroic. A Trappist Abbot openly offered himself to be the propagandist and apologist of both the writings and the virtues of this singularly holy child. The Superior General of a Missionary Order told how he had sent copies of the book to priests working in the mission fields where they had served to spread to clerics and laity alike the knowledge of the Little Way of Spiritual Childhood. There seems to be almost a note of irony in the fact that a specially bound copy was laid at the feet of Leo XIII, at whose feet Thérèse herself had knelt and begged so ardently to be allowed to enter the convent at fourteen years of age.

Edition after edition of the book were poured out of Lisieux to be sent to all parts of the world, pictures of Thérèse herself, very carefully doctored pictures that made her look like a French version of Little Lady Bountiful, were posted off to enquirers everywhere, while her sister Céline, known as Sister Geneviève in Carmel, was sewing up rose petals that had touched her clothes into little sachets what were offered to the faithful as mementoes of the one who had prophesied that after her death she would let fall a shower of roses.

The statue of the Blessed Virgin that had stood by Thérèse's bedside when she had been ill as a child and that Thérèse claimed had come to life and spoken to her, and that later had been placed by her bedside as she lay dying, was placed on a pedestal near her old cell in the convent. Very soon people were writing in, sending small donations to the convent funds, and asking that a candle might be lit in front of the statue. Up to the year 1910 there was an average of about twenty a year, but five years later it was three hundred and fifty. Pilgrims from all parts of the world commenced to flock into Lisieux, particularly in the spring and summer months, from all classes of society. One Whitsuntide within a year or two of her death over a thousand people visited the house where she had been born at Alençon and knelt to utter a prayer for her aid in the little room where she had first seen the light of day.

It is important to remember that all these things were completely unofficial and received no active encouragement or official sanction from the Catholic Church. The only publicity was the book itself, the conversations between those who had read it, and a consuming desire among the thousands who became her devotees long before the church had even considered the question of her Cause.

Anglican priests, nonconformist preachers, publicists and politicians in Great Britain were among her early followers. There were the sceptics, of course, those who said that the Carmelite Convent at Lisieux had landed itself a money spinner and were bamboozling everyone they possibly could into believing they had housed a saint in their cloisters. There were the inevitable cynics who poured scorn on the book and hurled abuse at anyone who dared to defend its author.

By the year 1907 many strange stories had been sent to the convent telling of how Sister Thérèse had intervened in moments of crisis in other people's lives. The remaking of broken homes, the healing of broken hearts, the mending of broken bodies, the conversion of sceptics to the Catholic Faith, these were but a few of the tales that the post brought in from sundry places in Europe, Africa, Asia and in the Americas.

Some told how in a moment of grave crisis in their lives, remembering Sister Thérèse's words that she wished to spend her heaven doing good on earth, that had prayed that she would use her influence on their behalf, and almost immediately had been aware of the whole atmosphere around them being pervaded with the scent of roses. Their troubles were over, their prayers had been answered and they were sure, no matter what anybody might say that Thérèse of Lisieux was a saint.

Others would actually claim to have seen her, to have felt her hand on their shoulder and to have heard her voice as she spoke to them, bringing healing and consolation to their troubled hearts and minds. There was at this stage no proof of any of these things, they might well have been the superstitious babblings of mystery mongers who were always ready to believe what they were told in a gypsy's booth at any fairground. They were all slightly hysterical, say some; they were all subject to minor bouts of religious mania, whispered others; but could they all be unbalanced, given to hallucinations or subject to vivid day-dreams? the answer, even if we take the easiest frame of reference of all, the law of averages, must be no, for even if ninety-nine were taking part in a gigantic hoax, carefully sponsored by a small group of unscrupulous nuns at Lisieux, and cleverly engineered by their agents that they had placed in every quarter of the globe, the hundredth was not, and with that hundredth the element of the miraculous becomes part of our tale.

Before turning for a moment to consider the pros and cons of miracles as such let me remind you of the words of a very eminent Catholic theologian, the Benedictine monk Don Chapman, who wisely remarked, 'The impossibility of miracles is another way of saying that everyone can act in the world except the Creator'.

What do I mean by the word miracle? My own definition would be that it is an extraordinary event that cannot be wholly explained by reference to the natural order. This does not mean that in a miraculous event or occurrence we establish the fact of a breach in the natural law, but simply that powers are brought into being that by their nature supersede the limits of natural law. If I make an object I am not interfering with its nature if I destroy it but am merely using my natural right to discard the thing that I have made. If, having made another object, I then decide to act in such a way as to change its nature I am not denying the principle that underlay its original creation but am merely calling into play other factors that lead in turn to its transformation.

If I stand in a valley surveying the countryside all around me and my companion climbs to the top of a high tower and looks across the same landscape, we are both looking at the same vista but we are each seeing a different thing because of the point from which we are viewing it. If my friend, pointing in front of him, calls out to me, 'Look at that tiny hamlet nestling in that clump of trees,' it would be folly of me to say because I cannot see it from where I am standing that the hamlet is not there, that it does not exist, that it is only a fiction born of my friend's demented observations. We are all familiar to a greater or lesser degree with those areas of inexplicable experience that at some time or other impinge on our own consciousness, and few of us would be audacious or foolish enough to deny the existence of powers operating below or beyond the fields of normal consciousness that do not bring the miraculous very near to our own doorsteps.

I find that so many people who claim to be open-minded materialists, first of all say miracles never happen, then when you give them facts, evidence and data, add that the whole thing has been concocted by a gang of religious rogues, and if you succeed in completely cornering them by bringing them face to face with an indisputable case, vouched for by doctors and verified by scientists, will look at you and answer, 'Well, I don't believe it anyway'.

Before bringing you face to face with what Joseph Conrad defined as 'the cold silence of fact', I suggest we take a closer look for a few moment at what some of the critics have called the growth of the Lisieux Legend.

In June 1897, only a few months before Thérèse Martin's death, her sister Pauline had written to her the following words:

> The saints in heaven can receive fame and glory until the end of the world, and they favour those who so honour them. Ah well, I shall be your little herald; I shall proclaim your feats of arms; I shall endeavour to bring others to the service of God through all the illuminations, which He has vouchsafed to you and which shall never pass.

The words are either a profound obeisance to Pauline's knowledge of the sanctity of her little sister or a bold attempt to make sure that she has left a clearly defined statement about what her own aim was to be henceforth as far as Thérèse is concerned.

There are some who claim, among them Ida F. Goerres in her book *The Hidden Face*, that without the unceasing labours of her three sisters who survived her and lived on in the convent at Lisieux Thérèse Martin might have died as she had lived, a comparative nonentity in the eyes of the outside world. I cannot agree with this verdict, for in spite of the endless labours Pauline, Marie and Céline put in to proclaim their sister's message and to promote her cause, Thérèse would, I am convinced, in her own right have triumphed in the end

While I have no desire to deny or to belittle the constant labours of Pauline in striving to further the world's knowledge of her sister's name and sanctity, or to underrate the part that both Marie and Céline were to play for the next quarter of a century, I would also like to stress that it was on the merits of her life, her teaching and her miracles that Thérèse Martin succeeded in becoming raised to the altar of the church. Even when the court was sitting to examine the case for the entry of the cause one of the nuns who had known her in her convent days said quite openly, 'I could understand it if such a fuss were made of Mother Geneviève (a founder of the convent at Lisieux) or Sister Adelaide. But, Sister Thérèse of all people. Why is she not left in concealment among the Innocents? What has she ever done to claim any more attention?'

Another nun was much more outspoken in her criticism of the entry of her cause: 'No question about it, all this has been instigated by her sisters. But let us wait and see, the truth will be made known.' Well, what had she done? What was the truth that was made known?

In the Grand Seminary of Bayeux, during the hours of recreation when the students debated quite openly on any topic of the day that might interest them, the merits and demerits of the nun who had died a few years previously in the convent at Lisieux became an almost daily subject of conversation. When tales were told of the wonders that had been accomplished by invoking her aid and intercession there were heated discussions among the students gathered in the communal hall. The youngsters of those days were in many ways very like those of a similar type today. Some of them scoffed openly at what they considered to be old wives' tales that were better forgotten, others passed cynical remarks about the need the convent had for funds and how well it had done since the fame of Thérèse Martin had been spread abroad. A few of them, the intensely devout who are always ready to believe anything that verges on the unusual or the miraculous, spoke loud and long in her defence, but one of them who later became the Abbé Anne, and who was himself a native of Lisieux, spoke very simply and with complete sincerity of the little he had learned about her from the door to door gossip in his native town.

This young man had always enjoyed robust health and none were more surprised than his superiors when in 1904 his health began to fail. The doctors who saw him at this time put his illness down to his age and simply said he was probably outgrowing his strength . . . a common enough diagnosis for the ills of late adolescence in those days.

Nowever the young student grew gradually worse and on 20th August, 1906, he completely collapsed after a violent haemorrhage. Doctors were summoned to carefully examine him again and after a careful consideration diagnosed that he was suffering from consumption in a very advanced stage, and that there were large cavities already in both of his lungs. A few weeks after this a burning fever set in, the sick man had an aversion to food of any kind and the doctors solemnly declared that his death was imminent and that no power on earth could save him.

A novena to invoke the aid of Sister Thérèse was begun and one who was a regular visitor to the dying man's bedside obtained a relic of Thérèse

Martin which was hung round his neck. Despite these things, neither constant prayer to her for aid nor the relic touching his bare flesh were of any apparent avail and gradually the man grew weaker and weaker until his death seemed merely a matter of hours.

A nursing sister, who was sitting by his bedside, was certain that his last hour had arrived and implored the young cleric to make a willing sacrifice of his life as Thérèse Martin, whose aid had been sought, had done before him. There was however a stubborn streak in the patient that even the imminence of death could not destroy. He asserted quite frankly that he did not wish to die, that he knew that Sister Thérèse was with him, and that she had no wish for him to die either but was anxious to return him, completely recovered to his troubled family in order that he might continue in the service of the church for many more years to come.

Suddenly seizing the relic with both hands he pressed it to his heart and cried out, 'Sister Thérèse, you are in heaven, of that I feel sure. I am on earth where there is good to be done. *You must cure me.*'

A few minutes later, to the amazement of the sister sitting by his bedside, the dying man sat up, his struggling for breath ceased immediately, he was no longer in pain, his temperature was normal and the fever had completely left him. All he wanted to do was get up immediately and carry on with his normal duties. The doctors who had examined him previously, and who only a few days earlier had stated his case as hopeless, were summoned to see him once again. They examined him, shook their heads in astonishment, and stated that as far as they could see he was in perfect health. The story does not end there however. The diseased lungs were replaced by healthy new organs, the renewed normal respiration gave new vigour to his whole system, and the young cleric lived on for many years, eventually becoming a priest at the hospital at Lisieux where he dedicated himself to serving the spiritual needs of the patients.

The next case I would like to quote to you is one taken from miraculous events that occurred in the mission fields of Africa. The work of the Vicar Apostolic of Ubangi was being seriously hindered by a severe attack of rheumatism, of a type that in the year 1910 was liable to render him permanently unable to carry on with his labours. I feel that in this case I cannot do better than quote his own account of what happened to restore him to normal health and enabled him to continue with his work in the mission field for many years.

Two years ago (this account was written in 1912), I was confined to my room for three months by very painful rheumatism which caused me great suffering. During this time I had an opportunity of reading the Life of Sister Thérèse of the

Child Jesus and Holy Face, and was deeply edified. One evening when the sufferings had increased, I besought the dear Carmelite to ask God for my cure or my death, for I had no wish to remain a burden on my mission. Having reflected during the night I withdrew this petition, and said to the little sister, 'Let me suffer since such is the will of God. I ask nothing for myself but save Father X (naming another of the missionaries) from death.'

The missionary in question had been attacked by the fatal sleeping sickness which had claimed so many victims in the Congo and in those days was considered incurable. He was sent back to France where he was examined by the Pasteur Institute and was pronounced to be completely free of any microbes of the terrible disease. He returned to the Congo and from that time onwards enjoyed perfect health.

To crown all, I myself, who now asked nothing for myself was completely cured the day after I had withdrawn my own petition.

During the years since Sister Thérèse's death and the writing of the above statement, a complete record had been kept at the convent at Lisieux of all miracles, all prayers answered and all favours attributed to Sister Thérèse which by this time ran into thousands.

You will recall how they had found rose petals scattered round Thérèse Martin's head one day as she lay very near to death, and how the dying nun had told them to preserve these rose petals as they might prove to have a great value one day. In the year 1910, in the month of May, a man, Ferdinand Audry, aged sixty, entered the Home for the Aged kept by the Little Sisters of the Poor at Lisieux. He was in a terribly weak condition following a serious attack of paralysis. In August the sister noticed that ulcers were developing on his tongue, and towards the end of September the tongue itself commenced to split. The doctors attending him could do nothing to cure this complaint and could do little to alleviate his suffering. The Mother Superior of the Order who spent many hours sitting at the wretched man's bedside read to Audry the story of Thérèse Martin. As he listened to Sister Thérèse's own account of her life the sick man grew confident that if only he prayed to Sister Thérèse she would help him. In spite of his hopes and prayers he grew steadily worse and more fragments of his tongue fell away. It was obvious that this member was rotting with gangrene caused by some form of malignant and incurable ulcers.

On the 28th September when the invalid was in a pitiable condition the Sisters went along to Carmel and begged for one of the rose petals that Thérèse had been so certain would have a very significant value after her death. They were given a small sachet containing one of these precious petals and as soon as they handed it to Audry he tore it open, applied the petal to his tongue and with great difficulty managed to swallow it.

At once he said he felt better, appeared to be starting to recover, and on

2nd October told the Sister who was nursing him that he was cured. So much of his tongue had been destroyed by the terrible ravages of the disease that he could barely articulate the words properly and the sister had hard work to understand what he was saying.

The doctors who came to see him a few days later were surprised to find that he had been cured, that the last traces of the ulcers had disappeared, but had to break to him the sad news that his tongue was almost completely destroyed and that he would never be able to talk properly again. Audry continued to pray to Sister Thérèse for assistance and to the amazement of the doctors who were still attending him three weeks later his tongue had grown again and he was as normal in every way as he had been before the growth of the ulcers had commenced to rot it away.

Let us consider a case much nearer home. In 1909 a Mrs. Dorans, living in Glasgow, was suffering from an abdominal tumour. Towards the end of April she was examined by several doctors who all agreed that an operation would be useless as the tumour was already too deeply rooted in the flesh. The weeks passed, her complaint grew much worse and soon she was unable to partake of solid food of any kind. Surgery was impossible, the medicine seemed to do little to ease the constant pain in which she found herself, and even the prayers of her friends to the Sacred Heart and a novena to Our Lady of Lourdes was of no avail. On the 22nd August, 1909, the Protestant doctor who was attending her stated quite openly that she had not much longer to live.

On that same day a friend came to see her who told her about Thérèse Martin and suggested they should both offer up prayers to Sister Thérèse for assistance. 'Even if she does not restore you to health,' her friend said, 'she will without a doubt aid you to make a happy death.' All this happened on a Sunday. The two women commenced to pray. The sick woman grew gradually worse and by the following Thursday the doctor attending her said that she could not be expected to live until the following morning. At eleven o'clock that same night she was given a little ice to suck and this in its turn brought on a violent attack of vomiting. After this she fell asleep until half-past-five the following morning.

She was awakened by what she herself described afterwards as 'a light touch on my shoulder'. She was completely alone in the room at the time, as her daughter who had been sitting at her bedside had fallen asleep exhausted with the strain of nursing her for so long. Mrs Dorans sat up in bed. She could not understand what had happened but was aware of the fact that she had no pain of any kind although previously she had been in constant pain all the time. She put her hand down to feel the swelling where the tumour was and found there was none at all, in fact the tumour seemed to have disappeared.

Calling out to awaken her sleeping daughter she asked for something to drink and drank a large glass of soda water. A little later she asked for a cup of tea and something to eat. Her daughter, thinking that this was probably the last whim of a dying woman made her some tea and buttered her a roll of bread and gave it to her. She could hardly believe her own eyes as she watched her mother eating the roll and saw with what relish she was drinking the cup of hot tea.

The doctor arrived at ten o'clock in the morning expecting to find that Mrs Dorans had died during the night. Instead of this he found a woman sitting up in bed, talking in a weak but animated way to her daughter and obviously in excellent spirits. The poor doctor was nonplussed. He spent over an hour examing his patient and found that every organ in the body was working perfectly and that the large tumour had completely disappeared leaving a small lump the size of a marble. The doctor, a Protestant let us remember, gave Mrs Dorans a certificate stating that she was cured and she lived on and enjoyed normal health for many years.

These accounts you may say are all of events that have taken place some years after Thérèse's death when the upholders and camp followers of her cause were ready to accept anything and everything as proof of her sanctity. Let us therefore examine now a case that happened less than six years after her death and before her fame had spread over the whole world as it had done by the year 1910.

In 1903, Madame Jouanna, the wife of a gardener at Marne-le-Coquette was operated upon for a double strangulated hernia. She almost died under the operation and remained an invalid long after her recovery. A year later she had appendicitis, complicated by general peritonitis. The local doctors who were called in said quite bluntly that there was no hope at all for her, but in spite of their verdict a surgeon was summoned from Paris. He opened the sick woman's abdomen and found such an abscess and quantity of pus that he abandoned the idea of operating, sewed up the wound caused by the incision he had made and announced that she had at the most a few hours to live. The priest was called to her bedside immediately. He found her conscious but unable to speak, gave her absolution and slipped under her pillow a sachet containing one of the rose petals from the Carmel at Lisieux. Two days later she was out of danger. The doctors examined her and all expressed astonishment at her recovery.

Early in the year 1910 a copy of the life of Sister Thérèse had come into the hands of the Reverend Alexander Grant, a minister of the Free Church of

Scotland. He was, as were most men of his calling, an ardent anti-catholic; he was not particularly interested in nuns, he had no time for convents, and the only thing that led him to read the book at all was idle curiosity, mixed with a feeling that here, he might find another weapon with which to attack the Roman Church and all its Popish ways.

To his consternation he found that reading the life of a Carmelite nun who had died thirteen years previously in a convent in Normandy was having a very disturbing effect upon him. He could not sleep without finding himself distracted by thoughts about her simple sanctity. He could no longer preach without feeling in some way that his words were inadequate to spread the gospel of love to his half-somnolent congregation. He had no illusions about churchgoers. With most of them it was a habit they had been brought up to from their Sunday School days, and going to the kirk on Sunday was as regular a thing for many as going to the pawn shop on Monday morning was when times were hard. The Christian gospel was a hard gospel. It demanded so much and apparently gave back so little. Already there were malcontents about who were murmuring abuse against his church in particular and Christianity in general, and warning the people against the dangerous delusion of falling for such nonsense as 'pie in the sky'.

The months slipped by and the Reverend Alexander Grant found his mind growing more disturbed and his heart deeply moved when he thought of that simple life in that little town known as Lisieux. At last he called upon a Catholic priest, talked to him about the problems of faith that were commencing to trouble him and on 20th August, 1911, was received as a convert into the Catholic Church. It is difficult for us to conceive, looking at this situation as we do from the sceptical outlook of 1966, just how great a step this must have been for a man of the Reverend Alexander Grant's outlook and persuasion. It meant the end of his career. It spelt disgrace among his contemporaries. It demanded a break with all those things upon which he had built his life throughout the foregoing years. And yet he was prepared, largely through reading the life of Thérèse Martin to do all these things and later to offer himself and his wife wholeheartedly to her service as custodian and caretaker of the house at Alençon where she had been born and in which she had spent her infant years.

Writing to Pauline, who by this time had been re-elected Mother Prioress of Carmel, in a letter dated 23rd April, 1911, the converted Scottish minister said:

It is now more than a year since I became acquainted with the Autobiography of Sister Thérèse of the Child Jesus and Holy Face in its English Translation. I opened it at random, and was immediately struck by the beauty and originality of the thoughts. I found that the work of a genius as well as a theologian had fallen into my hands, the work of a poet too of the first order. I felt as one to whom the invisible world is suddenly revealed, and I said to myself: 'Thérèse is here in this room'. Her image came repeatedly before my mind; she refused to leave me and I seemed to hear her say, 'See how Catholic saints love Jesus Christ. Listen to me. Choose my little way, for it is a sure way, the only way.' I then commenced to invoke her aid with joy, a joy I shall not attempt to describe. One day, she said suddenly to me, 'Why do you ask me to pray for you, if you do not wish to know and to invoke the Blessed Virgin?' I realised immediately how illogical it was to invoke Thérèse and not accept the Mother of God. The light had come; I turned forthwith to the Blessed Virgin, the promptness of her response astonished me. All at once my soul was filled with impassioned love hitherto unknown, a love that has gone on increasing and is now an abyss.

Surely these words by the very depth of their sincerity convey to us the idea of a miracle of another order than those we have examined concerning physical healing. The Reverend Alexander Grant was the first minister of the Free Church of Scotland to become a convert to the Catholic Faith. He was willing to give up his career, to sacrifice the respect of his friends, to tear up his roots from his native land he loved so dearly, and to sail for France where as we have seen he became a devoted servant to the furthering of the work and knowledge of the one who had appeared to him, who had spoken to him, and who brought him into a heaven of peace such as he had never known in the past.

Thérèse's mission had been defined by herself as being to all people, and it is surprising to consider the testimony of an Anglican clergyman, given before the canonisation of Thérèse Martin took place, to see how she foreshadowed in her impact and influence upon people the move towards unity within Christendom that seems to some of us to be at last becoming a reality in 1966.

The Reverend Newman Guest was the well-respected Rector of the Parish Church of Stantonbury. He was very much what I would call a middle-of-the-way parson who abhorred the bigotry of the low church element in the Anglican Communion, but also sceptical of the value of the High Church faction who seemed to him to be destroying many of the things that had been achieved by the Protestant Reformation. In spite of this he wrote a very remarkable letter about the influence of the nun of Lisieux that I think is well worth quoting here.

I believe that one day the East and the West of England will be united in real unity. For the attainment of this end I count on the autobiography of the Little Flower of Jesus, this young soul, who will soon let us hope be canonised by the Church of Rome.

If we Anglicans and Roman Catholics could unite in the same prayer, and if a novena of our reunion through the intercession of Sister Thérèse were begun I have no doubt a happy result would come suddenly, as came the conversion of three thousand Israelites on the day of Pentecost. I say, cease your controversy and pray.

These stories of sudden conversions, pleas for greater religious tolerance, a seeking for the healing of the wounds of a divided Christendom could go on indefinitely. In Protestant Germany, in the United States of America, in the mission fields of Africa, India, Japan and China, in the British colonies people of all creeds and classes found a common bond in their devotion to this nun of Lisieux who had herself prophesied that after her death she would seek to help men of all races, of all creeds and of all colours. Who had herself, even when still a child set her seal upon this ideal by seeking as her first convert a convicted murderer who was both an agnostic and a blasphemer.

With all this activity going on in the world outside it was inevitable that many changes should also become necessary in the Carmelite House at Lisieux. Year by year the postbags delivered to the convent each week grew heavier and heavier. The Mother Prioress found a great deal of her time, when she was not directing the spiritual life of the community, had to be devoted to answering the apparently never ending requests for information, relics and souvenirs of her sister Thérèse.

From the year 1888 to the year 1915 more than 200,000 copies of the complete French edition of the Life had been sold and 700,000 of the abridged version. The book had been translated into Polish, English, German, Italian and Portuguese, while missionaries in various parts of the world had translated portions of it into the languages of the natives among whom they were living. During this same period over 8,000,000 pictures of Thérèse had been published and circulated and 1,124,000 sachets with relics of her had been distributed. Céline, who was in charge of seeing that these sachets were properly prepared, admitted that she had had to use up the sheets, the bed curtains, Thérèse's own clothing and finally the slats of the bed on which her sister had died to satisfy the needs of the supplicants who wrote to the convent.

The wide diversity of people and places from whom the requests came makes it impossible for us to explain this away as some form of mass hysteria or crowd hypnosis. As many of them were non-catholics as catholics, in fact quite a number of them as the examination of the relevant documents that have been kept show were unbelievers. Year after year new volumes poured off the printing press containing accounts of the miracles, the good works, the conversions, for which the intercession of Thérèse Martin was said to have been responsible, and faced as we are with such a mass of carefully checked and assiduously sifted evidence it is difficult to escape from the conclusion that many of us have reached, even against our own wills and desires, that Sister Thérèse of Lisieux was one of the greatest saints of all times.

The manifold changes that had taken place in what had once been an unknown Carmel at Lisieux were not accepted in a kindly spirit by all its inmates. It is true that after the name and fame of Sister Thérèse had spread abroad there was an endless stream of applicants hanging round the door seeking admission to the novitiate. What had once been a very much hand-to-mouth, poorly endowed convent was now growing wealthier year after year. Some of the older nuns, and nuns can be just as conservative in their ways and set in their outlooks as ordinary folk, objected to the constant upheaval that seemed at times to threaten the very stability of the Foundation itself.

The doubters were inside the walls as well as outside and quiet whispers could be heard in the cloisters suggesting that the Mother Prioress might serve her position better if she gave more time to the daily running of the convent and less to seeking to promote the cause of her sister who had died there twelve years ago. Thérèse had been a nice, quiet little thing, she had been an admirable nun and had come out with some pleasant sounding phrases about the spiritual life, but there were hundreds of nuns living lives of humility and obedience and all of them were constantly voicing pretty little spiritual homilies that no doubt were a great help to the novices in the various religious orders.

This, then, was very much the mood in the year 1910 when the initial stages of the process that were to lead to Thérèse's canonisation thirteen years later were begun. Thousands outside the convent had already canonised her in their own hearts. There were some who said that the Church itself was much too slow in opening up its preliminary examination of her merits. The nuns themselves were divided in their opinions but then they were much more used to seeing people striving to live a religious life up to its highest point than the rest of humanity.

The first thing the commission, set up under the Bishop of Bayeux, had to do was examine the writings of Thérèse Martin to assure both themselves and the Church that these contained nothing of a heretical nature, nothing that in any way contravened the moral teaching of the Church, and that nowhere in them was there anything that contradicted its basic theological teachings.

To some all this may sound very trivial and unimportant, but we must realise that this first step meant that the Catholic Church with its full majesty and authority, in the full panoply of its spiritual and temporal power was embarking on a road that might lead to the point where one of its members who had only died a comparatively short time ago would be elevated to the altars of the church itself. None knew better than her the danger of local cults and hysterical, miracle mongering. Each syllable, word, sentence must be considered, and if the writing passed with the full approval of the council who were considering them, then, and only then could the process move on to its next stage, a critical examination of the person's own life, death and whatever any claimed had followed after. Whatever public opinion might say and whatever private individuals might think the fact remained that the glory of the church was that she claimed to be infallibly guided when it came to matters of faith and morals, and what could be more a matter of faith and morals than an open declaration that a human being was a member of the Elect of God, a Pillar in the House of the Lord who should go forth no more!

Seventeen months later, in December 1911, the Sacred Congregation of Rites issued their decree of approbation of Thérèse's writings, and less than two years later on 10th June, 1914, Pope Pius Xth signed the decree for the introduction of the Cause itself. The winds of destiny were blowing round the convent walls at Lisieux, but in Europe itself the storm winds of war were already stirring up a conflict that was to lead to the devastation and carnage of the First World War.

On 6th September, 1910, the nun's body had been exhumed from its grave in the public cemetery at Lisieux. As she herself had foretold, nothing remained but a handful of bones and these were placed in another coffin in a leaden casket and placed in a cemented vault a little distance away from where the original grave had been. Once more those who were present at the exhumation told how the air was filled with the scent of violets and roses when the coffin was being unearthed, and upon opening, in spite of the fact that all the flesh had rotted away there was no smell of death or decay in the crumbling wooden coffin in which the body had originally been buried.

War is no respecter of persons be they Popes, prelates or politicians, and as those frightening four years dragged on to their ruthless and indecisive close little was heard in the outside world about the Cause that was being tried in the little Normandy town. It is true that Thérèse was still carrying on her mission. Soldiers, nurses and doctors on both sides of the Front were constantly testifying as to how she had intervened and saved a soldier's life, aided in healing another's wounds, or had appeared by the bedside of one who was dying and had led him gently and lovingly from the shadows of this world to the light of the next.

Like her Master before her one can claim that to her there was neither

Jew, Gentile nor Greek, but that English or German, French or Prussian, Belgian or Italian, they were all as one to her when they invoked her aid. Love was her only weapon and love was a strange and bewildering challenge in a Europe filled with exploding bombs, bayonet charges and rifle fire. The parsons might claim that God was on the side of the Allies, the priests might equally well claim that He had given His blessing to the German Army, might had become right, and what place had the voice of a gentle nun who for eighteen years had been trying to win men and women of all races and creeds to the way of love in the babel of propagandists who were seeking to harness the Christian outlook to the side on which they happened to be serving? The fact was, as G. K. Chesterton was to wisely remark later on, that 'Christianity had not been tried and found wanting, it had been tried and found difficult so people had decided to leave it alone'. Any sense of Christian morality in the absolute sense, and that is the only level on which it makes sense at all, was ruled out on 4th August, 1914, and was not allowed to raise its badly battered head again until 11th November, 1918. There were some who tried to warn mankind that modern warfare was a luxury no civilised people could any longer afford. There were others, and a few priests and parsons could be numbered in their ranks, who stated quite openly that war was not merely a denial of Christian morality but was a destructive element that would endanger in every way the dignity and decency of man. The rest, including the prelates and the politicians, the princes and the presidents, all plunged into the horrors and bestiality of modern warfare little realising that the bells that rang out the Armistice in 1918, far from being the bells of victory, were bells clanging across a Europe whose lights were going out.

The warriors on the battlefield, and there were noble and fine and brave men on all sides, were being used to stifle the message of a warrior whom they had enslaved in the chains of their own shortsightedness, their own hypocrisy, their own shortcomings lest a voice should call out to them quietly and insistently that her heaven on earth was a walking in a way of perfect love among the many who had set their feet in the pathway of hatred.

You may very well be wondering what the Great War of 1914 to 1918 has to do with the life and death and canonisation of Thérèse Martin. The first point I would like to make is that it was during that war that we had convincing evidence that she was no partisan and that she was acting as a very lively witness indeed to the universality of the love she had lived and died to teach all mankind. Her wartime miracles, and they ran into hundreds, all of which have been carefully recorded and filed away in the bureau at

Lisieux, manifested themselves among friend and foe alike, as the world in which she now lived and moved knew none of the geographical boundaries or taking of sides that always seems to have been a basic factor in man's limited vision. The second factor to be considered is that the impact of the war on all our lives made propaganda through the press an inevitable part of this mad game of arrant nationalists in which truth is always the first casualty.

It is a sad, but nevertheless true, thought that virtue has little or no news value. A particularly loathsome murder case, a juicy story of abduction and rape, a scandal in the divorce courts, or a theft that appears to touch the level of high adventure like the Great Train Robbery is far more significant to the alleyways of Fleet Street, than a simple story of silent heroism or the telling of a tale in which virtue proves itself to be triumphant. The fact of the daily impact of the war on the popular press made what was happening at Lisieux and Bayeux fade into comparative insignificance.

It must be remembered that the making of a saint is no automatic thing, it is not a device the Catholic Church uses to foist one of her children as being more worthy than the rest of mankind upon her unsuspecting adherents. The wheels of time grind slowly indeed, as a general rule, between the time when a cause is first examined and when the Church gives her final verdict upon the matter. Two, three or four hundred years can pass before a definite decision is reached, and even in modern times, with rare exceptions, it can take about one hundred years for the Council considering the case to reach its final conclusions and recommendations.

The saints are the Friends of God. They are those men and women, who within their own lifetime, have so perfectly aligned themselves with the Will of God that after death they have the power to intercede with Him on behalf of their fellow human beings who may have sought their aid. They are our friends at court, those who have trod the roadway we are trying to travel and knowing its rocky paths and hard places are ready and willing to assist us in any way they can to fulfil life's journey in as virtuous and victorious a manner as possible. They see us, as it were, through the eyes of God for they are partakers in the celestial vision.

It must also be stressed that no single saint has ever performed a single miracle, but that they have been the channels of grace through which a divine power has flowed to accomplish what seems to us in our normal outlook upon life an impossibility.

Let us consider for a moment how the idea of saints came into being. In the early centuries of the church martyrdom was common enough among practising Christians. They were looked upon as dangerous men, as the enemies of the state, as dabblers in mysteries that were dangerous to the life and wellbeing of the body politic. Those who survived and who handed on the stories of the heroism their comrades had shown in the arena, or when they were stoned, crucified or burnt at the stake, looked upon them as the friends of God, as those men and women who had become as 'a pillar in the house of the Lord who should go forth no more'. In the first and second century the church consisted of small groups who formed local communities, each subject to the authority of their governing bishop, who in his turn was responsible to and directed from the central authority in Rome. It becomes obvious that in a period when travel took years that now would take weeks, when methods of communication were slow and tedious, that it was inevitable that the bishops exercised in some ways greater power over their scattered flocks than they do today. The Papacy would establish the principles in matters of faith and morals, just as it does today, and then leave it to the bishops and through them the local clergy to see that its teachings were upheld and carried out.

By the beginning of the fourth century the making of saints by popular acclammation was being replaced by the consideration of the case of the person who was supposed to have lived a life of particular merit by the councils presided over by the bishop who would then declare their findings that were binding upon the faithful. Here then we have the beginning of the Process of a Cause that set the pattern by which it is carried out at the present time. Later no final decision could be declared by the bishop and the council without the consent of the Pope, who after all was then as he is now, the infallible voice of the church when it came to defining a matter relating to faith and morals. It was only in 1922 that the whole business of considering the evidences for and examining the life of the person who was to be raised to the altars of the church was given its present form in a decree issued by the Sacred Congregation of Rites acting upon the authority of the Supreme Pontiff himself. Another important fact that must be stressed here is that the Catholic Church does not claim that the only saints are the men and women whom it has found to be worthy of canonisation. There are probably thousands more who have lived perfect lives, who had fought the good fight heroically to the end and who now enjoy the felicity of God in all its glory.

I know that to those outside the Catholic Church, who have never given any thought as to how and why it operates in this way on these matters, the whole business may seem phoney, littered with hocus-pocus of all kind, and that miracles become looked upon as a sort of celestial sleight of hand largely organised by unscrupulous clerics to bamboozle their simple-hearted and unthinking flock. They are not prepared to consider the fact that the theologians of the highest intellectual attainment, philosophers who have specialised in the logical consideration of facts, scientists who are only interested in the pursuit of truth and doctors who have been trained in surgery and diagnosis, are all called upon to take part in the deliberations that form every step on the way to veneration, beatification and canonisation.

Nor must it be assumed that canonisation, which after all is setting the seal of a heavenly authority on an earthly decision, is an automatic thing that can be invoked as easily as the aged witches and ancient warlocks were supposed to summon up the unseen powers to their assistance. Many names that are set forward for consideration are thrown out without causal process being opened at all, and of the remainder many remain at the Venerable and Blessed stage for many years before their names are placed on the list of those saints who can be honoured throughout the universal church.

In the case of Thérèse Martin, it would be unjust and untrue to suggest that the demand for her being elevated to the altar called forth universal affirmation. There were those, Catholics and non-Catholics alike, who were either indifferent to or actively opposed to her case being opened up and considered by the bishops and cardinals who form the legislature for such proceedings. The Prioress of an Irish Carmelite Community openly stated after reading *The Story of a Soul* that if this justified Thérèse Martin in being canonised then all the nuns in her own convent would undoubtedly qualify for it as well when their time came. An Austrian nun of the same order stated that in her house Thérèse's obedience would have called forth no special approbation as it was the common way that all the inmates followed in obedience to the rule to which they had given a lively allegiance. Then there was the hospital director who wrote and said that he could name dozens of his Protestant hospital nursing sisters, 'in whose lives and at whose deathbed I have seen the same conduct'.

What each of these critics failed to recognise was that Thérèse Martin had lifted the ordinary rule of obedience to a supernatural level, that she had sanctified her suffering by consciously striving to offer it up for the good of all mankind, that she had written in the simplest possible terms of her Little Way because she knew that this was the one path that would have a universal appeal to lost souls who were seeking their way back to God.

After her writings had been examined and had been declared as being in full harmony with the teachings of the Church and without heretical content, the first Tribunal, that was to hold the initial enquiry into her heroic life and noble death, was set up under the Bishop of the diocese of Lisieux and Bayeux. The purpose of this enquiry was to establish first of all an open court before which anyone who wished to do so could give evidence if they had reason to oppose the furtherance of the Cause of Thérèse Martin. The Tribunal would then move to Lisieux where it would examine every member of the Carmelite Community who had known Thérèse during her lifetime, and also any of the local people both from Alençon and Lisieux who had been acquainted with Thérèse and her family before she had entered Carmel. Not only had the Tribunal to be satisfied that her written words contained nothing in them that was a danger to or a contradiction of the teaching and the authority of the Church, it must also be equally certain that nothing in her life, actions, or spoken words to the novices and nuns had led them into erroneous views.

The Church has never denied the possibility of private revelation between man and God or God and man, but in its wisdom it has always guarded against personal interpretation of such revelations in case, in the process of their filtering through the layers of consciousness in the human mind, they should become distorted and lead to self and group deception.

The political witch hunts of our own time have proved to every sane human being the danger of elevating private judgement to the point where it is looked upon as Divine inspiration. The horror of Nazism, the terror of the Klu Klux Klan, the wickedness of the Exclusive Brethren are all obvious examples that spring to mind. How wise the Church is then, when she is exercising her Supreme Authority in examining the cause of anyone whom it seeks to raise to its altars in insisting that evidence must be sifted and sorted, examined and re-examined, stated and challenged all through the months and years that such a critical study of the facts may take.

The Bishop of Bayeux and many of the learned men who sat with him at the preliminary hearings were aware that there had been many rumours and a great deal of gossip about many of the things that had happened in the four walls of the Carmel at Lisieux. Had not some of the nuns themselves openly suggested that this whole business of trying to get Thérèse Martin canonised was largely a family conspiracy being carried on by the Prioress herself and her two surviving sisters, Marie and Céline who were also nuns in the same enclosure? Was it not common knowledge that Mother Agnes had tampered with the manuscript of her own sister's life and had carefully edited it before letting it see the light of day? Could anyone deny that even the photographs of Thérèse Martin had been retouched, and that paintings of her had been reproduced for public circulation that were anything but a true likeness and might easily deceive people into accepting someone quite different to the actual person these things were supposed to represent? Unimportant questions, insignificant details you may be inclined to say, but were they? The Bishop knew that unless these matters were cleared up at the outset they would move like dark shadows across the pages of future history and that in later times men might reject their findings because they had ignored these questions in their deliberations.

Let us look at the points at issue one by one. The tampering with and editing of the manuscript of *The Story of a Soul*. The facts are these: the book was being printed at the expense of the convent whose funds were limited and was for private circulation only as a memorial obituary volume of interest to the inmates of Carmel. It was only when popular demand forced it to be published for wider circulation that the question of editing became relevant. Let us suppose Mother Agnes had prepared a different version for the public to the original version in the first place, then she would have been charged with altering the book to suit the changing winds of circumstance. She gave the world what the convent had read and later allowed the story to be added to *from the original manuscript* as it was printed in more and more countries in the world. Finally the whole manuscript was translated by the late Father Ronald Knox. Anyone interested in pursuing the subject can now read the original version prepared by Mother Agnes, the later English version prepared and translated by the Reverend Father Taylor in which additional matter was added, and the full version translated by Father Knox.

The question of the retouching of the photographs and the publishing of paintings that bore little resemblance to Thérèse Martin presents us with a different and slightly more difficult problem. Once again, however, we must relate these things to the time in which they happened. Victorianism was not merely an English vice, it also had its French counterpart. The actual photographs of Thérèse Martin, and these can now all be obtained from the central bureau at Lisieux, might easily have offended the susceptibilities of the Catholics of the late nineteenth and early twentieth century. A nun who had written of the simple way of spiritual childhood, who had written sugary verses that have little value as poetry and less as piety even today, must appear, so her sisters thought, in as palatable a form as possible, so by a little judicious retouching the photographs gave much more the appearance of Thérèse Martin as people thought she was than as she actually was in real life. As to the paintings, well, what family has not offered to posterity idealised portraits of their offspring, it is always the next door neighbour's children who are the ugly ducklings, never your own.

Personally I like the true photograph of the girl of twenty-three, who looked tired, wan and old and who appears to be racked with suffering, but if we look at the actual photograph of Thérèse Martin taken only a few hours after her death, we are forced to admit that there she does look young, childlike and charming and very like some of the retouched photographs themselves.

The major question however, and it is because it is the most important issue of all that I have left it until the last, is were the three sisters the three wicked ones who set out to build her life into a legend and so to bamboozle the Tribunal in particular and the world at large in general? They certainly devoted a great deal of time and energy to making her life, her outlook upon spiritual matters, the strange happenings that occurred after her death, including the miracles, known to as many people as possible. This is surely no crime any more than it was for the soldiers of the Crimea, who had known Florence Nightingale, to tell of the wonderful things that had been said by and done by the Lady with the Lamp. Sanctity cannot exist in a vacuum, and it was the duty of the three sisters to make sure that a truthful account of the life, death and after-death events connected with Thérèse Martin were broadcast to the world as widely as possible.

The preliminary hearing lasted from 1909 to 1916. Nearly two hundred witnesses appeared before it. The two essential miracles were carefully examined and the evidence for them subjected to a ruthless scrutiny.

One incident that happened the same night that her remains were first exhumed from the simple grave in the communal cemetery at Lisieux is worth recording here. The exhumation was carried out in strict secrecy. No one outside the small body of people immediately connected with this stage in the proceedings had been notified that it was taking place. On the night before the exhumation the Prioress of a Carmel in Gallipoli, Mother Carmela, saw an apparition of Sister Thérèse, and this figure in her vision told her 'they will find nothing in my coffin but a handful of bones'. When the coffin was opened the next day that was all that remained of the physical body of Thérèse Martin, a handful of bones, a threadbare habit, and the golden palm they had placed in her dead hand before the coffin had originally been closed up and lowered into the grave. The bones, as we already know, were enclosed in a leaden casket and then placed in an oak coffin before being reinterred.

Month by month rolled by and still the tribunal were busy with the enquiry at Lisieux. The credentials of every witness must be checked and double-checked. Every statement made must be subjected to more careful scrutiny, and should there appear to be any flaw, any loophole through which error might have crept into the evidence the witness must be recalled and submitted to the most rigorous cross-examination. Ultimately the church, through the lips of the Supreme Pontiff, will speak and once it has spoken the matter will be settled both in time and eternity. Meanwhile however, the bishops and clerics both at Lisieux and Bayeux must study every recorded statement, consider every verbal utterance to make sure that here, at the heart of the whole business, is a flawless diamond of sanctity.

While these deliberations were going on the convent was being besieged with letters from every corner of the globe reporting on favours received through intercession to the Little Flower, the diminutive and to me somewhat misleading name that had been given to Thérèse Martin by many of her devotees. The 'Shower of Roses' as it has been called form an essential part of the Process that, as we have seen, was moving through its first phases at Lisieux. The Vive-Postulator of the Cause, more familiarly known as the Devil's Advocate, was very doubtful as to its outcome. 'I knew,' he wrote,

> that any Carmelite Cause was hopeless in Rome. The Congregation of Rites were weary of Causes in which it was easy to prove that virtue had been heroically practised, but where authentic cures were invariably wanting. The last canonisation of a Carmelite happened centuries ago. But I saw from the outset in this case that matters were different, so after my appointment I gathered together the medical testimony on behalf of several outstanding cures, attributed to the intercession of Sister Thérèse. Taking the documents to Rome I submitted them to the Congregation of Rites who admitted that here was something substantial to work upon, and who after examining the evidence assured me that all that was needed now was the episcopal signatures to the evidences.

The daily miracles attributed to the intervention of Sister Thérèse now fill over thirty closely printed volumes that are kept at the central bureaux at Lisieux. They cover such a wide field that it is almost impossible to select a representative group to illustrate how well she was fulfilling her promise and was spending her heaven doing good on earth. Conversions to the Catholic Faith, physical and mental ailments cured, families reunited, agnostics turned towards a reconsideration of the Christian Faith, young men inspired to offer themselves for the priesthood and young women seeking to serve God both in the enclosed and the external orders. Even if we discount nine-tenths of these cases the residue are sufficient to make us pause and ask ourselves 'how did these things happen?'

On 14th August, 1922, the first decree was issued stating that the Servant of God had practised heroic virtue, and thus opening up the way for the completion of the Process. The Decree of Approbation of the Miracles was promulgated on 11th February, 1923. His Holiness Pope Pius XI, who, like his two predecessors had taken a vital interest in the case of Thérèse Martin said on this occasion, 'This silent flower, these petals of resplendent hue, this perfume that fills the air, this beauty that displays itself only for the eyes of God, is not this the little Thérèse of the Child Jesus?'

Before the final ceremonies could take place at Rome there were still other formalities that had to be fulfilled including the re-exhumation of the lead coffin containing the mortal remains of Thérèse Martin and transferring these to the Carmel at Lisieux where they would be both formally and officially identified. They would then be separated into several parts, each part being enclosed in a reliquary. The Catholic Church of Brazil had presented one very beautiful reliquary of solid gold encrusted with jewels and in this an armbone was placed. This can still be seen in the church built in the Saint's honour at Lisieux. A marble figure was carved of Thérèse Martin, reclining with her face a little to one side and a crown of white roses on her head as she had appeared when they had clothed her in her habit after her death. Several bones were placed in and sealed up in this figure that lies on its couch in the chapel of the Carmel at Lisieux.

Over fifty thousand pilgrims had arrived at the little Normandy town on 26th March, 1923, the day fixed for the re-exhumation of the coffin and the verification of the relics. By special permission of the Bishop of Bayeux a poor woman who had travelled from Angiers to be present on the occasion was allowed to stand inside the cemetery enclosure while the coffin was being lifted from the grave. In her arms she carried a sickly looking child who had been paralysed from birth. Doctors who had examined the malformed infant had told the woman there was no hope of anything being done to cure him. As she stood, watching the proceedings, she laid the child down on the soil that had been thrown in a heap at the side of the grave. A few minutes later the child sat up, stood up on its legs of its own accord and with stumbling footsteps staggered towards its amazed mother, completely cured.

The coffin was placed on a richly decorated trolley and taken in pageantry and splendour through the streets of Lisieux back to the Carmel in which Thérèse had spent the final years of her earthly life. There must be no public acclammation of any kind but the air was filled with a murmur like the buzzing of a million bees as men, women and children all intoned quietly and reverently the decades of the Rosary. Many miracles occurred amongst those who were watching this wonderful spectacle. A soldier who had lost the use of his legs found that he could walk normally as before, a lady from Paris suffering from an ulcer that caused her a great deal of pain and made it difficult for her to take either food or drink returned home to be told by her own doctor that she was completely well again, a blind girl received her sight as the cortege passed by and the first thing she saw with her newly opened eyes were the relics of Thérèse Martin passing along on their triumphant journey.

There was a deep sense of joy, a feeling of abiding happiness not only in the town of Lisieux itself, not only in the province of Normandy, but throughout the whole of Catholic France at the thought that soon now another saint would be added to those illustrious names that studded French history. On 29th April, 1923, the formal pronouncement of beatification was made by which the little Carmelite nun became known as Blessed Thérèse of the Child Jesus and Holy Face.

There were already those within the church who doubted the wisdom of allowing the newly beatified Carmelite to become too closely linked with the image of the Little Flower that had been built around her name and memory. It was a misleading epithet. It suggested only a minor saint and yet here was a women who was undoubtedly to prove herself one of the greatest saints of modern times. Father Piroy, preaching at a mass held in her honour leaves us in no doubt at all about his attitude and feelings upon this matter: 'Little Thérèse of the Child Jesus, let us defend you against those who represent you as walking at your ease through a fragrant rose garden. I want to tell the world that your soul was above all else virile; I wish to tell them that you could take your place between St Joan of Arc and St Margaret Mary. I desire to make known that your combats against self were the combats of God. I would declare you heroic among heroines, because you have chosen the way most contrary to nature, the way of little ones. I desire to say that if every knee of earth bends before you, if your name has become the most renowned in the modern world, it is not alone because you bring roses, but because, with the Crucified for whom your flowers have exhaled their fragrance, you have been obedient even unto the Cross.'

Just over two years later, on 17th May 1925, the Pope raised Thérèse Martin, Sister Thérèse of the Child Jesus and Holy Face, to the altar of the universal church. Henceforth she would be known as Saint Thérèse of the Child Jesus and Holy Face. It is difficult looking back across the years to capture the rapture and the serenity of that solemn and splendid spectacle at St Peter's. Hundreds of people from every part of the world had assembled there for the ceremony. And yet its central motif, its underlying theme, had within it all the simplicity and majesty that belongs to one of the most solemn moments in the liturgy of the Catholic Church. The singing has ceased, the music had been silenced. Not a cough can be heard, nor does the rustling of paper disturb the solemnity of Michelangelo's wonderful Basilica. Quietly, and yet with a clarity that causes his voice to echo throughout the building the Secretary of Briefs commands, 'Arise; Peter is about to speak by the mouth of Pius'. The rustling of silk and velvet gowns, the heavy crinkling of vestments, the low murmurs of approbation break the stilled atmosphere for a moment, then all is silence again. A silence deeper than silence, a quietness beyond quiet, a sense of peace that does in fact pass all human understanding filled the expectant air.

The voice of the Supreme Pontiff can be heard speaking proudly and distinctly as he delivers his infallible pronouncement whose ruling and judgement will be binding on the Catholic Church until the end of time.

'In Honour of the Holy Trinity and each of the Divine Persons; for the exhaltation of the Catholic Faith and the progress of Christian religion, by the authority of our Lord Jesus Christ, of the holy Apostles Peter and Paul and our Own, having carefully deliberated and frequently implored help from God, having taken counsel with our venerable brethren the Cardinals of the Holy Roman Church, the Patriarchs, Archbishops and Bishops present in the city, we declare Blessed Thérèse of the Child Jesus to be a Saint. We define as such she is. We inscribe her name in the catalogue of saints, and We decide that each year on the day of her birth in heaven, that is 30th September, her memory shall be, ought to be commemorated by the Universal Church.'

The pilgrimage that had commenced at Alençon on the 2nd January, 1873, and had reached its triumph in Rome on 17th May, 1925, had moved from the quiet garden of the cloister at Carmel to the wider reaches of the world and its needs in the twentieth century. Here was a warrior who had fought for the good of all men and for the wellbeing of all mankind. Would she escape from the chains, would the future submerge her in the Little Flower or would it elevate her to levels of greatness that would take her work far beyond the boundaries of even the Catholic Church itself? This is a question that none of her biographers have tried to answer, and yet it is the one question that must be answered if we are to fully justify her own prophecies and visions.

CHAPTER XI

A Pillar of Fire

> Orthodoxy to the orthodox; heresy to the heretic;
> but the scent of the rose belongs to the heart of the
> perfume seller.
>
> EASTERN PROVERB

In many ways St Thérèse of Lisieux seems the most improbable saint the Catholic Church should have raised to the altar in the first quarter of the twentieth century and there are still many people who question the wisdom of naming her as one of the greatest saints of all times. Her attitude, her outlook, her life and death hardly seem to fit into a period of time when religion was facing the greatest challenge it had ever met, the rising tide of materialism that threatened to engulf it from all sides. Surely what the church needed was a philosopher saint such as St Thomas Aquinas, or a scholarly mind like that of the founder of one of the greatest teaching orders, St Dominic, or a man possessing the unrivalled skill at carrying the battle into the enemy's camp such as the founder of the most loved and hated of all religious communities, the Jesuits, St Ignatius Loyola. The mettle of these men would have been able to meet materialism on its own ground and challenge both its premises and its conclusions. Why then a comparatively unknown girl whose childish prattlings, as some have called them, have irritated many devout catholics who find so many things about her going very much against the grain?

The challenge inherent in the miracle and message of St Thérèse is in the fact that she cut across and through all the diverse elements that were proving a source of pain and bewilderment to a divided Christendom. Her graces were bestowed freely on men and women of all nations and of all creeds who interceded with her for assistance. Her miracles of healing were performed on the participants of both sides in the two world wars that have ravaged our own day and generation. Her message has been profound enough to challenge the thought of some of the greatest theologians of our time, and yet simple enough to meet the needs of ordinary people who have neither the education nor the understanding to delve into the deep waters of moral theology. Christianity to her was love in action, not a sloppy or sentimental feeling that made you comfortable inside, but a practical application of love in the spirit of 'if a man ask for thy coat give him thy cloak also'.

Hers was the philosophy of the extra mile, the widow's mite, the lost coin, the Magdalene's phial of sweet oil, the washing of the feet, the sweat and agony of a garden and the loneliness and desolation of a cross. Perfection consisted in the washing of pots, the scrubbing of floors, the cooking of a meal, the devout offering of a prayer, the joyous rendering of a thanksgiving. Her first question was not, do you understand the mystery of the Trinity? or, do you accept the authority of the Catholic Church? or, have you been to church this morning? but, do you really love your neighbour as yourself, have you really forgiven seventy-times seven, have you said every time you hear or read of someone in trouble or distress, 'there but for the grace of God go I'? Lip service is not love but life dedication is, and love in itself and by virtue of its unity will lead you to the only truth that can set you free and that is that God's Church is as a city set upon a hill that all men may see it, and know it, and love it for what it seeks to accomplish for the well-being of all mankind. Once we grasp these facts we recognise that we have seen a life and death of majestic splendour, a life that has opened up to all men who shall follow after a way into the veritable City of God itself.

Today we are seeing for the first time in human history a living witness to the underlying unity of Christian belief and experience. Catholics and Protestants, Nonconformists and Quakers, East and West are all seeking to emphasise the factors they share in common and out of this are seeking to gradually cut away the things that keep them apart. In this we see a lively witness to the living spirit of Lisieux and what it really stands for. Among the confusion of tongues that has for so long divided us we are hearing a simple message, 'Little children, love one another as I have loved you'. I do not believe there is any magical formula that will bring about reunion all round, but I am convinced that we stand at the beginning of a newly orientated vision of the message of Christianity, a cutting away of the dead wood in order that the new branches may thrive in harmony together.

The sneering taunt 'look how these Christians love one another' has driven thinking men and women of all denominations to a reconsideration of the issues that divide them. Most of these recognise that they are at one in essentials and that the things that divide them are largely irrelevances that have crept in with the passing of the centuries. The difficulties arise when they seek to find a point of unity; the dangers arise when they stress too much the need for uniformity. Is there one voice that can speak out clearly and authoritatively to which all intelligent Christians will be prepared to listen?

As I write these words, a Jesuit priest, Father Thomas Corbishley, has, at the invitation of the Dean and Chapter, preached at a service in Westminster Abbey. It is the first time this has happened since the Reformation. It is true there were a few dissenting voices raised in protest and that a letter was sent to the Queen asking her to intervene as the Protector of the Protestant Faith in this country. The leaders of the Anglican and Nonconformist bodies all openly disassociated themselves from these cranky hecklers, thereby showing a willingness and tolerance towards the Roman Catholic Church that has never been shown hitherto.

The voice of the Pope is becoming universally listened to and respected. He is being seen as a spiritual leader whose common voice carries a message for all humanity. The leaders of other Christian denominations respect and praise his integrity. The statesmen of all nations are prepared to consider the suggestions he puts forward to help to create a better understanding among men and women of all races and of differing political ideologies. Rome has become a transforming pivot, a living centre of universality and while I am not suggesting that everybody will become a Catholic overnight, I am asserting that the principle of catholicism in religion, in politics and in philosophy is a very important contribution indeed to the needs of our time, and I am sure that much of this can be traced to a Carmelite cell in a small convent in Normandy.

St Thérèse of Lisieux was born in 1873 and died in 1897 when Leo XIII was on the throne of St Peter. Her Cause was introduced during the pontificate of Pius X, who reigned from 1903 to the year of the outbreak of the First World War, 1914. The decrees stating that she had lived a life of heroic virtue was promulgated when Benedict XV was Pope and her beatification and canonisation was ratified when Pius XI was the incumbent of the See of Peter. On the 3rd May, 1944, Pope Pius XII declared her the joint patron saint of France along with St Joan of Arc.

It is important as we glance quickly over the lives of the popes who had ruled during the years of St Thérèse's life and in the period leading up to her canonisation to note the tremendous changes that were taking place in the attitude of the Catholic Church, both to its own needs and to the needs of the larger world outside of which it was becoming more and more an integral part. The days of its splendid isolation were over. Its battlefield was for the conquest of the human spirit and it saw clearly that this could only be achieved by tolerance and love. There were the diehards within the church, the conservative element who saw those who sought for a more liberal interpretation of the church's teaching the spawn of the devil, but these were in the minority. The time was arriving when something must be done about the warring members, when Jerusalem, Athens, Canterbury and Rome must seek to move closer together and find some common bonds of harmony that would unite as they set out to face the challenge of an ever increasing materialism that was threatening to destroy the soul of man and surrender him to new forms of political slavery.

A new life seemed to be permeating the body of the church itself, and a new spirit of love seemed to be demanding allegiance from all members of the Christian community in every part of the world. A hundred years previously no one would have been able to foresee or to forecast these changes in emphasis. The church of Christ was on the march again and at the forefront of the procession was a Carmelite nun, who in her life and death had striven to make all things new by love and for love alone.

Let us consider the words of Benedict XV, spoken on the day he raised Thérèse Martin towards the altar, naming her 'Venerable' in the eyes of the faithful. 'Duplicity and crafty stratagem are only too characteristic of the day. It is not therefore to be wondered at, that piety towards God and charity towards one's neighbours should so have waned. May all this soon be changed. To the deceit, the fraud, the hypocrisy of the world may there be opposed the sincerity of a child. With this sincerity, under the guidance of the Carmelite of Lisieux, may there be also cultivated the habit of always walking in the presence of God, and the resolution to let oneself be guided by the hands of His Divine Providence.'

Speaking some years later in 1922, Pius XI made a much more definite statement about the role that the new saint was destined to play in the modern world. After talking of her life and virtues and of her miracles he said, 'We commend to her intercession not only our poor humble self, not only the Carmelite missionaries and the missionary work so dear to her heart – the work that inspired her high hopes and burning words – but we commend to her the Universal Church, the whole of the vast family that the heart of God has entrusted to our own heart, and from that heart of ours we bless each one of you.'

In another sermon that Pius XI preached on her in May 1925 he made it abundantly clear as to the high place St Thérèse held in his heart and in the heart and mind of the Catholic Church. He told his listeners that she had had 'that superabundant share of divine light and grace enkindled in her, so ardent a flame of love that she lived by it alone, rising above all created things, till in the end it consumed her, so much so that shortly before her death she could carefully avow she had never given God anything but love. Evidently it was under the influence of that burning charity that the Maid of Lisieux took the resolution of doing all things for the love of Jesus, with the sole object of pleasing Him and of consoling His Divine Heart, and of saving a multitude of souls that would love Him eternally. We have proof that on entering into Paradise she began at once, there also, this work amongst souls, when we see the mystical shower of roses which God permitted her, and still permits her, to let fall upon the earth as she had ingeniously fore-told.'

The underlying spirit of these noble words carries with it a message of hope and consolation for men of all creeds and of none. The words of men may fail us, the message of the church itself may at times seem inadequate to meet our needs, but a Friend of God of our own time has, of her own voli-tion offered herself until the end of time to work with Him and with us for the healing of men, for peace among the nations, and for the bringing into being of the rule of universal love among all mankind. I say deliberately of all creeds and of none, for in her perfect life and heroic death St Thérèse proved that all humanity was her mission field, and there are many miracles recorded that proved to non-Christians as well as to Christians that her services were for the common good of all people. Like her Master before her she did not ask, 'Is this woman a prostitute, is this man a thief, is this man a believer?', but merely through the benevolence of her ever-increasing love saw his need and gave of her heart that his soul might be healed.

The second quarter of the twentieth century is looked upon today as the age of despair. The aftermath of war was proving to people in all parts of Europe that four years of bloody carnage had not taught the peoples of Europe to know the things that belonged to their peace. Life seemed to be wrapped up with a pall of hopelessness and anyone who paused for a moment to con-sider the situation into which the post-war world was drifting found them-selves lost in a miasma of universal despair. The League of Nations, looked upon as the white hope of the Utopians soon proved to be simply the league of the victorious nations each in turn struggling to get their pound and a half of flesh. Discontent, frustration, and a feeling of helplessness were the prevalent mood in both the conquered and the victorious nations. In fact, it would be true to say that had any group of sensible men sat round a table and discussed the international issues that faces them they would have been forced to the conclusion that the price of modern war was simply an uneasy and an uncertain peace.

In a defeated Germany poverty and prostitution strode the streets hand in hand. In France there were obvious signs of a renewed conflict between the Catholic Church and the agnostic state, coupled with signs of an intellec-tual revival in Christian thought led by the famous philosopher Jacques Maritain. In England the first faint rumbles of the economic crisis that was to plunge the country in the tragedy of mass unemployment could be heard. The peasants of the Basque country in Spain, groups of anarchists who sought a co-operative way of life for their mutual wellbeing, were ready to rise in revolt supported in their endeavours to find an escape from the shadow of poverty that haunted all their days by many Catholic priests, who were sad at heart themselves at the starvation level at which so many of their flock had to live. In Italy the old power of the ancient Caesars was to be revived by that majestic and at times sad-faced clown of European politics, Benito Mussolini.

Religion had become irrelevant, morality was being thrown overboard and man was rapidly becoming a victim to the malady of his own making, universal despair. Poverty and destitution were there in every town and city in Europe. The old, the uncared for and the lonely ones were dying of slow starvation while the young and the frustrated were ready to follow the latest painted peacock who arose on the political scene, be it a Hitler, a Mussolini, a Franco, a Stalin, a Salazaar or a Sir Oswald Mosley. The screams of hatred could be heard on every side. Hatred of the capitalist, hatred of the negroes, hatred of the Jews, hate, hate, hate, a clanging bell of doom, accepted by many as the joyous bell carolling in a new era of might is right, little realising that it was in reality the funeral bell tolling their own death.

Dr Achille Ratti had been a scholar and a recluse, a librarian and a diplomat before he was elected to the throne of St Peter in 1922. Almost his first utterance after become Supreme Pontiff was a very clear analysis of the condition of the world at the time he had come to power. 'Neither individual men or human society nor nations have as yet found true peace since the disaster of the war. The calm, for which we all long, and which would give us new life and wellbeing is still sadly absent. It is true to say that the same conditions which caused our esteemed predecessor Benedict XV so much sorrow throughout his reign are still with us. It is logical that we should undertake the same plans and decisions that were his.'

Plans, what plans could even a man in the Pope's position make when he was faced with a church that made it obvious that it was entrenched in a nationalism in some parts of the world that must inevitably lead to divided loyalties. Decision, what decisions could he arrive at that would be universally acceptable to all members of his vastly different and widely scattered flock? Infallible, yes, but only in the defining of doctrine where such a definition becomes an essential part of faith and morals. He might advise disarmament but his words would be ignored by Catholic and non-Catholic alike. He might plead for the peaceful settlement of international disputes, but very few would be prepared to heed his words. He might call for an end of racial hatred and senseless persecution but even the Christians who looked upon him as their spiritual leader would choose hatred rather than love and nothing that Pius might say would bring about a change of heart. His was in many ways the voice of a broken hearted man crying to a Europe that had become a wilderness.

In his first Encyclical to the universal church in December 1922 he made his position and the role he hoped to fulfil in history perfectly clear: 'I was born under a Pius and under a Pius I came to Rome. Pius is a name of peace and therefore I shall carry that name.'

The new Pope saw quite clearly that the Church must leave its cathedrals, its churches, and must go out into the market place. It must enter the spirit of the home and uphold the dignity of family life. It must find its place in the workshops and teach men something of the true dignity of labour. It must sit in the bank and the board room, in parliaments and council chambers and must seek in every way possible to proclaim the word of reconciliation that alone could bring peace to the nations and hope to the human heart. It must brood like a benevolent mother over schools and universities and try to educate the growing children and the young men and women into the need for a virile morality that would be the mainspring of Catholic Action. In short, no matter what the cost and no matter how much the individual efforts of men and women might be derided it must live by the simple word of the Saint of Lisieux, love.

When Rosenberg, ideological propagandist for the vile dogmas of Adolf Hitler, spoke of the 'senile doctrines of Christianity' and reminded his hypnotised listeners that 'Universalist doctrines have long been abandoned as spiritual food', the Pope, weeping over the horrors being perpetuated against the Jews in Germany said, 'We cannot give our feelings better expression than to repeat the words of that rabbi who affirmed his sympathy and solidarity with the persecuted priests in Spain and Mexico, "We must regard our persecuted brothers as victims of the same persecutions and mourn them together".'

If I have painted the picture in dark colours it is merely to give emphasis to the fact that there were the few who were striving to bring a new vision of peace and love and unity into a disturbed and distressed world. From the beginning of the century there had been solitary voices in all denominations who had seen the folly and the fallacy of a divided Christianity. The one dominant hope of Pope Pius XI as he lay tired and ill in December 1938 was that he would live until the end of the following February in the hopes that out of the talks at Munich there might emerge a semblance of sanity. He might just as well have hoped for a gentle mood in a madly enraged bull as to hope to find any semblance of justice, mercy or peaceful intentions in the heart of Adolf Hitler.

This Pontiff, whom many today already regard as a saint, was in some ways a strange and bewildering creature. His years of reading and scholarly pursuits had given him a clear picture of the history of Europe. His envoys in each country had kept him fully posted with the tragic turn that events were taking in the late thirties. His own insight ought to have given him a clear understanding of the fact that a hazy, idealistic approach to peace could not bring it about. There was no peace in the church of Christ that was as a house divided, so how could the followers of Christ hope for peace in the world? There was no unity of purpose among practising Christians so wherein lay the possibility of them offering the solace that might help to bring about the healing of the divided nations?

Years earlier that often misunderstood and frequently misguided prophet of our age, D. H. Lawrence, had warned mankind that 'either a great wave of tenderness or a great wave of hatred was about to burst over our world'. Before the turn of the century the Saint of Lisieux had shown us all that we must rediscover for ourselves the simple way of love. Mass movements no matter how good their intent, and mass organisations no matter how strong the ideals that inspire them, are not sufficient to change men or change the world. In our own age we are faced with one of the greatest contradictions in history, that while on the one hand the whole trend in time is towards the denial of the individual man whom, it is affirmed, must fit into the mass pattern that is the underlying principle of social thinking, at the same time only the assertion by the individual of those things that are good and true and beautiful can give any real meaning to the mass pattern itself. Only a moral man can save an immoral society, and this is the one vital lesson that history has been striving to teach us from the dawn of time.

The Pope did not live, as he had hoped, until the end of February. As he lay on his deathbed he meditated on how much he had striven to achieve and how little he had really accomplished. What he had done, and what so many of his own followers in the Catholic Church ignored, was to assert throughout his Pontificate the supremacy of love, the significance of personal responsibility, and the futility of warfare and hatred to offer any solution to the many problems that were facing the modern world. In instituting Catholic Action he had forced his flock to try to face up to the relevance of Christianity to life, and had sought to emphasise that doctrine and dogma were not ends in themselves, but means, and that unless the proclamation and the practice of the Faith made for a happier and healthier society then it was failing in its impact on our own day and generation.

In all these things I am convinced that we see the spirit of St Thérèse of Lisieux at work. In the complexity of our times we all need a new simplicity that will bring about a synthesis of heart and head, and will lead us to see all men as one with us in the common bond and fellowship we share in Christ.

Pius XI's successor, Pius XII, was one of the most enigmatic Popes of modern times. As Cardinal Pacelli he had been the representative of the

Vatican in Germany and had been closely associated with the controversies about the Church's attitude to the Hitler regime and in particular its role in opposing the merciless persecution of the Jews. As I have already pointed out his predecessor, Pius XI, had quite clearly outlined his own position and that of the Church on this controversial issue. The Church had done a great deal to assist Jewry in the dark hour that had once more overshadowed it, and today thousands of Jews testify to the magnificent work that was done by the Vatican to assist them in their distress. As Papal Nuncio Cardinal Pacelli's first duty was to protect and uphold the rights of the Catholics in Germany to practise their religion without interference from the State. We must remember that it was not a Catholic country and would certainly under Hitler have tolerated no political interference from Rome. If, as some would claim, the Cardinal was not strong enough in his attitude to Nazism and all it stood for and had not suggested to the Vatican the proper course of action to take against Hitler himself, we must remember that he was balancing on one of the most delicate political tightropes in Europe. The church's attitude had been clearly defined, The duty of Catholics in Germany was to oppose all the evil things that the madman of Munich stood for. If Catholics failed in their duty this does not mean that the church itself was a failure, but merely that it was subject to the weaknesses and shortcomings of its members.

Let us look a little more closely at this man who had been Pius XI's successor. He was a quiet, shy, retiring, cultured man, a wise and kindly pastor of his flock, and a man who was well versed in the political arena in which he had laboured for so long. A diplomat and a realist, Pius saw quite clearly the inevitability of the Second World War. He was a man of peace and throughout the tragic four years in which the whole of the civilised world apparently went mad he had tried to bring to bear upon the sorry state of affairs a semblance of piety and sanity. Like Christ Himself, who had founded the church of which he was the supreme head, he recognised that the people of all the nations had failed to seek those things that belonged to their peace. Let me quote from one of his speeches in order to give to you a clear statement of his attitude to world events.

'We can no longer say "This is my body" without feeling not only the awful splendour of the resurrected Lord, but also the great suffering of his martyred body; the swollen limbs and faces of our brothers in Vietnam, in Korea, in the mines, in the steel mills, in the plantations, in the prisons of Kenya, Africa and Spain. And "the blood that is shed for all" is mingled with those innumerable pools of blood in the public squares, on the pavements, in the streets, in the convict settlements, and on the wheels of machines.'

Throughout the war the Pope remained a man of peace. He tried to guide all men into a fuller knowledge and a greater understanding of the meaning of love and of the need for brotherhood and in the last years of his life he was duly rewarded, not by men who failed in many ways to understand the pathway he was seeking to lead them into but by God Himself. One day Christ walked with him and talked with him in the garden of the Vatican and later, as he lay ill, came and stood by his bedside to give to the dying Pope a filial benediction before taking him to Himself.

Lisieux itself had been very heavily bombed, standing as it did so near to the Normandy beaches. The Carmelite Convent itself was hit and Mother Agnes, who was now approaching her eightieth year, shepherded her flock into an underground shelter, the crypt of the church that had been built in St Thérèse's honour. The Carmelite nuns all marvelled at the serenity with which their Prioress faced up to this disturbing element that was so alien in every way to their way of life. The daily discipline of the order must be carried on as usual. They might have been forced back into the world but they must still maintain an attitude of being in the world but not of it.

The ageing nun had mellowed and grown very wise with the passing of the years. In some ways she felt that the task to which God had set her hand had been accomplished. Her sister had been raised to the altar, the shower of roses was still falling everywhere where her aid was invoked, the miracle of love was hallowing all things and out of it was to emerge a richer harvest than even she had thought possible. The post-war pilgrimages had started and each year Lisieux received an ever increasing number of visitors. Some came to worship, others to investigate, others to sneer. They were of all denominations and of none, but most of them found solace and inspiration in the message of love that was the centre of all the processions and services that enlivened the little Normandy town. Love was the unifier, the breaker of chains, the charity that knew no boundaries, and this was the ever-abiding message that the Saint of Lisieux was giving to a war-scarred world. The ordinary men and women who could not understand the profundities of theology, or the endless controversies that had rent the church of Christ asunder, found in *The Story of a Soul* a simple affirmation of divine truth that broke down the barriers between Christian sects, and gave them a common allegiance to the suffering Christ who must be daily crucified to the end of time that His sublime purpose of winning all to Himself by love alone might be accomplished.

Quietly, and almost imperceptibly at first, a breath of new life was being breathed into the body of the Church Militant on earth. Pope John XXIII, who succeeded Pius XII, saw quite clearly that the mission of the church in the world of today was to bring Christians of all denominations together in order that in unity of purpose they might seek to reinterpret and relive the love of Christ that would alone unite them in a common cause, the bringing of all men back to the way of grace. The Catholic Church, the Protestant bodies, the Church of England and the Nonconformists must all look for what they had in common, for a church divided was a church in a state of semi-paralysis. He found opposition to his vision of a renewal of all men through the love of God both within the Church and without. Some looked upon his wise counsels as a trick to persuade all men to offer complete and unswerving allegiance to Rome. Others felt that he was surrendering part of his territory to the enemy.

Without deviation, he pursued the road to a clearer understanding among the separated brethren and then as a final gesture called the Vatican Council into being that it might make a study of the part the Catholic Church must play in the remaking of Christendom. For the first time since the Reformation non-Catholic observers from the various Christian bodies were invited to attend the sessions of the Council itself. The underlying theme of the three years that the Council was in session was renewal of the love of Christ in the hearts of all men of faith. The Catholic Church examined its internal structure in order that it might bring it in line with the needs of modern man. The Church Militant was a corporate thing, a united body of clergy and laity, and each had their part to play in making it a more effective instrument to meet the needs of all mankind. The teaching of the Church itself must be re-examined and reassessed in order that that too might take into account the changed circumstances of our age. The problems of the family as the natural and spiritual unit in society, the part the Church must play in the reconstruction of the social order, the emphasis that Christian thought must bring to bear on the national and international problems that face all of us; these things must all be taken into account.

Here we see the vision of the simple saint of Lisieux coming to its fruition. Just as her first conscious thoughts as she moved on the pathway to sanctity had been the salvation of one outside the church, so the church itself must now strive to win back by love all men of goodwill into the living fellowship of Christianity. Just as she had realised that simplicity must be the keynote by the way of love, so the church itself must strive to find a new simplicity in terms of love in its approach to the many difficult and thorny problems it would have to face in the Vatican Council. Just as she had devoted so much of her life and so many of her prayers for missionary work, where the priests must go out to the people to seek to bring them back through love and suffering to the fold of the Universal Shepherd, so the Pope himself tore down the walls that had imprisoned him in the Vatican that he might meet and mix with all sorts and conditions of men. Pope John had visited the sick, sat by the bedside of the dying, gone to bring solace to those who were in prison, moved freely among the poor, doing all these things in the true spirit of Christian charity, that is after all but another name for love, and that must lie at the heart of the ecumenical movement if it is to have any message and any authority for the men and women of today.

The warrior's chains were broken. St Thérèse of Lisieux had herself escaped from the rather tawdry sentimentality with which so many of her followers had striven to enslave her. In an age of gathering darkness she had become a messenger of light. In an age of hatred and destruction she had become a herald of love. In a church divided she had become the living and eternal witness of the unity that love alone can bring about.

This then, as I see it, is the meaning of her life, death and canonisation. In Alençon, in Lisieux and in heaven a new spirit was brought into being, a spirit that saw all men as brethren in Christ, and that in its earthly life and heavenly mission was and still is constantly striving to bring us all into the bondage of universal charity. You may not understand the Mystery of the Trinity. You may not be able to unravel the problem of evil. The fact of God made Man and being crucified to the end of time that He might win all men to Himself may puzzle and perplex you. These things matter, they are the basic principles of the faith that men have in Christ. We need the gift of grace that comes with baptism. We need the guidance of the Holy Spirit that is ours through the laying on of hands. We need the knowledge of forgiveness that is the solace of a humble confession before God of our failings and shortcomings. We need the ability to face death as the gateway to life if we are to fulfil ourselves as whole and complete persons. But more than all else we need love and tolerance and understanding. 'Though I speak with the tongue of men and of angels and have not love,' the words of Paul are re-echoed in the words of St Thérèse of Lisieux. The childlikeness she portrayed in her life is probably the greatest need of our age. It teaches us to love our enemies. It lifts us above the shifting sands and the quagmire of life and shows us clearly and decisively our Eternal Heritage. Until we too become as a little child we shall not enter the Kingdom of God.

Every saint that is born is God's promise that He is not yet dissatisfied with His world. Their life is a divine signature on temporal things. They are our signposts, our road maps, our light in a darkened place. In each age God has not been without the witnesses to His truth and in our age more than any other we need an awareness of their reality and an assurance of their presence in this ordinary world of unspectacular events. Their miracles are our guarantee that the world is the same yesterday, today and forever.

The dawn had just broken over the streets of Lisieux. The bells of the

Carmelite convent were calling the faithful to prayer. I walked along the cobbled road that led to the chapel and felt I was being wrapped in a peace that indeed passed human understanding. I lit a candle and knelt before the shrine where relics of St Thérèse were encased in the marble effigy of her lying in the splendour and solitude of her last sleep. There were labourers there who had come into the chapel on their way to work. There were peasant women from the farms in the surrounding countryside. There were students who spoke in a diversity of tongues. There was a bishop and a schoolteacher. Roses were scattered inside the grille that separated the sanctuary from the people all kneeling around it in prayer.

The miracle that St Thérèse had promised had been acomplished. We were all of one accord seeking to understand the love that she had proclaimed in her life and death and its hereafter. I could hear the soft voices of the nuns reciting the morning office. The lights were lit on the altar and we all joined in the love feast that brings the healing grace of Christ Himself to our souls.

A voice, gentle and insistent, seemed to murmur out of the grey and blue shadows of the convent chapel, 'Until ye become as a little child ye shall not enter the kingdom of heaven'. I moved out of the silence into the first golden rays of the morning sun. A white dove had settled on the corner of the wall of the enclosure. As I looked across to where it was sitting it took to the air and flew away into the blue dome of heaven.

BIBLIOGRAPHY

Saint Thérèse of Lisieux. The Little Flower of Jesus. A revised translation of the Definitive Carmelite Edition of her Autobiography and Letters. Rev. Thomas Taylor. 1930.
Collected Letters of St Thérèse of Lisieux. 1949.
Novissima Verba. The Last Conversations and Confidences of St Thérèse. Revised translation by the Carmelite Nuns of New York. 1953.
Two Portraits of St Thérèse of Lisieux. Etienne Robo. 1955.
Autobiography of a Saint. The Complete and Authorised Text of 'L'Histoire d'une Ame'. Translated by Father Ronald Knox. 1958.
The Photo Album of St Thérèse of Lisieux. 1962.

LIVES

Ste Thérèse de L'Enfant Jésus. Mgr Laveille. 1928.
St Teresa of Lisieux. The Reverend Vernon Johnson. 1936.
The Story of a Family: The Home of the Little Flower. Stephane-Joseph Pait OFM. 1948
Storm of Glory. John Beevers. 1950.
St Thérèse of Lisieux. Frances Parkinson Keyes. 1950.
Thérèse of Lisieux: The Story of a Mission. Hans Urs Von Balthasar. 1953.
The Secret of the Little Flower. Henri Gheon. 1954.
Saint Thérèse of Lisieux: The Making of a Saint. J. B. Morton. 1954.
The Hidden Face. Ida Friederike Gorres. 1959.
Thérèse. Dorothy Day. 1960.

THE MARTIN FAMILY

The Father of the Little Flower. Translated from the French by the Reverend Michael Collins, SMA. 1955.
The Mother of the Little Flower. Translated from the French by the Reverend Michael Collins, SMA. 1957.
A Memoire of my Sister, Saint Thérèse. Céline Martin. 1959.
Mother Agnes of Jesus. Obituary Memorial Volume to St Thérèse's Sister, Pauline. Translated by the Carmelite Nuns of New York. 1962.

WORKS ON ST THÉRÈSE

St Thérèse of Lisieux: A Spiritual Renascance. Fr Henry Petitot, OP. 1927.
St Thérèse: An Interpretation. Reverend J. F. Cassidy. 1932.
Saint Thérèse and her Mission. L'Abbé André Combes. 1956.
The Spiritual Genius of St Thérèse. Jean Guitton. 1958.

PLAY

Inquiry at Lisieux. Le Proces de Ste Thérèse de L'Enfant-Jesus. Marcelle-Maurette. 1964.

OTHER WORKS

Mysticism. Evelyn Underhill. 1911.
Saint Joan of Arc. V. Sackville-West. 1936.
The Eagle and the Dove. V. Sackville-West. 1943.
Mother of Carmel. E. Allison Peers. 1945.
The Theology of Crisis. Emil Brunner. 1929
The Word of God and the Word of Man. Karl Barth. 1931.
The End of the Modern World. Romano Guardini. 1927.
The Popes. Friedrich Gontard. 1959.

Acknowledgements

The author would like to express his gratitude and thanks to the Executors of the Eric Gill Estate and Messrs. Jonathan Cape for permission to quote from *Autobiography* by Eric Gill; to Messrs. William Heinemann Ltd for the quotation from one of the letters of D. H. Lawrence; to Messrs. Macmillan & Co. Ltd for the quotation from *The Canticle of the Rose* by Dame Edith Sitwell; and to Messrs. J. M. Dent & Sons, Ltd for the quotation from *Immanence* by Evelyn Underhill.

The photograph used as a frontispiece is from a painting of St Thérèse of Lisieux by Benedicta de Bezer and is published with the kind permission of Mrs Betty Morgan who owns the original painting.

Index